Golden Gate Metropolis

Spanish Discover San Francisco Bay
(San Francisco Arts Commission, Rincon Annex Post Office Murals, by Anton Refregier, 1941, 1945-49)

Golden Gate Metropolis

Perspectives on Bay Area History

Charles Wollenberg

INSTITUTE OF GOVERNMENTAL STUDIES
University of California, Berkeley
1985

The following publishers and individuals have generously given permission to use quotations and illustrations from copyrighted works:

On the Loose. Copyright 1969 by Terry and Renny Russell. Reprinted by permission of Sierra Club Books.

"Hands." Copyright 1929 and renewed 1957 by Robinson Jeffers. Reprinted from *The Selected Poetry of Robinson Jeffers* by permission of Random House, Inc.

Cover: Photographs of frescos painted in Coit Tower, San Francisco, in 1934 as part of the New Deal's Public Works of Art Project. Copyright 1981 by Don Beatty.

1934 San Francisco maritime strike photograph. Copyright 1963 by Hansel Hagel.

Photograph of Costanoan basket, circa 1800. Copyright 1984 by Glenn Matsumura.

Bay Area ancestry graphic. Copyright 1984 by the *San Francisco Chronicle.* "Progress Demands That the Bay Area Be De-Balkanized," cartoon by Bob Bastian. Copyright by the *San Francisco Chronicle.* Reprinted by permission.

Institute of Governmental Studies
University of California, Berkeley 94720

Library of Congress Cataloging in Publication Data

Wollenberg, Charles.
    Golden Gate metropolis.
    Bibliography: p.
    1. San Francisco Bay Area (Calif.)—History—Addresses, essays,
lectures. I. Title.
F868.S156W63   1985   979.4'61   84-12848
ISBN 0-87772-301-X

Design: Carolyn Sue Hughes
Production: Joan Lichterman

To my parents, Leah and Harold Wollenberg

Contents

Illustrations

Maps

Foreword

The Institute of Governmental Studies, established in 1919 and one of the oldest research units in the University of California, sponsors and conducts research on public policy, politics, urban-metropolitan problems, government, and public administration. Charles Wollenberg's book on Bay Area historical perspectives is an appropriate extension of the Institute's long interest in regional policy questions and the future of the San Francisco Bay Area.

In his opening remarks and Afterword, Wollenberg stresses the importance of a regional view, lamenting the fact that historians have not yet given adequate attention to the Bay Area's "shared social and economic conditions, and common experiences and lessons." Tracing the principal influences of the past can contribute to a fuller understanding of the contemporary scene and of what the future may bring. Wollenberg's book should aid newcomers and visitors as well as old-timers in seeing how the Bay Area came to be what it is— how topography and humanity, myth and reality, have blended in the peculiar amalgam of this unique, storied, and well-blessed region.

Stanley Scott
Editor

Acknowledgments

This book is the outcome of work jointly sponsored by Vista College and the Institute of Governmental Studies at UC Berkeley. It was an unusual cooperative planning effort involving a local community college and an arm of the University. An outline was prepared for a projected twenty-part television series on Bay Area history. Although funds for the series did not materialize, the Institute staff encouraged me to develop the outline into a series of historical essays, which form the substance of the book.

At Vista, I received valuable assistance from President John Holleman, Jerry Herman, the late Dick Ricca, and Beth Hackenbruch. At the University, Eugene C. Lee, director of the Institute, provided enthusiastic support and sage advice, as did Robert Peyton, also of the IGS staff. The manuscript was greatly improved by the painstaking editorial work of Stanley Scott, IGS assistant director, and Harriet Nathan and Joan Lichterman of the IGS editorial staff. Janice McCrear of the IGS publications staff performed heroic deeds in transferring my handwritten manuscript to the University computer. In addition, IGS publications coordinator Patricia Ramirez supervised the production effort and also did a substantial share of the computer work needed for successive proofs. IGS artist Carolyn Hughes worked diligently and creatively on the book's design and graphics.

I am also grateful to a small army of friends and scholars, including many already mentioned, who read and commented on all or parts of the manuscript at various stages of development. Richard Walker and T. J. Kent, Jr. made especially cogent criticisms and suggestions. I also greatly benefited from the thoughtful reviews of James Rawls, Richard Reinhardt, James Vance, Allan Jacobs, Mel Scott, Gunther Barth, Harold Gilliam, Gloria Bowles, Ted Bradshaw, Ora Huth, Neil Smelser, Wolf Homburger, Victor Jones, Tom Wolf, and Jacqueline and Harold Wollenberg. As always, the staff of the Bancroft Library efficiently rendered valuable assistance.

Another small army helped with production, providing advice or sifting through archives to enrich the book's visual presentation. Among the many others to be thanked are Harlan Kessel and Chet Grycz (UC Press), Jonathan Sharp (Chandler & Sharp Publishers), Malcolm Margolin (Heyday Books), Hansel Hagel, Fr. John B. McGloin, SJ, the Association of Bay Area Governments, CalTrans, the East Bay Municipal Utility District, the Bay Area Air Quality Control District, Judah L. Magnes Museum, UC's Lowie Museum of Anthropology, Pacific Aerial Surveys, the San Francisco Archives, San Francisco Arts Commission, the Santa Clara County Department of Planning and Development, Southern Pacific Transportation Company, the US Army Corps of Engineers/SF Bay Model in Sausalito, and the Wine Institute.

Charles Wollenberg

1 Golden Gate Metropolis

The Bay Area, 1868
The developed eastern section of San Francisco is portrayed larger than life, reflecting the city's dominance of the region at that time. Across the bay is the mouth of the Oakland Estuary, and behind it are the Oakland-Berkeley hills and Mt. Diablo. On the right, the San Francisco-San Jose railroad line makes its way down a foreshortened Peninsula. (Bancroft Library, UCB)

1

Golden Gate Metropolis _____

If I were king, I would declare a moratorium on the writing of individual city histories of San Francisco and other Bay Area municipalities. Instead, I would direct local scholars to concentrate on the region. This nine-county metropolitan area, stretching roughly from Santa Rosa on the north to Gilroy on the south, and from Antioch on the east to the Pacific Ocean on the west, encompasses nearly 7,000 square miles and more than 90 cities and towns. Its population of slightly over 5 million comprises the nation's fifth largest metropolitan region, more populous than most states of the union, or than many foreign countries. Its area is larger than that of the nation of Lebanon, or of the states of Connecticut and Rhode Island combined. Although the Bay Area is one of the world's great urban centers, it also includes several hundred thousand acres of wild park and watershed lands and about 2 million acres devoted to raising crops and livestock. In fact, the Bay Area produces more agricultural wealth than each of 14 states, including the "Garden State" of New Jersey.

In recent years, the Bay Area has developed a regional consciousness. There are several powerful regional governmental agencies that deal with such problems as bay fill, air and water pollution, and public transportation. But while the general public and even local politicians have gradually come to understand the regional nature of Bay Area life, historians continue to view the metropolis as a collection of separate communities, each with its own distinct past. Every year authors turn out still more books on the history of the city of San Francisco, and of other individual local communities, but the area's regional history is virtually ignored.

Lawrence Kinnaird's *History of the Greater San Francisco Bay Area* contains valuable information, but is primarily a factual history of the central city of San Francisco with little regional synthesis. Mel Scott's classic, *The San Francisco Bay Area, A Metropolis in Perspective,* is an excellent account of the physical development of the region, but does not attempt to cover the area's social or political history in any depth. Much the same can be said for James Vance's valuable interpretive study, *Geography and Urban Evolution in the San Francisco Bay Area.*

This volume is a collection of short essays on selected aspects of

Principal Place Names
(Carolyn Sue Hughes, from Vance, *Geography . . .*)

Bay Area history. Arranged in more or less chronological order, the essays concentrate primarily on the major population cores of San Francisco, the East Bay, and the Santa Clara Valley. Most of the essays are "present-minded"—using events and themes from the past to help explain current settlement patterns and social conditions. The book is not intended as a comprehensive regional history that gives detailed information on individual cities and prominent leaders. Nor does it attempt to assess the Bay Area's rich cultural heritage in art, literature, and music, or to place the region's past in the larger context of American urban development.

Instead, the aim is to present a number of useful perspectives on Bay Area history, demonstrating the value of studying the subject from a broad regional point of view. These essays should help residents see the main outlines of the history of the metropolis, and to understand how the growth of their particular communities fits into the larger scheme. It should also give nonresidents a clearer picture of the development of an important and fascinating urban region. Finally, the book should suggest to historians the rich potential that the field of regional metropolitan history offers for further research, writing, and interpretation.

□ □ □

2 The Environment's Impact

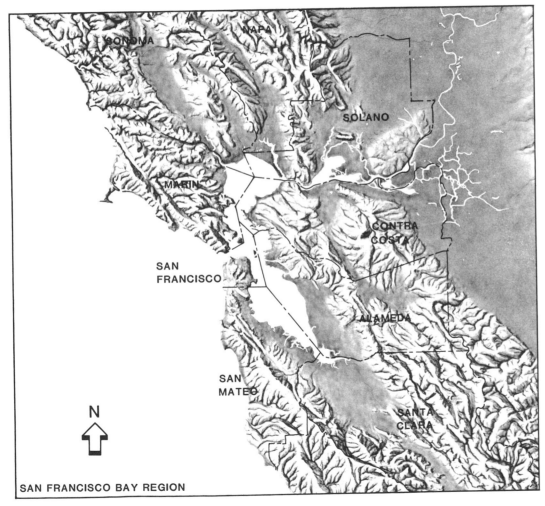

N

SAN FRANCISCO BAY REGION

Bay Area Topography
(Association of Bay Area Governments)

2

The Environment's Impact _____

Fifteen thousand years ago, barely yesterday on the geological time scale, San Francisco Bay did not exist. That was during the last ice age, when the world ocean level was 200 or 300 feet lower than today, and what is now the floor of San Francisco Bay was a series of dry valleys. Running through the northern portion of the valley system, the combined flow of the Sacramento-San Joaquin rivers emptied into the Pacific near the present-day Farallon Islands. Over hundreds of thousands of years, the rivers had carved three great gorges through the coastal mountains: the first at Carquinez Strait between what is now Vallejo and Crockett, the second at Raccoon Strait between Tiburon and Angel Island, and the third and largest at the Golden Gate. About 10,000 years ago, much of the world's ice cap began to melt, raising the ocean level, flooding the valleys, gorges, and rivers, and forming San Francisco Bay.

Significance of the Bay

The creation of the bay was to have an immense impact on the human history of this region. The bay is the region's principal and indeed defining geographical feature, and the piece of physical geography that has most affected the area's human development, from Indian times to the present. It is thus logical to begin this review of Bay Area historical geography with a discussion of the bay itself.

In 1850 the bay waters covered about 800 square miles at mean high tide, but today the bay is approximately 25 percent smaller than it was 130 years ago, primarily due to filling and diking of marshes and tidelands. Nevertheless it remains an impressive body of water. The volume of the daily tides through the Golden Gate is far greater than the average daily flow of the Mississippi River past New Orleans.

Strictly speaking, San Francisco Bay is not a single body of water, but an interconnected system of estuaries, including Suisun and San Pablo bays (an estuary is the meeting place of fresh and salt water). The main source of fresh water for San Francisco Bay is the combined Sacramento-San Joaquin rivers that merge at Antioch. The bay and its adjoining river and delta system occupy the only substantial gap in the otherwise solid wall of mountains that parallels the California coastline. Thus the Sacramento-San Joaquin river system drains a vast portion of interior California—including the agricultural heartland of the Central Valley, and the western slope of the Sierra Nevada. Nearly half the state's total annual surface water runoff flows through San Francisco Bay into the Pacific Ocean.

People have used the bay as a source of food, salt and other minerals, recreation, and, of course, as a major ocean port. It is, in fact, one of the world's great natural harbors, an attribute that attracted Spanish settlement in 1776. Equally important, the bay has also been a major river depot, providing a crucial water link between coastal and interior California before efficient land transportation was developed. When gold was discovered in the Sierra foothills, the bay-river system provided easy access to valley settlements such as Sacramento and Stockton, which were within a day's horseback ride of the diggings. When large-scale farming developed in the Central Valley, the harvests moved to international markets via the bay. In short, the Bay Area has been economically linked to the interior since the Gold Rush. In contrast, urban southern California developed, in Carey McWilliams' words, as an "island on the land," geographically cut off from the rest of the state by mountains on the north and deserts on the east. It is hardly surprising that Los Angeles' historical development is distinct from that of the rest of California. But largely because of the Bay Area's water access to the interior, its history is an integral part of the development of the whole of California.

Just as the bay helped connect the coast with the interior, it also linked the separate communities of the Bay Area to each other. San Francisco Bay was actually the region's first rapid transit route. By the 1860s an efficient ferryboat system already was in place, allowing the region to function as a single metropolitan unit very early in the process of its urban development. The ferries continued as important transit carriers until the 1930s, serving as agents of metropolitan regionalism for more than 70 years. Perhaps the bay's historical significance is best illustrated by the fact that even today more than 80 percent of the region's population lives on or near the narrow plain that surrounds the bay shore. Only in a few places, for example south San Jose or central Contra Costa County, are substantial population centers located more than what was once a short horse-and-buggy ride from San Francisco Bay.

The Hills

Although the bay has been the most important single geographical feature influencing the region's history, the hills have also played a significant role. Part of California's Coast Range Mountains, the highest summits of the Bay Area's "hills"—over 4,000 feet (Mt. St. Helena and Mt. Hamilton) and 3,800 feet (Mt. Diablo)—compare favorably with the elevation of Appalachian peaks. The Coast Range was a natural boundary between Bay Area and Central Valley Indian cultures. It was a major impediment to settlement during the Hispanic era. No Spanish missions were located east of the range, and the Mexican government was able to establish land grants in the interior valleys only in the final decade before the 1846 conquest by the United States.

Mt. Tamalpais, Marin County
(Mill Valley Public Library)

The hills continued to be formidable obstacles to transportation for the remainder of the 19th century. Only the invention of the cable car allowed urbanization of San Francisco's comparatively modest summits. Steam and later electric trains provided some access to the much higher elevations of Mt. Tamalpais, the Santa Cruz Mountains, and the Oakland-Berkeley hills, but in the 19th century construction of hillside homes and water systems was difficult and expensive. In many places it was impossible. This reinforced the tendency for the population to concentrate on the narrow bay plain. By the time automobiles, modern earth-moving equipment, and massive public water projects made hillside development possible, much of the region's highlands had been set aside for watershed, military reserves, and, increasingly in recent years, parklands. As a result, the Bay Area has much pleasant undeveloped open space situated very near the densely populated urban cores. But there are also tremendous development pressures on the bay plain and local valley floors, areas that contain some of the world's finest agricultural land. Particularly since World War II, much of it has been paved over for suburban housing tracts and the freeways and shopping centers that are their inevitable companions.

The Climate and Weather

The hills also profoundly influence the region's climate. Summer's intense heat in the Central Valley usually creates a low-pressure system over much of interior California, whereas along the coast the cool ocean waters and seasonal Pacific high-pressure zone keep the air heavy and moist. Since nature abhors a pressure differential, the cool, heavy coastal air is drawn inland, pushed along by prevailing northwesterly winds. Particularly in the evening hours, the damp coastal air condenses into clouds or fog, extending over San Francisco, into the bay, and often reaching the delta. But the higher hills pose fog barriers that are effective for most of a typical summer day. Thus summertime temperatures on the foggy western side of the coastal range can be 30 or 40 degrees cooler than those east of the summits. Even San Francisco's summer climate differs dramatically in the areas east and west of Twin Peaks. The foggiest western parts of the city were the last to be settled.

The more substantial elevations of the coastal hills in Marin and Sonoma counties, the East Bay, and on the Peninsula, are responsible for much greater temperature differences than are found in San Francisco. Further, the region's summer fog belt creates ideal growing conditions for artichokes and brussels sprouts along the San Mateo County coast, and provides moisture for the lush dairy pastures of western Marin and Sonoma. On the other hand, the hot, protected inland valleys are excellent sites for orchards and vineyards.

In the winter, however, the temperature differential is reversed, and the hills shield the inland valleys from the moderating climatic effect of the bay and ocean waters. Accordingly, just as the interior is warmer than the coast in the summer, it is cooler in the winter. The cold valley air often condenses into a thick, ground-hugging "tule fog" that frequently blankets the Central Valley, and may move through the bay towards the ocean. This winter fog has caused some of the Bay Area's greatest maritime disasters, and often creates monumental transportation difficulties in the Central Valley.

Rainfall and Water Supply

The hills play a similar role in distributing the region's winter rainfall. Although the Bay Area's Pacific storms usually originate in the

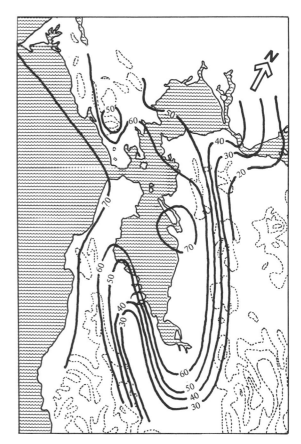

Summer Fog: Early Morning
Shows percent of time stratus cloud cover—the normal Bay Area "fog"—was observed at 2:30 a.m., in summer months. There is a striking pattern of widespread fog penetration. (Carolyn Sue Hughes, from Vance, *Geography . . .*)

Gulf of Alaska, the cyclonic, counterclockwise motion of the weather systems means that the storms tend to approach the mainland from the southwest. When the moisture-laden air is forced up and over the coastal hills, it cools and condenses into rain, which falls most heavily on the western slopes where the air rises most rapidly and cools fastest. This, by contrast, leaves the eastern slope as a rain shadow. Thus Ben Lomond, near the western summit of the Santa Cruz Mountains, averages more than 50 inches of rain per year, while San Jose, less than 20 miles to the east, receives under 15 inches annually.

In summer, all of the Bay Area, even the otherwise well-watered portions, suffers an annual six-month drought that characterizes most of California. During the summer months, the Pacific high-pressure system keeps Pacific storms to the north of California. This high usually dissipates in the fall, allowing the rains to return. Because of this seasonal weather pattern, the Bay Area gets more than 90 percent of its rainfall between the beginning of November and the end of April. Occasionally, when the high fails to dissipate, e.g., in 1976-77, the drought can continue into the winter as well.

In any event, fog ameliorates the summer drought on the west side of the coastal range, allowing redwoods, firs, and other coastal conifers to survive the dry months on "fog drip." But there is no respite east of the range, where tinder-dry grasslands and chaparral are prime candidates for fierce summer fires.

The annual summer drought makes the Bay Area a semiarid region, in fact the first such region in which Americans built a major city. Since the Gold Rush, development of water systems has been the key to Bay Area life. By the 1930s, when the Hetch Hetchy and East Bay Municipal Utility District systems were completed, the area was no longer able to survive on its own local water supplies and has increasingly tapped Sierra Nevada watersheds. The area's aqueducts flow from the Tuolumne, Mokelumne, American, and Sacramento rivers, and divert water from the delta. These great plumbing systems are the region's lifelines. Consequently Bay Area residents who self-righteously complain about southern California's diversions of Sacramento-San Joaquin delta water are hardly in a position to cast the first stone.

Earthquake Faults

In addition to its bay, topography, and hydrologic patterns, the Bay Area is well endowed with earthquake faults. The great San Andreas fault system passes through Tomales Bay and the Olema Valley in Marin, before crossing the Golden Gate west of the bridge. It puts ashore again near Lake Merced in southwestern San Francisco and continues into the San Mateo County spine, through Crystal Springs lakes and into the Santa Cruz Mountains west of San Jose. The region also

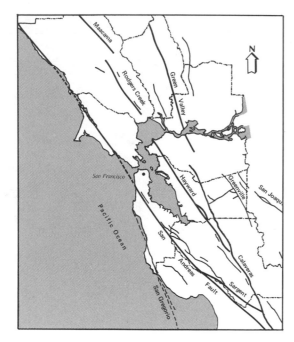

Principal Known Earthquake Faults
(Carolyn Sue Hughes, from a map by Darrel G. Herd, USGS)

has many other active fault zones, including the Hayward, along the base of the Oakland-Berkeley hills, and the Calaveras, in central Contra Costa County. The founders of the University of California's Berkeley campus and of Stanford University managed to locate both campuses squarely astride major earthquake faults. While proximity to an active fault can increase hazards, especially if structures actually cross a fault, no part of the region is safe from severe earthquake effects.

Several great Bay Area earthquakes have been recorded in historical times, but the 1906 San Francisco quake on the San Andreas fault is justly famous, having occurred after the region had been substantially urbanized. It was probably the greatest natural disaster experienced by a major American metropolitan region, and it also was a significant historical event, altering settlement patterns and even contributing to political changes. Geologists expect another earthquake of 1906 proportions to hit the region sometime during the next hundred years, and damaging quakes of lesser intensity are even more likely to occur. We still do far too little to prepare for serious earthquakes. Meanwhile life goes on, with a seismic clock ticking beneath our feet.

Assessing the Environment's Impact

Bay and hills, fog and rain, drought and earthquake—these are some characteristics of the Bay Area that have affected the region's human history. This chapter has looked at the "environmental impact" of our natural surroundings on human beings, rather than vice-versa. Perhaps one of the most difficult influences to assess is the effect of the region's geography on the minds of its residents. Bay Area Indians lived intimately with nature, and the landscape, wildlife, and climate affected every part of their religion and world view. Beginning in 1776, however, the region was increasingly dominated by people whose European-derived culture and values emphasized the need to exploit and control nature.

Since the Gold Rush, the Bay Area environment has been exploited and controlled with a vengeance. Nevertheless an appreciation for the beauty and significance of the natural environment has remained an important part of the regional culture. Perhaps the very pace of environmental change and destruction produced a strong conservation ethic among many 19th century Bay Area writers, artists, and teachers. John Muir found plenty of support when he established the Sierra Club in San Francisco in 1892. A few years later, Bernard Maybeck spoke for many Bay Area architects when he advocated building with nature rather than against it.

Poet Gary Snyder recently said that "Sometime in the last ten years the best brains of the Occident discovered to their amazement that we live in an Environment." This may be true for some parts of the "Occident," but not for the Bay Area, where contemporary environmental activism has a long heritage. It is fitting that novelist Ernest Callenbach made San Francisco the capital of his fictional environmentally utopian society, "Ecotopia." The late Terry Russell was expressing an ideal of Bay Area environmentalists, from Indian times to the present, when he said:

> We fear what we don't know:
> I know what the hills are there for and they
> know me.

□ □ □

3 First People

Mural Depicting Bay Area Indians in a Reed Boat
(San Francisco Arts Commission, Rincon Annex Post Office Murals, by Anton
Refregier, 1941, 1945-49)

3

First
People _____

The Bay Area's first inhabitants had at least one thing in common
with the region's current residents: they dumped their garbage on
the shores of San Francisco Bay. Anthropologists have identified more
than 400 bayside "shell mounds," Native American refuse piles, composed partly of shellfish remains. More sites undoubtedly existed, but
have been covered or removed by urban development. One of the largest mounds was in Emeryville, near the mouth of Temescal Creek,
measuring 40 feet deep, 270 feet in diameter at the base. For many
years it served as centerpiece of Shellmound Park, a private amusement
ground and dog-racing track. Eventually the park was abandoned and
the mound leveled to make way for an industrial site.

Evidence of the Shellmounds

To anthropologists, refuse piles such as the shellmounds are valuable sources of information about the ways of life of the people whose wastes are dumped there. University of California scholars studying the Ellis Point mound near Richmond concluded that it had been used continuously for at least 3,000 years, and noted subtle changes in toolmaking techniques and diet over the centuries. A modern historian accustomed to rapid change, however, may be surprised at how little material change there was in the lives of the mound users. The people inhabiting the shores of San Francisco Bay at the time that the Greeks were fighting the Trojan War, 1,000 years before the birth of Christ, apparently lived in much the same way as the native inhabitants at the time the Spanish settled here in 1776. For 30 centuries or more, Bay Area residents remained nonagricultural hunters and food gatherers, living in subtribal groups.

A remarkably successful adaptation to the Bay Area's natural environment underlay this cultural stability. Indian legends suggest that local Native Americans understood the principles of agriculture. Some local groups may have even cultivated small plots of native tobacco. But agriculture was not used for food production, probably because it was not needed. People gathered shellfish and caught salmon from the bay; they hunted rabbit, deer, antelope, elk, and a great variety of birds;

they dug edible roots and gathered a host of different berries, nuts, and greens. They ate insects and small rodents, and occasionally feasted on the blubber of whales washed up on the beaches. Acorn meal was an essential part of the native diet, the acorns being harvested and carefully stored as if they were a cultivated crop. Acorn grinding rocks and stone mortars and pestles were essentials in any Indian settlement. Given the mild climate, low population density, and tremendous variety of food sources, active cultivation was simply unnecessary.

The Major Groups: Miwok and Costanoan

At the time of Spanish settlement, there were two major Native American groups in the Bay Area: the Costanoan (or Ohlone) and the Coast Miwok. The Costanoan people, numbering about 10,000 in 1776, occupied the area from central San Francisco Bay south to Monterey Bay, including what is now San Francisco, San Mateo, Santa Clara, Alameda, and much of Contra Costa counties. Because they were a coastal people, the Spaniards called them *Costanos,* from which "Costanoan" is derived. (Some authorities, however, prefer "Ohlone," the native name of one of the region's Indian villages.)

The Coast Miwok, numbering about 3,000, are not to be confused with other Miwok people who lived in interior California. The coastal

Native American Villages
(Carolyn Sue Hughes, based on Kroeber, *Handbook of the Indians of California*)

branch of the Miwok family occupied much of the North Bay, including Marin and parts of Sonoma and Napa counties. In addition to the two major groups, other Indian cultures touched the Bay Area. Thus the Wintun and Yokut peoples of the Central Valley occupied parts of Solano and eastern Contra Costa counties, and the Wappo and Pomo of the Clear Lake area also ranged into parts of Napa and Sonoma. All told, in 1776 probably 15,000-20,000 native people lived in the nine Bay Area counties.

The Miwoks and Costanoans were not "tribes" in the sense of being well-defined social and political units. They were cultural groups, identified primarily by common or closely related languages. The social and political basis of Bay Area Indian life was a few hundred people occupying one or two villages in a well-defined hunting and gathering territory. Within the broad Miwok and Ohlone cultures, there were scores of such subgroups.

The headman, whose office was inherited, was usually the major village political figure. But his authority was limited by the need to obtain consent on major decisions from important people in the village, and by the potent force of tradition, which even the most powerful individual could not violate. Bay Area Indian societies tried, with apparent success, to resolve or reduce individual conflict and to promote joint cooperation and a sense of community. Within the villages there were strict divisions of labor and cultural role assignments, based on sex, age, strength, and skill. Moreover all were supposed to be working for a common goal, the survival and comfort of the group. The worst punishment was banishment, for that meant the individual lost his essential identification with "the People."

Village groups often fought each other, but conflict was usually limited in scope and damage. No Bay Area Indian cultures bothered to develop weapons *per se*. Instead they fought with hunting implements, sticks, stones, and barrages of well-chosen insults and expletives. People of neighboring villages might cooperate in joint hunts and ceremonies, and also intermarry. Trade between groups was common, and trade networks extended throughout California, with goods passing from village to village.

A "Stone Age" People

The Bay Area natives were "Stone Age" people, only in the narrow sense that they used natural materials to make a variety of ingenious tools, hunting and fishing implements, and household goods. During warm months everyday clothing was sparse, even nonexistent, but abundant clothing was often worn in cool and wet weather. Ceremonial costumes were elaborate. Community buildings—the ceremonial round houses and the sweat houses that were the special preserve of adult

Costanoan Basket, Circa 1800
(de Saisset Museum, University of Santa Clara, from the collection of the Department of Anthropology, Smithsonian Institution; photograph © 1984 by Glenn Matsumura)

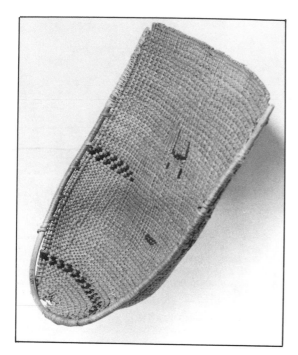

Costanoan Basket, pre-1900s
Basket used in removing chaff from wheat. A distinctive Costanoan "hidden design" is created by changes in the weaving pattern, forming two subtle and hard-to-see diamond shapes in the flattened part of this basket. (Lowie Museum of Anthropology, UCB)

men, for example—were constructed of large branches covered with mud and rocks, and often dug a few feet into the ground. Families built small, practical thatch houses for their personal use, and during rainy months these dwellings might be covered with rabbit-skin blankets to provide additional warmth and weatherproofing. When a house became too smelly or lice-filled, the family burned it and quickly built a replacement. The thatch construction was well suited to earthquake country: a whole house could collapse on its inhabitants without causing injury.

Like most California Indians, native peoples in the Bay Area were expert makers of all sizes and manner of baskets. Baskets were so tightly woven they could hold water, and even were used for cooking, hot rocks being inserted in a basket full of acorn mush or stew. The baskets became outlets for artistic creativity, and the weavers, usually women, decorated their handicraft with elaborate designs. The baskets also served as containers for every conceivable item, and were used as hats and clothing. With their extensive range of basketry, Bay Area Indians had no need to develop pottery. In a sense, even Indian boats were large baskets: they were canoes made of woven reed and thatch, propelled by double-edged paddles.

The native religions emphasized the close relationship between human beings and their natural surroundings that underlay the whole Indian way of life. Animals and landmarks had divine status. There were complex ceremonies for various stages of life, and a whole range of taboos and forbidden activities. The priests or shamans were often also doctors or healers. Each village had a large body of oral literature—tales, legends, and historic and religious myths—that was carefully passed from generation to generation.

The traditions preserved by this literature were essential to native California culture. Continuity and custom were important cultural values in a world where little or no observable change might occur in an individual's entire lifetime. A north coast Indian legend tells of Earth-maker and Great Grandfather creating the world and teaching the First People language and rituals, hunting and fishing techniques, how to make houses, tools and boats, the boundaries of their territory, and all the other things that go to make "The Way." Since then, since the beginning of the world and the time of those First People, nothing has changed. The legend is thus based on a theory of history that, in effect, denies the occurrence of significant change. If the evidence of the shellmounds is correct, that theory was consistent with the experience of countless generations of Bay Area native peoples.

A Disastrous Clash of Cultures

The very slow pace of change, the fact that California Indian cultures had little understanding of the concept of "progress," is one reason why the state's native people have so often been described as "primitive." Certainly the Bay Area Indians were primitives, if by this one means a nonagricultural, hunting and gathering people with no written language or monumental architecture. This definition is based on reasonably precise material criteria. But problems arise when we also assign other values to such words as "primitive," so that they carry connotations like "backward," "underdeveloped," "lowly," or "inferior." If "civilized" individuals are supposed to be intelligent, polite, and sophisticated, "primitive" people may be considered oafish and crude, and primitive cultures may be thought of as having less worth or virtue than those that are more highly civilized.

These kinds of value-laden, culture-bound, and self-serving assessments of the "primitive" nature of the Bay Area Indians and their way of life are themselves important parts of the region's history. The Spaniards used such thinking to justify their attempt to destroy native culture and convert Indians to Christianity. The Mexican *rancheros* used it to justify the employment of forced Indian labor as part of the "civilizing" process. The Anglo-Americans, in turn, used it to rationalize the physical removal of native peoples as an inevitable requirement of "progress."

But European-style "civilization" and "progress" proved disastrous for the Bay Area's first people. Entire cultures were destroyed in a remarkably short time. For California as a whole, the Indian population fell from 300,000 in 1776 to only about 20,000 in 1900. The major cause of this devastating decline was not warfare or murder, though these certainly took place. Rather, the effects of European diseases, and the resulting disintegration of traditional native values and institutions, were the principal causes. In the Bay Area the decline of the Indian population was even more drastic than in California as a whole.

In 1850 the United States Indian agent was able to find only one native inhabitant of San Francisco, an old man who explained, "I am all that is left of my people—I am alone." In other parts of the Bay Area, more people of Costanoan blood survived, and even prospered, but they did not perpetuate the native culture. The last speaker of an Ohlone language died in 1935, and there seem to be only a very few authentic Costanoan baskets left. In the less densely populated areas of the North Bay, however, more of the Indian way of life has survived, particularly among the Pomo people.

Today, the Bay Area probably has twice the Native American population it had in 1776, but the great majority of present-day Indian residents have migrated here from elsewhere in the United States. After World War II, the Bureau of Indian Affairs encouraged people from reservations throughout the western US to resettle in cities such as Oakland and San Francisco. Some of the new arrivals successfully made the difficult transition from reservation to urban life, but many others did not. Indians remain among the most economically impover-

Pomo Indian in Dance Regalia, with Bird-Bone Whistle, 1931
(Lowie Museum of Anthropology, UCB)

ished and socially deprived of the region's ethnic minorities. The 1969 Native American occupation of Alcatraz was a symbolic protest against two centuries of accumulated grievances, but few if any of the participants were Ohlone or Miwok.

The world might be a better place if the distinctions between "primitive" and "civilized" cultures were seen as differences in kind, rather than in quality and virtue. Latter-day Social Darwinists may argue that the terrible fate of the Bay Area native cultures simply demonstrates that they were not up to competition with the more vigorous peoples who came after 1776. But if real Darwinian "survival-of-the-fittest" is the final test, a lesson of the shellmounds is also worth noting: "primitive" native cultures lasted more than 3,000 years on the shores of San Francisco Bay, while our western "civilization" has so far survived here barely 200 years. Robinson Jeffers probably expressed the lesson best in his poem "Hands":

> Inside a cave in a narrow canyon near Tassajara
> The vault of rock is painted with hands,
> A multitude of hands in the twilight, a cloud of men's palms, no
> > more,
> No other picture. There's no one to say
> Whether the brown shy quiet people who are dead intended
> Religion or magic, or made their tracings

In the idleness of art; but over the division of years these careful
Signs-manual are now like a sealed message
Saying: "Look: we also were human; we had hands, not paws.
        All hail
You people with the cleverer hands, our supplanters
In the beautiful country; enjoy her a season, her beauty, and
        come down
And be supplanted; for you also are human."

□ □ □

4 Missions and Presidios

Father Narciso Durán with an Indian Child
Durán, administrator of Mission San Jose, was one of the ablest Franciscan missionaries, and his mission was the Bay Area's most economically productive. (Bancroft Library, UCB)

4

Missions
and
Presidios_____

In 1769 Captain Gaspar de Portolá and Father Junípero Serra led a joint military-religious expedition to California, with orders to establish settlements in San Diego and Monterey. After founding a mission and presidio in San Diego, Portolá and a small group of men set off on foot to find Monterey. Unfortunately, they walked right past their intended destination, and on November 2, 1769 found themselves on what today is Sweeney Ridge, in Pacifica. When members of the expedition crossed to the eastern slope, to their surprise they saw a vast body of water stretching out below them. By this fortuitous accident, Spaniards "discovered" San Francisco Bay. For more than two centuries before Portolá's expedition European ships had been sailing along the California coast, but with the possible exception of the British pirate and navigator Francis Drake in 1579, apparently none of the sailors had noticed the great estuary. This is not surprising given the seasonal fogs, the configuration of the coastline, and the narrowness of the Golden Gate. But Captain Portolá undoubtedly would be the first to testify that San Francisco Bay is mighty hard to miss on foot.

Portolá's accidental find ultimately was also to mark an imperial dead end for Spain in America. The Bay Area was as far north as Spanish settlement ever got in the New World, and just a half century after the Portolá expedition Mexico won its independence, ending Spanish rule in California. The history of the first Hispanic settlers around San Francisco Bay is thus little more than a footnote to the three-century epoch of Spanish colonization in the Americas. Nevertheless the Bay Area missions and presidios provide a microcosm of Spanish imperialism, an excellent case study of Spain's colonial theory and practice.

Spanish Imperialism

Spanish colonial concepts differed greatly from those of the English in New England. Spain sent only a small number of colonists to occupy California, whereas tens of thousands of English eventually settled in Massachusetts. New Englanders worked the land themselves, having little use for the native inhabitants, while Spanish colonists expected to be a small master class, living off the labor of a large native workforce. Spain did not intend to wipe out Bay Area Indians or pen them up in reservations. Instead, the success of Spanish colonies would depend on the native peoples' fitting into a European economic, social, and political system.

In "civilized" parts of Indian America—e.g., Central Mexico or the highlands of Peru—the Europeanization process was simplified by the fact that the Spanish could establish themselves at the top of a functioning system. Indians were living in agricultural settlements and were already part of complex economic and political structures. By contrast, however, the entire California Indian way of life had to be changed. The Spanish had to transform hunters and gatherers into farmers, herdsmen, and craftsmen. Members of fairly egalitarian tribal societies had to be made into subjects of a vast authoritarian empire.

In California the chief instrument of the transformation was the mission. The religious convictions of most Franciscan friars were undoubtedly sincere, as was their commitment to converting Indians to Christianity. While attempting to convert Indians, however, the friars were also serving the Spanish government's purpose of transforming native peoples into useful subjects. As part of this process, the missions were political and economic institutions, as well as religious communities. Today, all that is usually left of the missions is the restored church or chapel. But the mission establishments also included dormi-

California Missions
The dashed line indicates the route of "El Camino Real," the largely unimproved trail that linked the missions. The thin solid line running along the edge of the Sierra foothills indicates partial mission influence. The missions' full influence did not reach beyond the western edge of the Central Valley. The map also shows presidios and pueblos of the Spanish era, as well as Fort Ross, the Russian settlement. (Carolyn Sue Hughes, based on Donley, et al., *Atlas of California*)

Fort Ross

San Francisco Solano

San Rafael Arcángel
San Francisco Presidio
San Francisco de Asís

San José de Guadalupe
San José Pueblo
Santa Clara de Asís

Santa Cruz
San Juan Bautista
Monterey Presidio
San Carlos Borromeo
de Carmelo
Nuestra Señora de la Soledad

San Antonio de Padua

San Miguel Arcángel

San Luis Obispo
de Tolosa

Santa Inés
Virgen y Martir
La Purísima Concepción
San Buenaventura
Santa Barbara
Santa Bárbara Presidio
San Fernando
Rey de España
San Gabriel
Arcángel
Los Angeles Pueblo

San Juan Capistrano
San Luis Rey de Francia

San Diego de Alcalá
San Diego Presidio

tories, barns, shops, and stables. At Mission San Jose, for example, such buildings occupied a 50-acre plot adjacent to the chapel. In short, the friars operated institutions that were the economic and political heart of Spanish California, as well as its religious soul.

The presidio was the inevitable companion of the mission. Although Spain established only four formal presidios or forts in California, soldiers always accompanied the friars. Each mission had a small military garrison to protect the community from Indian raids and rebellion, and to enforce the friars' rule over the mission neophytes. The garrison was under the ultimate command of the nearest presidio. In the Bay Area, this was the San Francisco Presidio. The soldiers had the added duty of defending the colony against foreign enemies, and the military commanders also served as local civil authorities.

The Spanish government had used the mission-presidio combination to pacify and hispanicize several Latin American frontiers, and the system was two centuries old by the time it reached the Bay Area. In theory, the system would eventually self-destruct, for at some point the native population would become indistinguishable from the other lower-class Spanish imperial subjects, and the colony would no longer need the special talents of mission friars and presidio soldiers. In California, the Spanish government intended for this to occur after only 10 years, but in fact, the mission-presidio system was still going strong at the time of Mexican independence in 1821.

Exploration and Settlement

Portolá's successor as military commander in California, Pedro Fages, twice explored the eastern shore of San Francisco Bay, in 1770 and 1772. In 1775, Juan Manuel Ayala sailed the first Spanish ship through the Golden Gate and made an extensive survey of the estuary. Reports of the expeditions impressed the viceroy in Mexico City. Juan Bautista de Anza, a frontier military officer, was then preparing to lead about 240 colonists and assorted livestock and supplies on a remarkable trek from northwestern Mexico to California. The viceroy ordered Anza to establish settlements around the bay. He finished his 1,500-mile trip in 1776 and, leaving most of the settlers in southern California and Monterey, proceeded to San Francisco Bay. As a soldier, Anza first sought a strategic location for defending the bay from foreign attack. One logical place was a mesa on the northern tip of the San Francisco Peninsula, commanding the entrance to the estuary. This was where Anza founded the San Francisco Presidio in June of 1776, and it has remained on the site ever since.

With the presidio located on the west side of the bay, it made sense for the first mission in the region to be nearby. Anza picked a site about three miles south of the presidio, along the banks of a creek called Arroyo de Dolores. The soil and climate were better than those at the presidio, and the creek and a nearby lagoon provided adequate fresh water for the mission's needs. Father Serra formally named the new mission after St. Francis of Assisi, but from the beginning it was popularly known as Mission Dolores. In 1777, the governor at Monterey chose sites for Mission Santa Clara and for the pueblo or civil town of San Jose at the south end of the bay. Both settlements experienced minor location changes due to flooding, but they eventually prospered in the Santa Clara Valley's fertile soil and pleasant climate. In the 1790s, Indians from the mission linked the two settlements with a tree-lined road that still is known as the Alameda.

Not until 1797 did colonial authorities establish a settlement on the eastern shore of the bay. This was Mission San Jose, located in what is now the city of Fremont. It eventually became the most successful of the Bay Area missions, but at the time it was founded, the east side of the bay was already called *Contra Costa,* a term meaning "opposite" or "other" shore. Use of the term implied that the western side of the bay was *the shore,* the place of greatest significance and prestige. In a sense the East Bay has suffered from a "contra costa" syndrome ever since, and relations between residents of the two sides of the bay are still affected by settlement patterns and images dating from two centuries ago.

The governor at Monterey did not recognize the need to settle the north shore of the bay until after 1812, when the Russian American Fur Company established settlements at Fort Ross and Bodega Bay, along the Sonoma County coastline. The Russian colony was primarily a business venture rather than a territorial claim, but Hispanic authorities feared a possible Russian advance toward San Francisco Bay. The establishment of Mission San Rafael in 1817, and Mission San Francisco Solano (Sonoma) in 1823, thus in part represented a "defensive expansion" to protect the Bay Area's northern flank. The friars also intended these missions to serve as hospitals for sick neophytes from Mission Dolores. The San Rafael Mission was the northernmost advance of Spanish-era settlement in the New World, and the Sonoma Mission was the only one established during the Mexican period, which began in 1821.

The Missions and the Indians

By 1823, there were seven Hispanic settlements around the bay, five of them missions. This indicates the missions' importance in the Spanish colonial scheme, and their key role in establishing and maintaining the Hispanic way of life in the Bay Area. Theoretically, the friars were to persuade Indians to come to the missions, rather than force them. During the early years, at least, the Franciscans acted in accord with this principle, engaging in tremendous recruiting efforts. Gradually the neophyte population grew, and by the early 19th century, five or six thousand Indians lived and worked in Bay Area missions. Once an Indian was baptized and took up residence, all pretense of voluntarism ceased. The missions were designed as authoritarian institutions where friars gave orders and Indians obeyed. If necessary, soldiers enforced the friars' authority.

Mural of Farming and Preaching at Mission Dolores
(San Francisco Arts Commission, Rincon Annex Post Office Murals, by Anton Refregier, 1941, 1945-49)

Inevitably, some of the neophytes rebelled, and running away was the most common form of protest. Garrison soldiers spent a good deal of time tracking down escapees, as the friars wanted to avoid a precedent of easy escape, and because runaways were sometimes the most dangerous Indians. They had learned European ways, including a taste for beef and a desire for other Spanish products. Sometimes they also adopted "civilized" methods of warfare, including use of horses and firearms. The most famous Bay Area Indian rebel was Estanislao, a runaway from Mission San Jose. In the 1820s his band of men carried out a number of daring raids on Bay Area missions and ranchos, before finally being subdued by a force led by Mariano Guadalupe Vallejo. Stanislaus County and the Stanislaus River are both named for this mission-Indian rebel. Whether seen as a brave freedom fighter or as a cruel bandido, he was by no means unique as an Indian who resisted Hispanic rule.

In addition to Indian resistance, there was also Indian compliance and cooperation, without which the missions would not have survived. At a typical mission, two friars and perhaps a half-dozen soldiers were in charge of 1,000 or more Indians. The friars created a force of Indian middle managers, overseers, and foremen, who directly supervised mission activities and communicated the friars' orders to the neophytes. (Estanislao occupied such a position before leaving the flock, so the friars may sometimes have promoted leadership potential that came back to haunt them.) In any event the loyal Indian overseers were essential to the missions' success, and many of the neophytes developed affection for the friars and became devout Christians.

Indian rebelliousness seemed to increase as the Indian population declined. As disease reduced the mission Indian population, the workload of the remaining neophytes inevitably increased. Perhaps this led to greater dissatisfaction and a greater likelihood of rebellion. While the Spanish certainly did not wish to decimate the Bay Area natives, European diseases took a terrible toll, as happened everywhere in the Americas. The friars may have increased the effect of the diseases by gathering Indians into close proximity with whites, interfering with traditional Indian sanitary practices such as daily bathing, and enforcing other drastic cultural changes that may have reduced the will to live.

Mission Dolores was a particularly disease-ridden community. In 1816 a measles epidemic killed 234 neophytes, and a similar outbreak in 1824 caused even more deaths. The Indians also suffered greatly from smallpox and venereal disease. In 1818 the mission had 1,500 neophytes; five years later the number was down to 230. As we have seen, San Rafael and Sonoma were established as hospital missions for sick Indians from San Francisco, and in those sunnier and more fertile locations the death rate seems to have been lower. But inept administration of the Sonoma Mission produced an Indian uprising in 1826.

As noted earlier, the most successful Bay Area mission was San Jose, in present-day Fremont. During its 37 years of operation it achieved over 8,000 conversions, the second highest total of all 21 California missions. It led northern California missions in the production of wheat, corn, beans, and fruit, and by the 1820s, ran more than 20,000 head of livestock. For most of its history, Father Narciso Durán, ablest of Bay Area friars, administered Mission San Jose. Durán not only supervised the economic and religious life of the community, but also wrote church music and conducted an Indian orchestra, some of whose instruments were made in the mission shops. Yet even Mission San Jose suffered from outbreaks of disease, and Estanislao was Durán's most famous neophyte.

Despite their problems, and the tragic decimation of the Indians, the Bay Area missions effectively played their assigned role in the Spanish colonial plan. In a remarkably short time, thousands of hunting and gathering people were transformed into agricultural workers, herdsmen, and, in some cases, people who were adept at skilled European crafts. Their labor formed the basis of the colonial economy and allowed California to become a self-sufficient unit within the Spanish Empire.

The End of Spanish Rule

The presidios were also successful in their assigned role. The soldiers effectively enforced discipline at the missions, and were able to control if not prevent raids on Spanish settlements. The presidios also proved effective deterrents to European invasion, although their actual ability to resist such attack was minimal at best. In 1806, for example, when a Russian ship entered the bay and fired a friendly salute, the Presidio soldiers had to row out to the ship to borrow the powder needed to fire a polite reply. Despite this evidence of Spanish California's military limitations, the Russian settlements established five years later were carefully located north of the line of actual Spanish occupation. The Presidio's presence meant that foreign settlement on the bay itself would involve an exchange of shots, and thus an act of war that could activate vast alliance systems. The San Francisco Presidio was thus a trip-wire to general European war, and foreign powers did not consider the region worth the risk of such an eventuality.

Spanish rule was ended not by foreign invasion or Indian revolt, but by the Age of Revolution that swept the Western World in the late 18th and early 19th centuries. The United States declared its independence the same year that Juan Bautista de Anza established the San Francisco presidio and mission. Thirteen years later an even greater revolution erupted in France. Another decade later the Napoleonic Wars began, and by 1810 Latin America's wars for independence were under way. In 1821, after a decade of civil strife, Mexico declared its freedom from Spain, ending the Spanish era in Bay Area history.

The Spanish era may seem unimpressive from the perspective of the late 20th century. Spanish settlements in the Bay Area consisted of only four missions, one presidio, one pueblo, a few hundred Spanish-speaking residents, and a few thousand mission Indians. But the influence was profound. Spanish imperialism in the Bay Area meant the introduction of agriculture, livestock, the use of metals, woven cloth, sail power, and the wheel. It also brought European religion, language, philosophy, and world view. Finally, it began the very rapid decline and extinction of thousands of years of Bay Area Indian life. While the Spanish fully intended to destroy Indian religion and culture, the missions and presidios also brought about an unintended, precipitous decline of the native population—in effect, the virtual destruction of the Indians themselves. Those tiny Spanish settlements caused the most drastic change in the human history of the Bay Area.

□ □ □

5 Ranchos and Pueblos

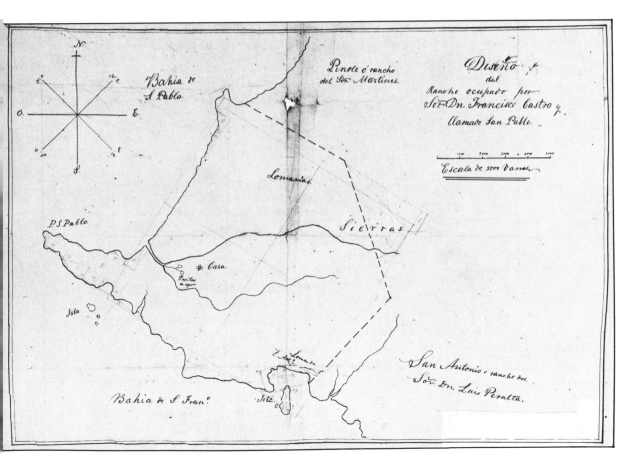

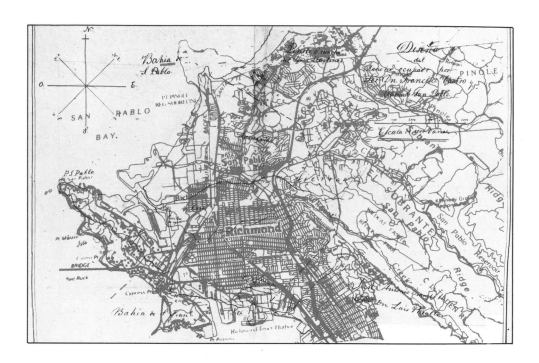

Rancho San Pablo
This rough map or diseño of Rancho San Pablo has been overlaid on a modern map to show how the Castro family's property included territory presently occupied by the cities of Richmond and San Pablo. Adjoining the Castro property were Rancho Pinole and Rancho San Antonio, owned by the Martínez and Peralta families, respectively. These three ranchos covered substantial portions of today's Contra Costa and Alameda counties. The map was used in the San Antonio land grant case litigated for 25 years in US District Court. (Bancroft Library, UCB)

5

Ranchos and Pueblos

While California may have been officially a colony of Spain until 1821, functionally it was attached to Mexico. Political decisions came from the viceroy in Mexico City, not the King in Madrid, and California's economic links with the rest of the Hispanic world were via the Mexican port of San Blas. Except for the Franciscan friars, most of the "Spanish" settlers were in fact natives of Mexico, usually of lower class and of mixed racial and ethnic origins. As long as Mexico and California were both part of the Spanish empire, this caused no problems. After Mexican independence, however, California had no way of maintaining a separate tie with Spain, and the province logically became a part of the new Mexican nation, remaining so until the American conquest in 1846. There were substantial social and economic changes in

Spain (1769–1821)

mexico (1821–1846)

Bay Area life during those 25 years, the most important being the entry and growing influence of English-speaking foreigners.

The Californios

A new generation of California Hispanic residents had come of age by 1821, with only an abstract allegiance to the Spanish crown and with little knowledge of Mexico. Chaotic conditions in Mexico City after independence, and the autocratic methods of the new national government, further weakened any loyalty that the Californians might have developed for the new Mexican nation. The Spanish crown had at least been a symbol of authority and legitimacy. No similar symbol took its place. California's Spanish-speaking residents began to think of themselves as *Californios,* a home-grown aristocracy whose loyalty was owed to its own local interests and territory, rather than to Mexico. No matter how humble their social origins, the Californios were the founding fathers and mothers of the Hispanic way of life in the province. Although willing to give formal allegiance to the new Mexican nation, by 1821 they were also ready to assume effective leadership in California.

Like most 19th century Hispanic-American elites, the Californios wished to control the local land and labor. Their chances of achieving this were enhanced when the Mexican Congress passed the Colonialization Act of 1824, authorizing governors of frontier provinces like California to make free grants of unoccupied land to worthy residents. In some respects, the Colonialization Act was a Mexican forerunner of the United States Homestead Act. In both cases, the aim was to promote economic development and population growth. But American laws restricted land grants to no more than 160 acres, while the Mexican act allowed allocations as large as 11 square leagues, or nearly 50,000 acres. The grantee had only to build a house and put the land to some use, such as cattle grazing, to receive the property free and clear.

Although amended many times after 1824, the Colonialization Act continued to provide a way for Californio families to acquire vast amounts of land. The Franciscan missions, however, controlled most of the promising territory in the settled areas of Hispanic California—the coastal plains and valleys from San Francisco Bay to San Diego. The missions also virtually monopolized the province's chief labor force, the neophyte Indians. Clearly, the missions stood in the way of the Californios' ambitions.

Secularization

We have seen that even under Spanish colonial theory, the missions were to be phased out when frontier conditions were a thing of the past. The friars' position was further weakened by Mexican independence and the production of liberal constitutions that—theoretically at least—gave citizenship to Indians and separated church and state. Under these circumstances, the Californios argued, the government no longer could justify Franciscan control of the Indian neophytes and of the best land in the settled parts of the province. The Mexican Congress responded by "secularizing" the missions in 1833: providing that the friars could retain the mission chapels and serve as parish priests, but stripping the missionaries of all authority over the Indians and all control over mission lands.

Governor José Figueroa issued an implementation decree that allowed about half the mission lands and most of the system's other assets to remain with the former neophytes, to be owned and worked communally as in Mexico's Indian villages. The remainder of the land was immediately available for colonization grants.

Figueroa appointed influential Californios to administer the secularization process at each mission, and to protect the rights of the new Indian citizens. Obviously, however, the Californios had a conflict of interest, as they stood to gain from diminution of Indian rights. Moreover even if the administrators took their jobs seriously, it was hard to protect the Indians' interests. The missions had taught the neophytes to follow the friars' orders, rather than to act like self-reliant citizens of a European society. Many Indians must have also preferred to return to their old hunting and food-gathering way of life. Others were easily swindled out of their land. Still others simply died, continuing victims of disease, as well as of social and cultural dislocation. Thus for a variety of reasons, the Indians soon lost control of any significant share of the former mission land. By 1846 virtually all such property in the Bay Area was included in private land grants.

Some of the mission Indians passed with the land into the hands of Californio masters, becoming workers on the new estates. If the former neophytes had been baptized, spoke Spanish, and wore European clothes, they were indistinguishable from *peones* throughout Latin America. Physically, they might resemble many Californios or lower-class Mexicans who emigrated to the province during the 1830s and 1840s. Many of the California *vaqueros*—cowboys justly famous for their spectacular horsemanship—were probably former mission neophytes or their children. For some Indians, then, the land grants were more effective hispanicizing forces than the missions. But secularization also was accompanied by increased Indian alcoholism, vagrancy, and new outbreaks of banditry and rebellion against Hispanic rule.

The land grants were the origins of California's "old Spanish ranchos," which were neither very old nor very Spanish. Before 1821, the Spanish government approved fewer than 30 grants. After independence the Mexican government made more than 600 grants. In short, 95 percent of the ranchos were of Mexican origin, and were less than 25 years old when the United States occupied California in 1846. The majority were actually less than 13 years old at the time of American occupation, as most of the grants were made after the 1833 secularization.

The development of the ranchos represents a fundamental change in California society. Whereas the Franciscan order controlled most of the productive land and labor in the Spanish period, control had shifted to the Californios by the end of the Mexican period. A new national institution, the rancho, had replaced the old colonial institution, the mission, as California's center of wealth and power.

The Rancheros

Petaluma Adobe
This turn-of-the-century photograph shows the headquarters of Rancho Petaluma, a 66,000-acre land grant that comprised less than half of the total Vallejo family holdings in the North Bay. (Bancroft Library, UCB)

The Bay Area's most prominent ranchero was Mariano Guadalupe Vallejo, the California-born son of a soldier who came from Mexico in

the 1790s. A friend and supporter of Governor Figueroa, Vallejo obtained an appointment as administrator of the secularization process at Sonoma. Not surprisingly, most of the former Sonoma mission land eventually ended up in Vallejo family hands. When Don Mariano wanted a vineyard, he simply ordered the vines at the old San Rafael Mission removed and replanted on Vallejo property in Sonoma. He became the Bay Area's largest landholder, owning more than 175,000 acres in the North Bay region. His brothers and other close relatives controlled thousands of acres more. An able, well-educated man, Vallejo combined wealth with political and military influence, becoming the most important figure in Bay Area life during the Mexican period.

Unlike Vallejo, Luis Peralta was one of those very few Californios who received his grant during the Spanish period. Don Luis had come to California as a young boy with the Anza expedition of 1776. He followed his father into the army, serving at the San Francisco Presidio and various other Bay Area locations. His last years on active duty were spent in the garrison of the San Jose pueblo, and he became one of the town's leading citizens. In 1820, after 40 years of service, Peralta retired as a sergeant and requested a land grant as a reward for loyal duty. He hoped to receive a parcel near San Jose, but land in that area was either claimed by the town or by Mission Santa Clara or Mission San Jose. Accordingly he consented to accept Rancho San Antonio, nearly 50,000 acres of East Bay land that now includes the entire cities of Oakland, Berkeley, Alameda, Albany, Emeryville, Piedmont, and part of San Leandro. Peralta received his grant only a year before Mexican independence, and to be sure of his title, he successfully reapplied under Mexican law.

Don Luis never lived on the rancho himself, but sent his four sons north from San Jose to bring the land into production. Eventually, each son built a modest adobe house on a part of the grant, and Rancho San Antonio in fact became four adjoining ranchos. Each brother occupied approximately 12,000 acres, probably close to the average size of a Bay Area grant. Such a rancho would support about 1,000 head of cattle, but as large as these figures may seem, they were small compared to the great haciendas of Mexico, or even to the holdings of leading Californios like Vallejo. Nevertheless, the simple fact that the Peraltas had a land grant meant they were members of Mexican California's elite, and they married daughters of other land-holding Californio families.

The Peraltas began to have neighbors in the 1830s. To the south, the Estudillo family received a grant they called Rancho San Leandro. To the north, the Castros occupied Rancho San Pablo, while further north and east was Rancho Pinole, owned by the Martínez family, another particularly powerful Bay Area clan. Directly east of the Peraltas, the Moragas and Bernals started Rancho de la Laguna de los Palos Colorados (Ranch of the Redwood Tree Lagoon), the name referring to the great groves of tall trees that once stood on the hills between Oakland and Moraga. One large East Bay tract remained unoccupied, being considered "el sobrante" (the surplus). Eventually, one of the Castros acquired it as a land grant, calling it Rancho El Sobrante.

This same process of dividing the land into ranchos went on throughout the Bay Area: on the San Francisco Peninsula south of the region reserved for pueblo and presidio purposes, in the South Bay adjacent to San Jose, and in those North Bay territories not already claimed by the Vallejos. Virtually all portions of the Bay Area that today are well-populated or agriculturally valuable were once part of somebody's rancho.

The Beginning of Capitalism and Foreign Influence

The ranchos were the real beginning of capitalism in California. The missions had been primarily self-sufficient institutions, interested in supporting themselves and perhaps helping feed nearby presidios. The ranchos, however, were privately owned businesses whose owners wished to make a profit and accumulate wealth. Their cattle were valuable at the time principally for their hides and tallow, which could be shipped long distances via the sea. The rancheros concentrated on such market products. Because Mexico had plenty of hides and tallow, the ranchos sold to foreign markets, particularly the growing leather and soap industries of the eastern United States and Britain. Thus during the Mexican period, California became like a typical "third world" developing country, exporting unprocessed primary goods to the economically developed parts of the world, and receiving manufactured items in return. One major difference in living standards between the land-grant holders and the rest of the Hispanic population was the ranchero families' far greater access to goods from England and the United States.

The rise of the ranchos and the beginnings of export trade contributed directly to the growing influence of foreigners in the Bay Area's economy. The first foreign intrusion in the Bay Area, that of the Russians on the Sonoma County coast, occurred before the end of the Spanish period. As noted earlier, Fort Ross and the Bodega settlement were primarily commercial enterprises. When the fur-bearing sea otter and sea lions were virtually wiped out, the Russian American Fur Company left California, selling its assets to John Sutter in 1841. Meanwhile neither Spain nor Mexico formally recognized the right of Russians to settle in California, although unofficially Bay Area Hispanic residents carried on a lucrative trade with Fort Ross.

This gave Californios early access to American goods, since Yankee traders, headed for China, called at Fort Ross to purchase Rus-

Fort Ross, 1835
Russian American Fur Company Settlement, Sonoma County Coast. (Bancroft Library, UCB)

sian furs. The Russians then traded with the Californios, offering goods from Boston and New York for food and supplies. Soon, however, New England ships were stopping in California waters to hunt otter directly, rather than to deal with the Russians. American whalers also appeared in the Pacific, and both they and the otter hunters traded for provisions with Bay Area residents.

These early commercial contacts were dwarfed by the massive hide and tallow trade that developed in the 1830s. In *Two Years Before The Mast,* Richard Henry Dana immortalized the trip around the Horn from Boston to San Francisco Bay, and described commerce in "California banknotes," as the hides were called. British vessels also played a major role in the trade, and before long a few young Americans and Englishmen settled in the Bay Area to serve as middlemen in the increasingly lucrative exchange. Names such as Gilroy, Livermore, and Hartnell recall some of the earliest British residents of the region. Both British and American settlers often married into local Californio families and obtained land grants of their own. An American, William Heath Davis, married the daughter of Don Joaquín Estudillo, and another American, Jacob Leese, became Mariano Vallejo's brother-in-law. Some ranchero families eagerly sought such unions, for the Anglo merchants were important men in the regional economy. They could drive hard bargains with ship captains and had access to credit from British and American banks.

Richardson and Yerba Buena

During the early Mexican years the Bay Area's most important foreigner was an English seaman, William Richardson. Apparently he jumped ship in 1822, and Mexican authorities allowed him to stay in California if he could find something useful to do. Being resourceful, Richardson soon was operating a small cargo boat on the bay, and hiring himself out as a pilot for the growing number of British and American ships entering the Golden Gate. He became an indispensable middleman in the early hide and tallow trade, serving as go-between for Anglo ship captains and Californio rancheros, and arranging for bribes to be paid in lieu of Mexican duties. Eventually, Richardson married the daughter of Don Ignacio Martínez and purchased a land grant called "Rancho Sausalito" (Ranch of the Little Willow Grove), situated on the shores of the bay that still bears Richardson's name.

In 1835 Richardson asked the governor to allow him to open a mercantile business on the shore of a cove on the San Francisco waterfront, between Telegraph and Rincon hills. This inlet—now filled in and built upon—was named Yerba Buena after the mint-like herb that grew wild on the nearby sand dunes. It was a favorite anchoring place for trade ships. The authorities not only agreed to Richardson's request, but also decided to establish Yerba Buena as a formal civil pueblo, or town.

Yerba Buena was not, of course, the Bay Area's first pueblo. That distinction belongs to San Jose, founded by the Spanish government in 1777. Under Spanish law, a pueblo was given its own land grant of about 20,000 acres, to be owned communally by the citizenry as a whole. Small plots of the land were apportioned to families for house lots and gardens, and some property was set aside for public purposes. But most pueblo land was kept as common pasture for use by the community. The pueblo also had limited self-government, the heads of households selecting a town council, which in turn appointed an *alcalde,* or mayor. Only one other successful California pueblo was founded in the Spanish era—Los Angeles—but in the 1830s Mexico established several new municipalities. Some of them, e.g., Yerba Buena, were intended to serve as centers for the regional hide and tallow trade. In 1835 the governor also created the pueblo of Sonoma, to serve as a residence for new colonists from Mexico and as a bulwark against possible Russian expansion.

San Jose continued to be an important agricultural community during the Mexican period, and Sonoma became the headquarters of Don Mariano Vallejo's North Bay fiefdom. But Yerba Buena emerged as the hub of the Bay Area's economy. Although it received a pueblo land grant, there was little agriculture or grazing within the settlement. Prominent Bay Area Californios served on the council and occupied the post of alcalde, but most of the actual residents of the village were foreigners like Richardson, who played key roles in the hide and tallow trade.

Richardson built his place of business about 100 yards from the beach, on what is now the corner of Clay Street and Grant Avenue. Within four years the settlement was large enough for the governor to hire a Swiss adventurer, Jean Vioget, to make a town survey. Vioget laid out a few streets on a grid pattern and reserved space for a town plaza, which today is Portsmouth Square. In the early 1840s authorities constructed a customs house on the square, thus reinforcing Yerba Buena's economic importance in the region. In short, Richardson's entrepreneurship initiated the beginnings of downtown San Francisco, and the area has remained the Bay Area's chief financial and commercial center ever since.

Yankee Settlers and "Manifest Destiny"

About a year after Richardson opened his business, American Jacob Leese opened a similar establishment a few yards away. Leese invited Bay Area residents to help build the structure, and in return threw a community celebration on July 4, 1836. The party, which lasted three days and nights, was not only the first, but perhaps the rowdiest, of Bay Area Independence Day celebrations. Standing side-by-side in

Yerba Buena, the businesses of Richardson and Leese symbolized the informal but important rivalry between Englishmen and Americans for control of California's hide and tallow trade. By the mid-1840s, the Americans had clearly won out over the British. Yankees were the local population's largest foreign element, and California had far more commerce with Boston and New York than with San Blas or Mexico City.

Virtually every American in Mexican California subscribed to the belief in "Manifest Destiny," a conviction that the United States should and would spread from "sea to shining sea," thus incorporating California into the Union. Many of the traders who had come by sea and integrated themselves into the Californio elite believed the Americanization process could be peaceful and evolutionary. They saw no reason why American rule would displace the ranchos or the Hispanic upper class. They tried hard to persuade the Californios that US occupation was not only inevitable but also in the province's best interests. Many were convinced by such arguments, including Mariano Vallejo, the most important political and military leader.

In 1841, however, a very different kind of American settler began arriving in California—overland emigrants who came primarily from the Mississippi and Missouri river valleys. They were offshoots from the far larger emigration to Oregon, and followed trails blazed earlier by American trappers. Many of these newcomers shared the intense anti-Mexican feeling that spread throughout the American frontier after the

Texas independence revolution of 1836. Moreover their aim was to establish small family farms, which almost by definition meant destruction of the large ranchos and of the Californio elite. In the midst of growing international conflict between the United States and Mexico, the new settlers' arrival in California increased social and political tensions.

John Bidwell led the first expedition of overland settlers, which arrived at John Marsh's rancho on the eastern slopes of Mt. Diablo in 1841. Marsh had come to California in the 1830s, and with phony credentials established himself as the province's doctor. Although he welcomed American settlement, he almost immediately quarreled with Bidwell and his party. Thereafter, the primary destination of American overland expeditions was New Helvetia, the remarkable settlement that John Sutter, the Swiss adventurer, was building in the area of what today is Sacramento. In 1839, Sutter had received the first land grant in the Central Valley, and by 1841 was turning it into a full-fledged fort and community. He had a knack for getting further and further into debt, and welcomed American settlers as potential customers for his various enterprises.

Sutter's Fort thus became the center of a new American community that believed strongly in achieving Manifest Destiny by any means possible. In June 1846, the presence of a small American military force led by John C. Fremont was all that was needed to turn sentiment into action. From Sutter's Fort the Americans fomented a rebellion aimed at establishing a California republic modeled on Texas. The rebels captured Mariano Vallejo and occupied Sonoma and Yerba Buena in the name of their "Bear Flag Republic." A few weeks later, however, the new "nation" ceased to exist when it was learned that the United States and Mexico were already at war.

In southern California there was violent opposition to American

Raising the Bear Flag, 1846
Also depicts the arrest of Mariano Vallejo and his brother Salvador. (San Francisco Arts Commission, Rincon Annex Post Office Murals, by Anton Refregier, 1941, 1945-49)

conquest, but such sentiment was almost nonexistent in the Bay Area. The region had already established strong ties to the United States, and many leading Californios such as Vallejo had long since accepted the inevitability of American rule. Military action in the Bay Area was limited primarily to a small skirmish in Marin between Bear Flaggers and Californios, and a somewhat larger battle on the Peninsula between American forces and Hispanic residents. Thus the actual military conquest in the Bay Area was something of an anticlimax, coming after American economic influence already was well established. The real transformation of life was to be brought about not by conquest, but by the discovery of gold at Sutter's Mill.

□ □ □

6 Queen City of the West

San Francisco Views, Mid-to-Late-1800s
Clockwise from lower left: Portsmouth Square, the plaza and heart of the original city, with the old city hall; the Crocker mansion (present site of Grace Cathedral); Market Street, looking eastward toward Yerba Buena Island; the Hopkins mansion (present site of the Mark Hopkins Hotel); and the Stanford mansion (present site of the Stanford Court Hotel). (Southern Pacific)

6

Queen
City of
the West ——————————————————————

In 1847, two prominent Americans, Thomas Larkin and Robert Semple, teamed up with Mariano Vallejo to promote a new town on the latter's land near Carquinez Strait. They named the community Francisca, after Vallejo's wife, predicting it would soon surpass Yerba Buena in population and economic influence. Businessmen in the latter community were understandably concerned. They asked Washington Bartlett, a naval officer serving as alcalde during the American military occupation, to allow Yerba Buena to change its name to San Francisco, identifying the town with the entire estuary, rather than just a tiny cove. Bartlett agreed, and to avoid confusion, Larkin and his partners rechristened their community Benicia—after one of Señora Vallejo's many other given names. Symbolically, at least, San Francisco was laying claim to Bay Area supremacy.

Gold Rush San Francisco

This was the first of many moves that San Francisco's business community made over the years to maintain the city's position as the region's major economic center. Such action proved particularly significant in 1847: just a few months later, in January 1848, James Marshall discovered gold at Coloma. The resulting Gold Rush fundamentally transformed California, bringing revolutionary demographic, economic, and social change.

The Bay Area was particularly affected. San Francisco, strategically located at the junction of ocean, bay, and river routes to the gold fields, was affected most of all. From a total population of about 600 in 1848, the community grew to 25,000 by 1849, and to over 40,000 by 1852. Using Gunther Barth's term, an "instant city" emerged, first dominating the gold-mining economy of California, and then the whole precious-metal frontier that stretched from the Pacific to the Black Hills of South Dakota. For a quarter-century after 1848, San Francisco was "Queen City of the West," the social and economic capital of a major American region.

The Gold Rush created a new kind of American frontier. Prior to 1849, the frontier had been principally agricultural, attracting people who came to put down roots, both literally and figuratively. In contrast, the Gold Rush attracted people who came to "get rich quick" and return home. They were not interested in establishing permanent communities, and they did not bring their families. By 1850, there were more than 10 men for every woman in California, as most of the wives, sweethearts, and mothers stayed home, while their young men came west to seek their fortunes.

Gold Rush San Francisco, the ultimate boom town, reflected these social realities. The "instant city" was in fact a giant encampment. The cove was cluttered with abandoned ships, and San Francisco was a community of tents, shacks, and shanties, since few bothered to construct substantial buildings. Merchants, traders, gamblers, bartenders, and prostitutes vied for a share of the wealth that poured down from the gold country. The biggest winners were men like Sam Brannan and James Lick, who speculated in real estate.

One of the earliest land investors was William Leidesdorf, probably the city's most important man in the years just before the Gold Rush. Son of a Danish father and a black West Indian mother, he had come to California in 1841, and had served as American Vice-Consul in Yerba Buena. Leidesdorf built the village's first hotel, organized its first public school, and invested heavily in town lots. He died of typhus in early

1848, being then about $50,000 in debt. By the time his will cleared probate, lots he had bought for less than a hundred dollars each were worth thousands, and his estate was valued at over a million. The Gold Rush transformed William Leidesdorf from debtor to millionaire, even while he lay comfortably in his grave.

The city's growth was explosive, but not entirely unplanned. In 1847, Alcalde Bartlett commissioned Jasper O'Farrell to improve and greatly expand Vioget's original town survey. When the great boom came, there was thus already a street plan in place for downtown San Francisco that could accommodate speedy growth. Bartlett had also approved the sale to private parties of water lots in the tidal flats of Yerba Buena Cove. Once the Gold Rush began, entrepreneurs quickly built wharves out to deep water, and owners of tidal properties rapidly filled the shallows with sand, rubbish, and abandoned ship hulls. The city expanded into the cove, and wharves evolved into streets. Today's Commercial Street in the financial district, for example, got its start as San Francisco's Long Wharf.

From Boom to Bust

The boom lasted as long as thousands of Americans, Europeans, Latin Americans, Australians, New Zealanders, Hawaiians, and Chinese believed it was possible to strike it rich in California. In fact, the mines

Gold rush
1848 - 1853

were already overpopulated by 1850, and in 1853 the rush came to an end when surface deposits of gold rapidly disappeared. The economic boom turned to bust, and the mid-1850s was a period of depression. The hard times had redeeming effects, however, as the failure of many weak and speculative businesses ultimately strengthened the economy, and the depression finally drove down the extraordinarily high consumer prices of early Gold Rush days.

Most of the gold-seekers were lucky if they returned home with as much money as they had originally brought to California. Some of them, however, stayed on to become farmers, urban workers, storekeepers, and businessmen. Most of those who remained either married or brought their families to California, and began laying the foundations of communities that were permanent, if less exciting than those of the early 1850s. Mining, largely an individual or small-scale adventure in 1849, became a business that large operators increasingly dominated. By the late 1850s most of the remaining miners were wage earners, rather than independent prospectors.

From Encampment to City

San Francisco changed along with the mining economy. The city suffered six serious fires between 1849 and 1852, and, after each conflagration, San Franciscans rebuilt their homes and businesses in a bit more durable fashion. Masons constructed brick and stone buildings, including Henry Halleck's massive Montgomery Block, located where the Transamerica Pyramid now stands. Sturdy family houses, some shipped in pieces from New England, appeared along the city's streets. By the end of the 1850s, Rincon Hill, today the anchorage for the Bay Bridge, emerged as San Francisco's first elite neighborhood, graced with substantial homes of the city's social establishment. On the slope of the hill, George Gordon built South Park, a group of expensive row houses arranged around a neighborhood park in the manner of London town houses.

The emergence of an elite neighborhood was part of a general process of districting that occurred in the late '50s. As the cove was filled in, shipping and related industries naturally located along the waterfront. But banking and investment houses remained on Montgomery Street, at the old shoreline, which by then was several blocks from the bay. Retail business originally had crowded around Portsmouth Square, the old town plaza, but began moving to more spacious quarters nearer Market Street, and later to Union Square. The old area around Portsmouth Square was destined to become Chinatown, as well as the home of other immigrant groups and the hangouts of writers and artists in an early "Bayside Bohemia."

The new large-scale mining operations needed heavy machinery, and Peter Donahue's blacksmith shop near the foot of Mission Street began its evolution into the giant Union Iron Works. The city's first gas plant was located nearby, thus establishing the South-of-Market area as an early industrial district and working-class neighborhood. Meanwhile on the North Beach waterfront, Henry Meiggs built a large wharf and lumber yard. Although "Honest Harry," as he was often called, absconded with a substantial share of the city treasury in 1855, his initial development of the North Beach area attracted industry, shipping, and commercial fishing.

By 1860 San Francisco had become something of a real city. In addition to its various districts, the community had a network of volunteer fire departments, a neighborhood public school system, several churches, and two synagogues. As early as 1856, San Francisco even had a well-developed political machine, closely aligned with Democratic Senator David Broderick.

Hindsight suggests that the hard times of the mid-'50s were a virtually inevitable part of San Francisco's transformation from encampment to city. At the time, however, the process caused much pain and suffering. Not only did weak businesses fail, but also some of the city's leading firms went bankrupt. During the same period, Joshua Norton's bankruptcy transformed him from a prosperous merchant into San Francisco's legendary eccentric, Emperor Norton, the much-loved imperial panhandler.

Violence, Corruption, and Vigilante Action

It was a time of depression, with business failures, substantial unemployment, and declining local government revenues. In such an atmosphere, Bay Area citizens became particularly sensitive to problems of law and order. Gold Rush California was hardly an orderly place, being a society of primarily unattached men out to get rich quick. Regular civilian government had been established only after California achieved statehood in September 1850. Moreover the population was divided by national and ethnic rivalries and prejudices. In short, the ingredients were present for substantial social upheaval. Crime was rampant: between 1849 and 1856, San Franciscans committed more than 1,000 killings, or some 10 to 20 times the per capita murder rate of the early 1980s.

The financially extravagant, often corrupt city administration seemed unwilling or unable to control crime and violence. This prompted the citizens to take action, producing a tradition of do-it-yourself government. For example, in 1851 a Vigilance Committee led by businessmen Sam Brannan and William Tell Coleman briefly seized power from the legal authorities and hanged, jailed, and banished some alleged criminals. But this had little permanent effect, and by 1856, in the midst of economic hard times, crime and corruption were again rife. When a local politician shot and killed the city's best-known newspaper editor, Coleman organized a second and more powerful Vigilance Committee, which controlled the city government for more than three months, holding trials and dispensing its own brand of justice. This committee was not an unruly lynch mob, but a determined, well-organized, and wholly illegal rebellion led by some of San Francisco's most influential citizens. When the governor of California ordered them to cease and desist, the vigilantes fortified their headquarters and created an armed militia that was more powerful than anything the state could rally against them. In the Vigilance Committee's own words, it had created "a businessman's revolution," designed to make San Francisco safe for trade and commerce.

Even after the committee voluntarily disbanded, Coleman and others organized the People's Party, which dominated local government for nearly a decade. The party was concerned not only with local corruption and crime but also with the cost of government. Its major accomplishment was the San Francisco Charter of 1856, which separated the city from what became San Mateo County. Within the boundaries of present-day San Francisco it established a unique kind of consolidated city and county, eliminating a whole layer of government, reducing the number of officeholders, and, the sponsors hoped, also reducing taxes and the opportunities for graft. Despite these reforms, politics in San Francisco were generally as disreputable as in most late-19th century American cities. Nevertheless the "businessman's revolution" did sig-

Pictorial Lettersheet of Vigilance Committee Actions
In May 1856 Casey and Cora were tried, found guilty, and hanged. McGowan fled, and Sullivan committed suicide. (Bancroft Library, UCB)

nify the presence of a well-organized economic community that was willing and able to intervene in public life to protect its interests.

Prosperity and New Mining Frontiers

Prosperity had returned by 1860, due partly to the expansion of a reorganized California mining industry. But the recovery was also attributable to the opening of new precious-metals frontiers throughout the far west. For more than two decades after 1849, a portion of the American frontier reversed its classical westward push, establishing an eastward movement from California to mining communities in the Great Basin, Rocky Mountains, and even the Black Hills. San Francisco's hinterland expanded as the city became the chief financial and commercial center for this vast mining region. The most dramatic of all the post-1849 "rushes" was that to the Comstock Lode in Virginia City, Nevada, during the early 1860s. Some of the biggest names in San Francisco's economic history, Adolph Sutro, George Hearst, and William Sharon, among others, made fortunes in the Comstock.

California had taken a few years to shift from an economy based on individual prospectors to one emphasizing large, industrialized mining operations. In Virginia City and many of the other new mining frontiers, however, this process occurred almost overnight. The large mines depended on Montgomery Street banks and securities dealers for capital, and speculation in mining stocks was a San Francisco pastime. The city's stock exchange became one of the nation's largest, dealing not only in mineral-company shares but also in stock of industrial enterprises that were stimulated by the regional economic expansion.

Ralston and the Palace Hotel

Merchants and real estate investors had profited heavily from the early Gold Rush of the 1850s, while the new mining boom of the '60s favored industrialists and transportation entrepreneurs. Among these, William Ralston was the most important personal force in the Bay Area economy during the 1860s. Along with Darius Ogden Mills, Ralston founded the Bank of California, and developed it into the west's most important banking house, underwriting a significant portion of the economic growth of the 1860s, and helping to establish San Francisco's historic status as a major banking center for the west. He enjoyed playing the role of a merchant-prince, subsidizing San Francisco theaters and concerts, and Napa and Sonoma counties' fine wines. At his great country estate in Belmont—now the College of Notre Dame—Ralston entertained European royalty, American politicians, and famous artists and actors.

Ralston's most ambitious project for San Francisco was the Palace Hotel, a hostelry planned to equal the luxury of the great resorts of Europe and the eastern United States. Unfortunately, as the Palace neared completion in 1875, California was increasingly affected by a major national economic depression. Credit was tight, and western miners suffered from eastern attempts to manipulate markets in precious metals. Nevertheless, Ralston tried to gain control of Comstock silver production, using his bank's assets to buy mining stock at inflated prices. The bank failed, and Ralston resigned as president. The next morning, during his customary swim off North Beach, he suffered a fatal stroke. Tens of thousands of San Franciscans turned out for his funeral.

By the time of Ralston's death, the mining era that had created San Francisco was coming to an end. New economic forces were at work: in 1875 the transcontinental railroad was already six years old, and agriculture had passed mining as California's biggest business. New western metropolises were appearing. Soon Seattle, Portland, Los Angeles, Denver, and even Oakland would challenge San Francisco's position as the far west's sole urban center.

Today only a few direct connections with the mining era remain. For example, the Homestake Mining Co., the only large-scale gold producer left in the United States, still has its headquarters in San Francisco. Homestake's major mine is in Lead, South Dakota, thus suggest-

Palace Hotel and Lotta's Fountain, 1880
Entertainer Lotta Crabtree gave San Francisco this three-tiered fountain, which supplied drinking water for horses, people, and dogs. (Southern Pacific)

ing the geographic extent of San Francisco's historic domination of the US precious-metals industry. But the most dramatic monument to the mining era is still William Ralston's Palace Hotel. Burned in 1906, the Palace was redesigned and rebuilt in its original location. Today, the Sheraton chain manages the hotel for its Japanese owners, a sign of the San Francisco economy's present-day dependence on outside capital and ownership. But the Palace still retains some of the opulence and nouveau riche pretension that was so much a part of the Queen City of the West.

□ □ □

7 New Patterns on the Land

View of Oakland in 1853
According to the original caption, "this delightful little village [viewed from the foot of Broadway] is rapidly gaining favorable notoriety . . . as a resort for a day of leisure from the strife of business and the hum of city life." (Bancroft Library, UCB)

7

New
Patterns on
the Land

After gold was discovered, Don Luis María Peralta advised his four sons to stay on the family's vast East Bay land grant. "Let the Americans go [to the mine fields]," he counseled. "You can go to your ranch and raise grain, and that will be your best gold, because we all must eat while we live." While the statement is often cited as evidence of the old gentleman's wisdom, the recommendation did not prove helpful to the Peralta brothers, who did indeed stay home and try to maintain their hold on Rancho San Antonio.

Soon the Peraltas were dispossessed of their land by squatters, speculators, and a cumbersome if not outright hostile legal system. The Peraltas, like most of the region's Californio families, were prime victims of the social and economic upheaval of the Gold Rush era, which created dramatic new land ownership and settlement patterns in the Bay Area.

"Squatter's Rights"

In theory the Californios had no reason to fear for their land, as the 1848 Treaty of Guadalupe Hidalgo—ending the Mexican War and recognizing American sovereignty in California—protected the "inviolability" of the land grants. Moreover, the treaty made Hispanic Californians American citizens, with full constitutional protection of life, liberty, and property. But these treaty and constitutional provisions conflicted with the old US Anglo frontier tradition of "squatter's rights." Frontier settlers had always occupied "vacant" land. If they were still in possession of it when governmental authority finally caught up with settlement, they usually received formal title to the property.

Most of the new American residents of the Bay Area probably believed that the ranchos were in fact "vacant" land. After all, the ranchos were not fenced nor had the land been visibly improved. It seemed downright un-American for a family to control 50,000 acres or more, particularly if it were a "greaser" family whose former country had just lost a war to the United States. The state Legislature did its part with a law of doubtful constitutionality that further encouraged squatting by allowing individuals to claim up to 160 acres of "vacant" land. There was a basic conflict between treaty and constitutional provisions on the one hand, and frontier traditions, profit, and prejudice on the other. Unfortunately for the Californios, their rights established by treaty and Constitution lost, hands down.

By the end of 1849, disappointed gold seekers were already coming back from the Sierra foothills, tired of trying to eke out a living in the mines. With food prices at astronomical levels, many of the disillusioned miners looked for cropland with easy access to San Francisco's urban market. Thus three former gold seekers were farming and cutting lumber on Peralta property by the end of 1849. In 1850 the Peraltas finally forced them to pay rent, but by that time the family faced a much more serious challenge. Edson Adams was squatting on what is today a portion of downtown Oakland. Vicente Peralta and several vaqueros paid Adams a visit, suggesting that he farm elsewhere. Edson decided that he needed a lawyer, hiring Horace Carpentier, just off the boat from New York. Carpentier recognized the potential of Adams's location, and formed a land development partnership consisting of himself, Adams, and a third American named Andrew Moon. The partners hired their own band of armed men, and a shooting war was averted only when Carpentier theoretically agreed to pay rent to the Peraltas.

In fact, the partners then filed claims on the land under California law, had a surveyor lay out streets and lots, and persuaded the Legislature to incorporate the area into a new town called Oakland. Carpentier was instrumental in creating Alameda County, which was separated from Contra Costa County in 1852. That same year he won election to the state Assembly, receiving 590 votes, although a census made two months earlier had shown only 130 voters in the district.

The Land Commission and the Courts

Californios faced similar problems throughout the Bay Area. Squatters appeared wherever there was good cropland or a likely town site with easy water access to San Francisco. State and local authorities either would not or could not protect the rancheros' property rights, and it fell to the federal government to enforce the treaty and constitutional provisions. In 1851 Congress established the California Land Commission to resolve the disputes over property rights, requiring those who claimed to own land to appear before the commission with supporting evidence. If the Californios wanted treaty and constitutional protection for their land, they must first prove that the property was legally theirs.

Most of the ranchero families welcomed the chance to resolve the conflicts, and the Peraltas were among the first to appear before the commission. The commissioners did in fact approve the great majority of the land grant claims, including some which later proved fraudulent. For example, José Ives Limantour received approval for a grant that included much of downtown San Francisco, even though in a court appeal it was eventually discovered that he had forged the documents and bribed a former Mexican governor to postdate his signature. In this instance the court overturned the commission decision, but not before Limantour had fled to Mexico with several thousand dollars collected from San Francisco businessmen who wished clear title to their city lots.

If the commission had been the only legal hurdle, many Californios (and some swindlers like Limantour) might have held onto a substantial part of their land. However, commission decisions could be appealed to the federal district court, and if no one else made such an appeal, the United States government did so on grounds that land not legally part of a valid claim was public property. Moreover the district court decision could be appealed to the United States Supreme Court, and after the justices rendered their decision, someone might challenge the precise boundaries of a claim. During Mexican times, a *diseño* or rough map showed only the general, unsurveyed extent of the land grant, whereas precise and often conflicting surveys were now debated in court. Finally, legal battles sometimes erupted among members of the landholding families. In the case of the Peraltas, Don Luis had willed his land to his four sons, but he also had five daughters. Striking an early blow for women's rights, the Peralta sisters sued their brothers,

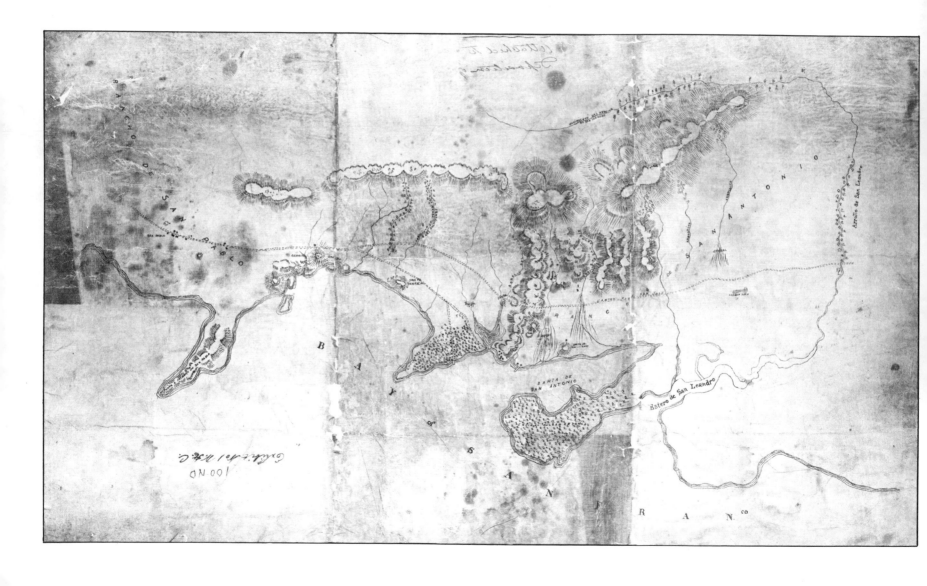

contending that all Don Luis's children should share equally in the inheritance.

The average California land grant case took 17 years from the filing of the original claim with the commission to the final court decision. The Peralta case dragged on for a quarter-century, and it was by no means the longest. Meanwhile, the rancheros were burdened by legal fees, property taxes, and squatters. The Peraltas, located just across the bay from San Francisco, were further plagued by massive cattle rustling. Like most rancheros, the Peraltas were forced to sell off their land long before the court rendered the final verdict on their claim. In 1853, Antonio Peralta sold Alameda to a group of San Francisco land developers, and by the same year his brother Vicente had sold much of north and central Oakland, including the area being developed by Carpentier and his companions, to another group of Anglo speculators. This created enormous legal problems, and land titles in central Oakland were in chaos for another 15 years.

In 1854, José Domingo Peralta disposed of most of his holdings in what is now Berkeley and Albany, keeping only 300 acres for himself. He received about $85,000 for the land, which barely covered his debts. In 1858 Alameda County seized the 300 acres for payment of back taxes, although Domingo managed to get the land returned. When he died in 1865, his family could not afford to pay the cost of his burial. They sold the last parcel of Domingo's land in 1868. Nine years later,

Diseño of Two East Bay Ranchos
This rough representation of the Castro family's Rancho San Pablo and the Peralta family's Rancho San Antonio was a US District Court exhibit in the San Antonio land grant case. (Bancroft Library, UCB)

the courts finally ruled that the original claim the Peralta brothers had made in 1852 was valid. By that time, Oakland was a city of more than 10,000, and the new state university had opened in Berkeley. The remaining Peralta family members probably held no more than a few hundred acres of the 50,000 acres that had once been Rancho San Antonio.

Speculators, Swindlers, and a Chaotic Process

Not all Bay Area Californio families lost their land in precisely the way the Peraltas had, but the result was usually the same. The Moragas and Bernals, for example, made the mistake of hiring Horace Carpentier as their attorney. For more than a decade, he represented them before the commission and courts, and when he finally reported that their claim had been confirmed, he also announced that he was occupying their land in compensation for thousands of dollars of unpaid legal fees. The Moragas fought a series of battles with the lawyer's hired gunmen, but in the end Horace Carpentier took possession of Rancho de la Laguna de los Palos Colorados.

Other speculators swindled the Berryessa family out of Rancho Milpitas near San Jose. John C. Fremont's men had senselessly killed three members of the family during the Bear Flag Rebellion, another had died in a dispute over title to the New Almaden quicksilver mine, and two additional family members were victims of an Anglo lynch mob. By the mid-1870s Don Nicolas Berryessa and his close relatives were penniless and homeless. Antonio Berryessa had good cause to complain about "the bad faith of the adventurers and squatters and the treachery of the American lawyers." The careers of Californio bandits like Tiburcio Vasquez and the legendary Joaquín Murieta were in part a violent expression of such understandable outrage. Just as Indian rebels such as Estanislao had attacked Hispanic Californios, now Californio rebels preyed on Anglos.

No Californio tried harder to adjust to the new era than Mariano Guadalupe Vallejo. Fremont had briefly imprisoned Vallejo and his brother Salvador at Sutter's Fort, but Don Mariano emerged from the experience committed to participating fully in the affairs of American California. He served as a delegate to the state constitutional convention in 1849, represented the North Bay in the state Senate, and was elected mayor of Sonoma. When his adobe Casa Grande in Sonoma burned to the ground in 1867, he built a typical wooden Anglo-American home to replace it. There was nothing Mexican or Californian about the new house.

Vallejo was not above a bit of land speculating himself. As we have seen, he developed Benicia along with Thomas Larkin and Robert Semple. The town served briefly as California's state capital, and obtained a secure economic base when the US Army located a munitions depot there. Another of Don Mariano's land developments, the town of Vallejo, also served briefly as the state's seat of government (so did San Jose) before the capital was permanently located in Sacramento in 1855. Like Benicia, Vallejo benefited from the military, as the Mare Island shipyard was established there in 1854. But in spite of his political clout and active career in land development, Mariano Vallejo did not escape the fate of most other Bay Area Californios. He, too, suffered mightily at the hands of squatters, speculators, swindlers, and lawyers.

Of course, the Californios were not the only ones affected by the chaotic process of establishing land titles. Anglo holders of land grants were afflicted by many of the same problems as their Hispanic counterparts, and the legal and procedural delays in settling title claims may have inhibited development of many Bay Area communities. The time-consuming process favored wealthy individuals and companies with the resources and legal talent necessary for the long series of procedures and appeals. Many of the original squatters had no better chance than the rancheros of hanging onto the land. Even the Catholic Church had to go through the commission and courts to win confirmation of title to the small plots where the old mission chapels were located. The towns of San Jose and Sonoma also made their ways through the procedural maze to establish rights to the pueblo land grants made by the Spanish and Mexican governments.

San Francisco's Case

The most important pueblo land case was San Francisco's.   We already have seen how "new patterns" began to be established on the city's landscape in 1847, when Alcalde Bartlett allowed the sale of town lots and commissioned the O'Farrell survey. O'Farrell straightened the original Mexican grid system and extended it west to what is now Leavenworth Street. His great innovation was to lay out Market Street on an angle approximating the old road between the pueblo and Mission Dolores. Consistent with Market Street's angle, O'Farrell created a new grid system, with much longer blocks, for the southeastern part of the city, thus establishing a street pattern that has persisted ever since.

In the early 1850s city officials filed claim for the pueblo land grant that the Mexican government had made to Yerba Buena. The claim did not include the southern half of the city, which had originally been mission land and was granted to several private parties after 1833. But the city did claim roughly the northern half of San Francisco, except for the military reserve of the Presidio. By 1855 the courts had approved this claim as far west as "the division," or Divisadero Street. The 1855 Van Ness Ordinances—named after a city alderman and future mayor—extended the grid system to this "western addition," and recognized the titles of squatters who occupied property in the area, minus land for streets and several small parks. In the long run, the Van Ness Ordi-

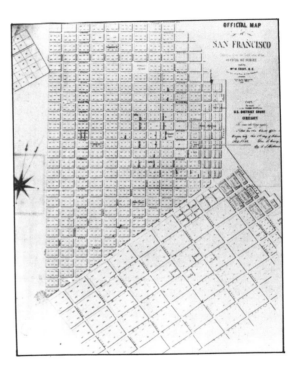

Official Map of San Francisco, 1850
This plat map was filed with San Francisco's claim for the pueblo land grant and shows the city's distinctive unconforming street pattern. (Bancroft Library, UCB)

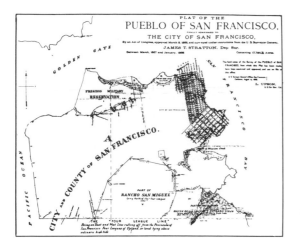

San Francisco, 1866
Map includes the "outer lands," and clearly depicts the relative compactness of the city's growth, and its isolation on the Peninsula's northeast tip. (McGloin, *San Francisco . . .*)

nances promoted the development of the Western Addition, but the immediate effect was to start battles, some legal and some physical, over who actually occupied many parcels of land.

In 1866 the city finally won title to the "outer lands" west of Divisadero. Again the Board of Supervisors recognized the title of those who occupied the territory, but now the city required the former squatters to assemble enough land to donate to the municipality a parcel of about 1,000 acres. Many leading citizens and distinguished visitors, including Frederick Law Olmsted, the creator of New York's Central Park, had lamented San Francisco's lack of recreational open space. The 1,000 acres of "outer lands" reserved by the city was supposed to solve this problem, although critics pointed out that it was primarily an area of barren, inhospitable sand dunes. The park's superintendent, William Hammond Hall, made energetic efforts to subdue the sand, successfully laying the foundation for one of the world's most attractive urban open space preserves. Golden Gate Park, a wholly man-made environment, is a dramatic symbol of the era when US society established new patterns on the Bay Area landscape.

Decline of the Californios

The most significant immediate effect of the process of change, however, was the destruction of the ranchos and, with them, the decline of the Californios. Gold Rush immigration quickly made the Hispanic Californians a small minority group, and destruction of their ranchos deprived them of valuable economic assets and of the ability to maintain the distinctive Californio culture and way of life. Today, there surely are more descendents of the old Hispanic families in the Bay Area than there were in 1846, and each year one of them, an attractive young woman, is named "La Favorita" to preside over San Francisco's birthday party. But the Californios have long since vanished as an identifiable ethnic group. The important Latino presence now found in the Bay Area has its roots in 20th century patterns of immigration from Mexico and Central America, not in the pre-1846 Hispanic population.

In 1875 Mariano Guadalupe Vallejo finished writing a massive history of the Californios, designed to show that the Hispanic Californians "were not indigents or a band of beasts." Another of his objects, Vallejo explained, was to assure that his people would not "disappear, ignored by the whole world." And yet, despite Don Mariano's efforts, to a great degree that is exactly what happened.

□ □ □

8 Golden Port

San Francisco Waterfront, 1900
This picture of California's "window on the world" shows a variety of vessels, including a scow schooner, a steam launch, and several sailing ships. (Bancroft Library, UCB)

8

Golden
Port

When Richard Henry Dana returned to San Francisco Bay in 1859, 24 years after the first voyage he had described so eloquently in *Two Years Before The Mast,* he found the region much changed. Yerba Buena Cove had been filled in to produce a deepwater port where "Clipper ships of the largest size lay at anchor. . . ." Dana also noted "capacious high-pressure steamers, as large and showy as those of the Hudson or Mississippi. . . ." His own arriving vessel had docked at midnight, nevertheless the city "was alive from the salute of our guns, spreading the news that the fortnightly steamer had come. . . ." The wharf was "densely crowded with express wagons and hand-carts to take luggage, coaches and cabs for passengers. . . ." The great majority of the people crowded on the dock were there simply "for newspapers and verbal intelligence from the great Atlantic and European world."

The Economic Foundation

Thus did Dana describe the Port of San Francisco, the vital depot through which passed most goods, people, and communication to and from California. In an age when water transportation was both cheaper and faster than land travel, the port was the economic foundation not only of the city, but also of the region and indeed the entire state. It was therefore no accident that in 1863 the California Legislature established a state harbor commission to govern San Francisco's port. The city's vast system of wharves and warehouses, and its extensive maritime industry, were crucially important resources for all Californians.

The Bay Area's maritime complex had already witnessed substantial development by the time of Dana's 1859 voyage. In the first months of the Gold Rush all kinds of vessels had sailed to California, but by the early 1850s most cargo from the east was hauled around the Horn by sleek clipper ships built especially for the California trade. In 1851, the clipper *Flying Cloud* made the voyage from New York to San Francisco in 89 days, a sailing-ship record that stood for decades. By the late '50s, as the extreme profits of the early California trade declined, New England began producing more economical "downeasters," ships built along clipper lines, but with more cargo room and smaller crews.

After the Civil War, California became a major exporter of wheat and other grains as the federal government disposed of Central Valley land, which formerly had been public. Much of it was obtained by large "bonanza" farmers, raising wheat for world markets. By 1880, British iron-hulled sailing ships dominated the grain trade, transporting California wheat to Europe and Asia. Since the grain was grown on Central Valley farms, communities near the Delta and river routes out of the valley were particularly affected by the trade. In the 1880s, Port Costa, between present-day Martinez and Crockett, became America's leading grain export depot. Martinez, Benicia, and Antioch also thrived.

The British ships brought English coal in exchange for California grain. Thus wheat effectively subsidized the growth of Bay Area industry. Coal was then the major industrial energy source, but except for small deposits on the northeastern slopes of Mt. Diablo, California had no coal of its own. The state depended on coal imports for which Central Valley wheat paid a substantial share of the bill. Wheat was also exchanged for pig iron and scrap steel, indispensable raw materials for the Bay Area's increasingly important metals industry.

Steam Takes Over the Passenger Trade

While sail power continued to dominate bulk cargo hauling for the remainder of the 19th century, steamships quickly took over most of the passenger trade. Unlike freight customers, passengers were willing to pay enough to justify the added costs of steam power. In 1848 the Pacific Mail Steamship Company began service from New York to San Francisco, via a land crossing in Panama. After suffering operational problems during the chaotic early Gold Rush years, the company developed dependable service and successfully fought off a competing Vanderbilt enterprise that used a Nicaraguan route.

In 1855, Pacific Mail built a railroad across the Isthmus of Panama, establishing the company as the prime mover of passengers between San Francisco and the east coast. As Dana's description illustrates, the arrival of the Pacific Mail steamer every two weeks was an important event in the Bay Area. The ship was California's main transportation and communication link with America's economic, cultural, and political heartland.

Completion of the transcontinental railroad in 1869 displaced Pacific Mail's role in coast-to-coast travel. The company was forced to seek new routes, and in particular began to emphasize transpacific service to China and later Japan. By the end of the 19th century, Pacific Mail had been joined in the Asia trade by many other Bay Area companies, including the Spreckels and Matson lines (which eventually merged). Greatest of all the California shipping enterprises was the Dollar Lines. Begun by "Captain" Robert Dollar as a fleet of schooners serving his lumber business, the line grew to a massive network of steamship routes linking San Francisco Bay with the entire world. A remnant of the system still survives as the American President Lines.

The Local and Coastal Trade

The growth of these great shipping empires was more than matched by the local bay, river, and coastal maritime industry. In 1847, William Leidesdorf bought the small Russian vessel *Sitka* and initiated steamboat service in the bay and river system. Reminiscent of BART in our own time, the *Sitka* was plagued by mechanical problems that turned its inaugural into a regional joke. But the Gold Rush made service to Stockton, Sacramento, and other river ports a big business. Hudson River captain Ned Wakeman, who was about to lose his new steamer to creditors, loaded the vessel with coal and set off around the Horn for California. Wakeman's riverboat not only completed the long sea voyage, but immediately went into service between San Francisco and Sacramento, soon to be joined by other steamers. In 1861, the California Steam Navigation Company's paddlewheeler, *Chrysopolis,* made the trip from San Francisco to the state capital in a record-breaking five hours.

As with the ocean-going vessels, sail power dominated bulk cargo hauling in the bay and river system for the rest of the 19th century.

Sacramento Waterfront Scene, 1868
Steamboats like the *Chrysopolis,* seen here, transported passengers between San Francisco and Sacramento, where they could board Central Pacific trains. The *Chrysopolis* was later rebuilt as a ferry and renamed the *Oakland.* (Southern Pacific)

Many of the new Bay Area communities that were formed in the early Gold Rush period served as ports linking important economic activities to San Francisco, via the bay. Redwood City and Oakland were initially lumber depots for logging operations in the Peninsula and East Bay hills. Napa and Petaluma also developed early, as agricultural goods

from the surrounding valleys could be readily transported to San Francisco down the Napa River and Petaluma Slough.

Union City and Vallejo were also significant depots for local farmers, but in the 1850s Alviso was probably the bay's major agricultural port. During the Gold Rush era, the Santa Clara Valley became a primary source of foodstuffs for San Francisco, and until completion of the San Francisco-San Jose railroad in 1862, Alviso wharves were the chief transportation link between the valley and the city's lucrative urban market. The ubiquitous, rectangular-hulled, shallow-draft "scow schooners," especially built for bay and delta traffic, were the region's most numerous waterborne cargo haulers. They were the bay's workhorses, playing a major role in linking dozens of bayside communities with San Francisco's urban core.

Coastal shipping was also vital to the region's economy. Eventually, regularly scheduled steamers provided passenger service to Los Angeles, San Diego, Portland, and Seattle. Sail-powered lumber schooners brought valuable cargoes from the Pacific Northwest and California's north coast, filling the tremendous demand for building materials caused by rapid Bay Area urban growth. Alaska Packing Company ships established a flourishing trade between the Bay Area and Alaska, while other Bay Area vessels sailed Alaskan waters in search of seals and mackerel. After the Civil War, much of the United States' whaling fleet moved to California. Consequently San Francisco Bay

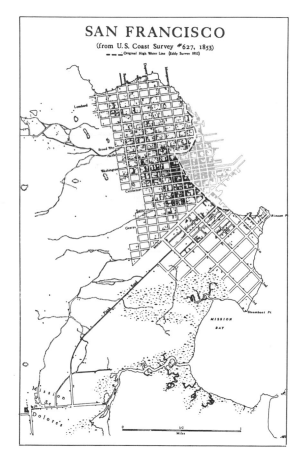

San Francisco, 1853
This map shows the original high-water line of Yerba Buena Cove, and subsequent landfill of the cove's mudflats (*screened area*). Except for the "Plank Road" across the marsh to Mission Dolores, on its landward side the city was framed by marsh, steep hills, or sand dunes. (US Coast Survey, and Vance, *Geography* . . .)

became the capital of the American whaling industry, and remained so until the development of California petroleum lessened the demand for whale oil in the 1890s. The nation's last whaling station operated at Point Richmond until 1971.

Fishing and Boatbuilding

Bay Area fishermen gathered a mighty harvest from bay and coastal waters. Italian and Dalmatian fishermen arrived in the 1850s, introducing lateen-sailed Mediterranean fishing boats to the region. The Chinese also played a major role, especially in developing the bay's shrimp industry. In Suisun Bay and the Delta, enterprising fishermen strung nets across river and slough channels to intercept millions of salmon and steelhead on their upstream migrations. The practice was so destructive of the fishery that it was eventually outlawed. By the turn of the century, several entrepreneurs had established a viable oyster fishery in the southern part of the bay.

The bay's great maritime activity naturally spawned an active shipbuilding and boatbuilding industry. In the early 1850s Pacific Mail started a ship repair facility on the Embarcadero, and by the end of the decade several other boatyards were operating along the San Francisco waterfront. In 1854, the Mare Island Naval Yard opened in Vallejo, giving the region its first taste of a "military-industrial complex." Later in the 19th century, boatyards appeared along the Oakland Estuary. In the 1880s San Francisco's Union Iron Works began producing metal-hulled steamships, and in the 1890s, Union built the *Oregon,* first modern battleship constructed on the Pacific Coast.

Mare Island Naval Yard, 1860
(Bancroft Library, UCB)

Maritime Labor and Capital

The corporate heartland of the region's maritime establishment was San Francisco's lower California Street, location of many of the steamship line headquarters. Shipping magnates like Robert Dollar wielded great economic and political power, and "Sunny Jim" Rolph, the city's most popular and longest-serving mayor (1911-1931), was also a steamship line executive. The industry affected the regional culture, and Jack London, who at his best was the Bay Area's finest writer, incorporated the local maritime heritage into many of his works.

If lower California Street was one foundation of the Bay Area's maritime economy, the infamous Barbary Coast, located alongside San Francisco's central waterfront, certainly was another. California did not have a tradition, like New England or Scandinavia, where young men looked to the sea as a career. Instead, the maritime labor force, largely comprised of immigrants, constantly had to be replenished. Most of the

Barbary Coast hotel, bar, and brothel operators were also labor contractors. By hook or crook they delivered more or less able-bodied crews for a price. The term "shanghai," as in "shanghaiing a sailor," originated in San Francisco. Although reformers often tried to clean up corruption and vice in the rest of the city, they made little effort to change the Barbary Coast, whose existence was considered crucial to the regional maritime economy. The district not only provided rest and recreation for merchant seamen, but also was the means by which a maritime labor force could be recruited and controlled.

The campaign to unionize maritime workers was opposed not only by powerful employers and business interests, but also by a significant section of San Francisco's underworld. If union hiring halls replaced bars and brothels as recruitment institutions, the Barbary Coast's economy would suffer. Not surprisingly, the fight to organize seamen and dockworkers was long, bitter, and often violent. Beginning in the 1880s and lasting until the early 1930s, it was basically a class struggle that was also the region's most dramatic conflict between labor and capital during the late 19th and early 20th centuries. The shipping industry was so crucial to the region's economy that Bay Area labor could be secure in its economic and political position only when maritime workers were finally organized.

Working conditions for merchant seamen in the 1880s had not changed much since the practices criticized by Richard Henry Dana on his first voyage 50 years before. Captains and mates still administered corporal punishment, sailors who attempted to escape from brutal conditions were still charged with the crime of jumping ship, and employers still regarded strikes as a form of illegal mutiny. Andrew Furuseth, like many of his compatriots a Scandinavian immigrant, led the early attempts at unionization. He organized several massive strikes, some of which virtually shut down the Port of San Francisco, but won few long-term victories.

Furuseth was more successful in publicizing the plight of merchant seamen. His lobbying was a major reason for passage by Congress of the La Follette Act of 1915, which substantially improved working conditions for American seamen. During World War I, maritime unions grew in numbers and influence, but after the war employers once again managed to break the organizations. And once again Andrew Furuseth was forced to bide his time.

A Time of Change

By the outbreak of World War I, the Bay Area maritime industry was experiencing great changes. As the operation of steamships became more efficient, cargo carriers underwent the shift from sail to steam power that had occurred in passenger traffic a half-century earlier.

Great sailing ships were sold for scrap, or used by the Alaska Packing Company to carry seasonal workers to Alaska canneries. On the bay, internal combustion engines replaced sails on scow schooners, fishing vessels, whitehall boats, and other small craft. Soon sailboats would only be used for sport and recreation. The maritime economy had completed its industrial revolution.

The Panama Canal, finished in 1914, further promoted the development of the shipping industry. Although it lacked the romance of the trip around the Horn, the new sea route from coast to coast via the canal saved both miles and dollars. The United States was now a Pacific power, master of the Philippines, Hawaii, and other island possessions, and San Franciscans assumed that their city would be the maritime heart of this new ocean empire. But other communities also had their eyes on the increasing Pacific trade. Seattle, Portland, and San Diego were growing rapidly. Within the Bay Area, Oakland's city fathers were discussing major port expansion. Most disturbing of all was the rapid development of Los Angeles's port facilities at San Pedro. Just as San Francisco was no longer Queen City of the West, its port was no longer California's sole window on the world.

Today most of San Francisco's central waterfront consists of outmoded and often deserted finger piers. Even its Fisherman's Wharf is far more of a tourist attraction than a working fish depot. Serious maritime activity has shifted to new facilities, some on San Francisco's southern waterfront, but most importantly at Oakland's giant container terminals. Stockton and Sacramento also have modern ports that are linked to the bay by deepwater channels. Richmond is a major oil depot, and, along with Redwood City and Benicia, has ambitious plans for future maritime development. Although San Francisco Bay remains an important port, and shipping is still a major part of the area's economy, the future of San Francisco's historic waterfront will probably be determined more by real estate developers than by shipping magnates.

□ □ □

9 Rails and Ferries

Terminus of the Transcontinental Railroad
This drawing depicts Central Pacific's Oakland wharf in the 1870s, where the national rail system met the local ferry and sail routes of San Francisco Bay. The Chinese laborers were probably waiting for transportation to interior California. (Bancroft Library, UCB)

9

Rails
and
Ferries _____

Theodore Judah was sometimes known as "Crazy Judah" for his obsession with building a transcontinental railroad. An engineer, Judah came to California in the 1850s and built the state's first rail line, providing service between Sacramento and Folsom. Soon he was consumed by the challenge and potential for profit of laying track across the Sierra Nevada.

Judah surveyed the general trans-Sierra route that is still used by the Southern Pacific, and joined the group of citizens who lobbied Congress for a federal subsidy to help construct a transcontinental railroad. The subsidy was essential because no private company was willing or able to raise the capital necessary for the job. Spanning the continent with rails may have been touted as a great accomplishment of the "free enterprise system," but it was free enterprise with a great deal of government help.

The Search for Subsidy

The concept of federal subsidies for transportation and communication links with the west was nothing new. The Pacific Mail Steamship Company and the Butterfield and Wells Fargo stage lines had received government assistance, as did the first transcontinental telegraph hookup. While the dollar value of the rail subsidy was far greater than that of these earlier enterprises, the size of the subsidy was not its major impediment to acceptance by Congress. The real problem was the north-south conflict. In the 1850s passage of a transcontinental railroad bill floundered, as did almost everything else in Congress, on the sectional struggle that soon was to ignite the Civil War. Only after 1861, when the Confederate states pulled out of the Union, was Congress able to pass a rail subsidy bill.

Judah had made several lobbying trips to Washington, was aware of these political realities, and in 1861 formed a corporation that would be in a position to receive a subsidy. He tried to get wealthy San Franciscans such as William Ralston to invest in the venture, but found the city's business establishment was more interested in land speculation, Comstock silver mines, and Bay Area industrial enterprises. Judah was forced to look elsewhere.

He sought backers in Sacramento, where he found such investors as Leland Stanford, a prosperous grocer, Charles Crocker, a dry goods merchant, and Mark Hopkins and Collis P. Huntington, partners in a hardware store. These proved good choices. In addition to being shrewd businessmen with available capital, they had important political connections. The four men were founding members of California's new Republican Party, and in 1861 Stanford was elected the state's pro-Union Republican governor. Since Republicans were also in power in Washington, Judah obtained an appointment to the staff of the joint congressional committee that wrote the railroad bill. Not surprisingly, his company was one of two that were granted land and credit subsidies to build the transcontinental railroad.

The Southern Pacific

Judah named the corporation the Central Pacific, but it eventually evolved into the Southern Pacific Railroad. By that time, Judah was gone from the scene. Ironically, he had died in 1864 in Panama of yellow fever while traveling to New York to raise money with which to

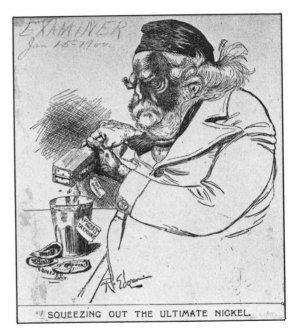

SQUEEZING OUT THE ULTIMATE NICKEL.

"Squeezing Out the Ultimate Nickel"
One of several cartoons that appeared during a *San Francisco Examiner* campaign against Collis Huntington and the Southern Pacific, 1900. Huntington had criticized Hearst for inciting the Spanish-American War, and it is believed that the *Examiner* campaign was Hearst's retaliation. (*San Francisco Examiner*)

buy out his four principal investors. Instead, the four gained undisputed control of the company, and thus of the state's most important emerging corporate force. Scratch the surface of Bay Area life in the late 19th century and you would find the influence of the "SP." It was, in the words of novelist Frank Norris, an "octopus" whose tentacles affected every aspect of the economic and political life of the Bay Area and of California.

When completed, the transcontinental railroad greatly reduced the problem of isolation and distance that had plagued California since Spanish days. The railroad cut travel time between the east and west coasts from weeks to days, thus completing California's effective integration into the American nation. The original subsidy bill provided for a rail line from Sacramento to Council Bluffs, and this was completed by joining Central Pacific and Union Pacific tracks at Promontory Point, Utah in 1869. But Californians realized that the transcontinental would not be truly finished until the railroad reached the waters of San Francisco Bay. Only then would rails actually link the two coasts and tie the west's one great city to the rest of the nation.

For the Bay Area, the immediate question was the location of the line's final terminus. San Franciscans naturally assumed their city would receive the honor, suggesting that the Central Pacific build around the south end of the bay and link up with a local rail line that already ran down the Peninsula to San Jose. The Central Pacific, however, considered San Francisco to be inconveniently located on the west side of the bay. Moreover the city's voters refused to support a local subsidy to attract the railroad. Vallejo also made a strong bid for the terminus, and already had a local rail link to Sacramento, but was far from the region's urban core. Further, the Central Pacific did not wish to deal with another railroad company.

The Rise of Oakland

Instead the "Big Four"—as Stanford, Crocker, Hopkins, and Huntington came to be called—picked Oakland, which has remained the Bay Area's major rail terminus ever since. By the end of 1869, the Central Pacific had built a line to Oakland via the Livermore Valley and Niles Canyon. In the late 1870s the railroad constructed a more direct line via Fairfield, Richmond, and Berkeley, including massive rail ferries across Carquinez Strait, between Benicia and Port Costa.

Oakland's geographical advantage was obvious: it was located in the central part of the region, adjacent to San Francisco, but did not require a water crossing or a long line around the bay. Equally important to the Big Four, Oakland was still a small community whose economy and politics the railroad could easily dominate. Oakland's mayor Sam Merritt—who a few years earlier had dammed an arm of the Oak-

Train Ferry at Port Costa, Early 1880s
The ferry *Solano* in Port Costa slip, shown shortly after the train-ferry began carrying passenger trains across Carquinez Strait, between Benicia and Port Costa. (Southern Pacific)

land Estuary to create "Lake Merritt"—engineered a complicated scheme whereby the town's waterfront came under railroad control. The Southern Pacific effectively dominated the Port of Oakland until the city finally asserted ownership over its waterfront in 1910. As long as the SP domination lasted, rival rail lines were unable to establish an Oakland terminal.

Bird's Eye View of Oakland, 1893
(Southern Pacific)

There was no joy in San Francisco when the railroad announced its decision in favor of Oakland. San Franciscans worried that it might cause a significant shift in power and influence, with Oakland becoming the new major center of Bay Area economic life, and San Francisco declining into a west bay "Contra Costa." In fact, the transcontinental's arrival marked Oakland's transformation from a modest bayside community into an integral part of the region's urban core. Its population increased rapidly after 1869, soon eclipsing Sacramento to become the state's second largest city, but Oakland has always remained San Francisco's junior partner. The Sacramento merchants who controlled the railroad accepted the prestige of the Queen City of the West and had no intention of undermining its supremacy. The railroad shops, yards, and roundhouses were built in Oakland, but its headquarters were in San Francisco. Blue-collar railroad workers moved into new West Oakland neighborhoods, but the Big Four built their monumental mansions on top of San Francisco's Nob Hill. Oakland might do the work, but the orders would come from San Francisco.

The new railroad terminals reflected Oakland's status. Along the northwest Oakland waterfront, the Big Four built a long wharf that extended nearly two miles into the bay. Freight trains traveled to the end of the wharf, transferring their cargoes to boats for the short voyage to San Francisco. The major passenger depot was the Oakland Mole, built on piers off Oakland's western shore so that railroad patrons could leave the trains and walk a few feet to San Francisco-bound ferries. Both terminals were designed on the assumption that most rail freight and passengers would continue to San Francisco, rather than stop in Oakland.

A Major Transit Link

Accordingly, the water route from Oakland to San Francisco became the Bay Area's major local transit and transportation link, and the railroad monopolized the route for the rest of the 19th century. When a tough Oakland merchant, John Davies, attempted to run a San Francisco ferry in competition with the railroad, the SP harassed him and finally drove him out of business. Davies eventually managed to parlay his notoriety into a successful political career, serving as Oakland's mayor for many years, but the SP retained its ferry monopoly.

By 1873, more than 2 million trips per year were being made on the East Bay-to-San Francisco ferry runs, and by 1877, the figure had grown to over 5 million. In addition to railroad passengers, the SP ferries served commuters who lived in Oakland or Alameda and worked in downtown San Francisco. The neighborhoods adjacent to Lake Merritt and on Alameda's South Shore were the Bay Area's first real commuter suburbs. While professional people often lived in these areas, working-class families were likely to have homes in West Oakland and in industrial districts along the Estuary. Like San Franciscans before them, East Bay residents quickly began segregating themselves into neighborhoods that reflected differences in wealth and class.

Local Railroad Development

In addition to the transcontinental route, several Bay Area companies constructed local railroads. As we have seen, the lines from San

The Ferry "Oakland"
Built in 1860 as the riverboat *Chrysopolis* and reconstructed as a ferry in 1875, the *Oakland* remained in use until 1940. The vessel was thus in service throughout virtually the entire period of significant riverboat and ferry activity in Bay Area transportation. (Bancroft Library, UCB)

Jose to San Francisco, and from Vallejo to Sacramento, predated the Central Pacific, but both were incorporated into the Big Four's system. The San Jose route stimulated some development on the Peninsula, and many wealthy businessmen emulated William Ralston by establishing substantial country estates there, the largest probably being Leland Stanford's "farm" at Palo Alto. But since San Mateo County rail fares were a good deal higher than those on East Bay ferry routes, there was not much suburban building south of San Francisco. On the other hand, the San Jose-San Francisco line effectively ended Alviso's brief career as a major bay port, for produce from the Santa Clara Valley or San Jose canneries could go to San Francisco by train.

Local rail construction in the East Bay also began before the arrival of the transcontinental route. By the time the Central Pacific was completed, local lines already linked Oakland with Hayward, San Leandro, and Alameda. Initially, the Big Four incorporated these lines into the SP system, adding a branch line to Berkeley in the late 1870s. The latter proceeded up Shattuck Avenue, thus forming the new university town's major thoroughfare.

In the North Bay, lines extended from Vallejo into Napa Valley, and from Sausalito and Tiburon into central and western Marin and Sonoma counties. These routes stimulated the further development of towns and agriculture, and opened vacation areas along the Russian River and around Sam Brannan's spa at Calistoga. By the early 20th century, these local rail systems had also been integrated into the SP network.

Of the various local lines, only the Peninsula route brought trains directly into San Francisco. The others built railheads on the bay from which they established ferry connections to the city. Vallejo, for example, was the major ferry depot for Napa and Solano counties. Sausalito and Tiburon were major terminals for the North Bay, their frequent ferry service allowing weekend retreats and even suburban housing to develop in southern Marin. When the Santa Fe finally broke the Southern Pacific's monopoly on Bay Area rail contact with the rest of the nation in 1900, it chose Richmond as its terminus. This not only produced a new bayshore community, but also a new ferry route from Richmond to San Francisco. Similarly, when Western Pacific built its rail line into central Oakland in 1910, it initiated another transbay ferry line. Just as most roads in France are supposed to lead to Paris, almost all ferry lines on the bay led to San Francisco.

Winehaven
The California Wine Association's winery and shipping terminal at Point Richmond, early 1900s. (Wine Institute)

Other Railroad Influences

The transportation boom of the late 19th century affected all of California, not just the Bay Area. The Southern Pacific opened up the Central Valley to large-scale farming, and by the 1880s California was the nation's leading grain export state. Bay Area agriculture, in turn, concentrated on intensive cultivation of fruit and vegetable crops, a trend that was followed by the Central Valley at the end of the century. The agricultural expansion opened major investment opportunities for Bay Area businessmen, and the founders of California corporate farming were 19th century San Francisco land barons like Henry Miller, Charles Lux, James Ben Ali Haggin, and Lloyd Tevis. While there were and are large numbers of small and middle-size farms in California, urban-based agribusiness interests have dominated the state's agricultural economy from the beginning of the 19th century land boom until now.

The agricultural expansion also influenced the development of Bay Area industry. Initial manufacturing growth had been in consumer fields, such as flour milling and brewing, or in industries dependent on mining, such as blasting powder, smelting, and mining machinery. By the 1880s, however, new industries related to agriculture were rapidly expanding. Canning became a major Bay Area activity. The region also developed a substantial agricultural machine industry. C. L. Best Company in San Leandro became one of the major farm implement manufacturers, eventually merging with Holt Brothers in Stockton to form Caterpillar Tractor. Caterpillar still operates a San Leandro plant.

Railroad construction promoted industrial dispersion. Manufacturing was initially concentrated in San Francisco, but by the 1870s Oakland and the East Bay were becoming important industrial locations. After the SP rerouted its main line along the northern Contra Costa bay shore in the late '70s, several powder companies located there, thus relieving urban residents' well-founded fears of damaging explosions in the midst of city neighborhoods. The existence of the Peninsula rail line similarly influenced the development of the industrial community of South San Francisco, which began in the early 1890s with the establishment of a large meat-packing plant.

The Southern Pacific also crossed the Tehachapi Mountains in the mid-1870s, tying southern California into the national rail network. This link brought rapid economic and population growth, particularly after the Santa Fe's 1887 arrival in the region. In 1870 Los Angeles had been "Queen of the Cow Counties," a rough, bilingual cattle town of 6,000, but by 1900 it had a population of over 100,000 and was a booming metropolis, ready and willing to challenge San Francisco's urban supremacy.

Transportation in San Francisco

The new transportation systems had a profound impact within San Francisco itself. The city had developed a compact settlement pattern in the Gold Rush period. Stage or omnibus service was offered to outlying

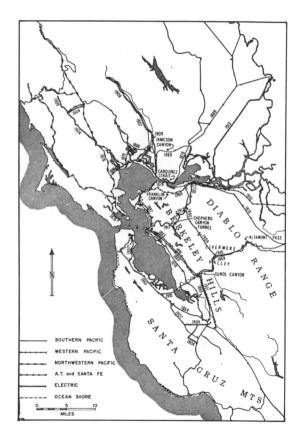

Steam Railroads and Electric Interurban Lines
(Vance, *Geography . . .*)

locations such as Mission Dolores, but within the small urbanized core people could easily walk to work, shopping, or recreation. By 1860, however, the city was big enough to need a transit system. Horse cars, animal-powered rail coaches, made their appearance, effectively serving the South-of-Market and Inner Mission districts. Similar vehicles began operation in and around central Oakland in the 1870s. Entrepreneurs also introduced small steam lines within the cities, including service to Ocean Beach in San Francisco via a route that eventually became Geary Boulevard. However, horse cars were not suitable for the steep hills north of Market Street, and steam trains were noisy, smelly, and not efficient for constant stop-and-go service within the urban core.

According to local tradition, a terrible horse-car crash on a San Francisco hill set local rope merchant Andrew Hallidie to thinking about a more efficient transit system for San Francisco. His answer was the cable car, relying on mechanical rather than animal power, and also avoiding the problems of steam trains for urban use. Hallidie's first cable system, the Clay Street line, begun in 1873, was an immediate success. Within a decade San Francisco had more than 100 miles of cable car tracks.

The new transit technology allowed development of hilltop residential neighborhoods north of Market Street. In 1868, entrepreneurs had excavated a large cut through Rincon Hill for a wagon road via Second Street to industrial property in the recently filled tidal flats of Mission

Bay. This action damaged the prestige of the old elite district on Rincon Hill, and wealthy San Franciscans looked for new locations north of Market. Leland Stanford began building his Nob Hill mansion at the same time that he invested in the California Street Cable Car Line, which served the hill. Soon he had neighbors, including the other members of the Big Four, as well as other wealthy San Franciscans. By the 1880s, Nob Hill was the city's most prestigious address, and its mansions were great, gaudy monuments to the wealth and power of a new generation of San Francisco magnates.

Cable car lines also crossed Van Ness Avenue, opening the Western Addition, Pacific Heights, and Cow Hollow to rapid development. Land prices were high, and 25-foot-wide lots were common. Developers often built narrow "Victorian" row houses in the new middle-class neighborhoods, which were linked to downtown by the cable cars. By the time of the 1894 Mid-Winter Fair in Golden Gate Park, the cable had reached the eastern edge of the park itself. Most of the lines carried passengers to Market Street, and many continued down that thoroughfare to the Ferry Building, the junction of San Francisco's internal transit system and the regional network of rails and ferries.

In 1898 the original barn-like wooden ferry terminal was replaced by a graceful steel and concrete structure surmounted by a good imitation of a Spanish-Moorish tower. Other large European and American cities built great railroad stations as symbols of the new urban industrial

The Ferry Building, Circa 1910
(Bancroft Library, UCB)

age, while San Francisco erected a ferry building far outclassing any train terminal the city was ever to build. This was appropriate, for the Ferry Building was one of the world's great urban passenger depots. By 1930 some 40 ferry boats operated on San Francisco Bay, and dozens of electric trolley and cable car lines ran to the great terminal at the foot of Market Street.

Today the view of the Ferry Building from the rest of the city is largely blocked by the bulk of the Embarcadero Freeway, a fitting comment on the way the automobile has destroyed the Bay Area's former transit systems. Bchind the freeway, however, the Ferry Building still stands, a monument to the original rail and ferry network that helped turn the Bay Area into a coherent metropolitan region.

□ □ □

Students of San Francisco's Chinese School
In 1871 the city excluded Chinese from the public schools, but when the courts prohibited this policy in 1884, San Francisco established a segregated institution for Chinese, which lasted well into the 20th century. (Bancroft Library, UCB)

10

Immigrant Metropolis _____

The Gold Rush, with its lure of quick wealth, attracted people of all races and many nationalities. French newspapers ran lotteries offering trips to California as prizes, and some of the winners may eventually have been part of San Francisco's prestigious "French Colony." Gold seekers from Mexico, Peru, and Chile caused a dramatic increase in the Bay Area's Spanish-speaking population, and like the Californios they were often victims of Anglo violence and repression. Immigrants from Australia, New Zealand, and Hawaii pioneered transpacific routes, and significant numbers of Chinese began arriving in 1852. While many of the early immigrants soon returned home, others stayed, and the Gold Rush produced a cosmopolitan, multinational population mix that has characterized the Bay Area ever since.

In 1880 about 60 percent of San Francisco's population was of "immigrant stock," people who were either foreign-born themselves or children of foreign-born parents. This was one of the highest such percentages of any American city at the time. The impact of immigration was not limited to San Francisco alone; the entire Bay Area was affected. Immigrants and their children were found at every level of society, but primarily they were members of blue-collar families. The early history of the region's working class is to a large extent a history of immigrants.

The Irish

The Irish were the Bay Area's largest foreign-born group by the 1880s, when they and their children made up nearly a third of San Francisco's entire population. The Gold Rush had come in the midst of the great migrations caused by the Potato Famine, and many of the new Irish-Americans eventually made their way west. "Eventually" is a key word here, for most of the Irish, like many other European immigrants to the Bay Area, apparently came west only after some years of residence on the east coast.

Some of California's wealthiest and most powerful people in the late 19th century were of Irish descent. James Flood and William O'Brien were San Francisco bartenders who teamed up with mining superintendents John MacKay and James Fair to speculate in Comstock silver stock. After the downfall of William Ralston, the four Irish-Americans emerged as the "Comstock Kings," the most powerful figures in Nevada's silver industry. The Bay Area's first major urban politician, Senator David Broderick, the son of Irish immigrants, brought to San Francisco politics an important Irish presence that lasted for over a century. Blind Chris Buckley, the city's infamous political boss during the 1880s, was of Irish descent, as was the major reform politician of the 1890s, banker James D. Phelan. This Irish political influence resulted in strong Irish representation in the municipal workforce, particularly in the police and fire departments. By the 1880s the Irish also dominated the region's powerful Catholic clergy and its parochial schools.

Despite the prominence of many 19th century Irish-Americans, most of the Irish immigrant population was working class. They did much of the basic labor that transformed the Bay Area into a major metropolitan region, and several of the most important leaders of the region's thriving labor movement were also of Irish descent. Working-class neighborhoods such as San Francisco's South-of-Market area were predominantly Irish, as was early Ocean View, the industrial and farming community that was to become West Berkeley. In fact, Irish were found in virtually every Bay Area community that was heavily populated by blue-collar workers.

Other European Workers

The Gold Rush coincided not only with the Potato Famine, but also with revolutionary upheavals in Central Europe that caused significant immigration from Germany and the Austro-Hungarian Empire. One of the founders of the Bay Area's wine industry, Agoston Haraszthy, was a self-proclaimed Hungarian nobleman. Germans were numerous and important in retail commerce and in the region's skilled trades. Oakland's Fruitvale district was the site of a well-organized German immigrant community that included German Protestant and Catholic churches, as well as strong ethnic institutions. Founders of a number of important Bay Area Jewish families, including Adolph Sutro, and the Stern and Haas families that have controlled Levi Strauss & Company, were also part of the larger German immigration.

Scandinavian and British immigrants were important in the maritime trades, serving not only as seamen but also as skilled boat and ship builders. The Bay Area's fleet of lumber schooners was called the "Scandinavian Navy," because of the birthplaces of most of the officers and crews. English and Scottish capital and entrepreneurial skill were also significant in the economic development of the Bay Area.

Most 19th century immigration to the United States came from Northern Europe, but by the end of the 1880s southern and eastern Europeans began arriving in large numbers. By the 1890s the Bay Area

Buena Vista Winery, Near Sonoma, Late 1870s
Founded by Agoston Haraszthy, a Hungarian who experimented with vine growing in the Bay Area. He is said to have imported cuttings representing some 140 European varieties. (Wine Institute)

felt the effects of this "new immigration." Portuguese, particularly from the Azores, played a major role in Bay Area agriculture as orchardists, dairy farmers, and cannery workers. They became an important part of the population of East Oakland, San Leandro, Hayward, and Half Moon Bay. Greeks, often working for the railroad or operating small cafes and stores, settled in the South-of-Market and West Oakland districts. Social and political upheavals in Czarist Russia prompted migrations of Polish and Russian Jews, including members of a remarkable community of socialist chicken farmers in Petaluma. Earlier upheavals had also caused the immigration of conservative Russian Christians, who settled on San Francisco's Potrero Hill and later in the city's Richmond district.

Greek Orthodox Church in Oakland
The Holy Church of the Dormition was built in 1919-1921 at the end of the major era of Greek immigration, which began about 1880. The message in Greek: "In Church God Is Worshipped." (Greek Orthodox Church of the Ascension, Oakland)

The Italians

The Italians comprised by far the largest of the "new immigrant" groups. A few northern Italian settlers had arrived during the Gold Rush, opening small businesses and restaurants. As we have seen, they and Dalmatian immigrants dominated San Francisco's fishing industry, introducing lateen-sail fishing boats to the bay, and establishing Fisherman's Wharf. In the 1890s this small Italian immigrant commun-

Fisherman's Wharf, Circa 1905
The lateen sails used by the fishing boats were the distinctive contribution of San Francisco's Italian and Dalmation fishermen. (San Francisco Archives)

ity was overwhelmed by a much larger Italian migration. While the bulk of Bay Area Italians continued to have roots in northern Italy, many of the newcomers immigrated from southern regions such as Sicily. By 1920 Italians had replaced the Irish as California's most numerous foreign-born group.

As was the case in many immigrant communities, tensions arose between the older, established Italian families and the great wave of often impoverished newcomers. The Bay Area's Italian community was split by old-country rivalries between north and south Italy and by political controversies imported from Europe. But along with conflict came mutually profitable cooperation. Established entrepreneurs such as Anthony Sbarbaro provided economic opportunity for hundreds of his recently arrived countrymen at the Italian-Swiss Colony winery at Asti. A. P. Giannini, another member of a well-established Bay Area Italian-American family, began his Bank of Italy by providing small loans to enterprising new arrivals. This gave Giannini experience in consumer-oriented banking that eventually helped him to build the giant Bank of America, despite opposition from the established financial elites of San Francisco and New York.

Like the Irish, Italians were found at every socioeconomic level of Bay Area life. But also like the Irish, Italians were primarily blue-collar workers. By the early 20th century, they practiced most working-class occupations. Moreover, working-class neighborhoods such as West

Oakland and West Berkeley were becoming increasingly though not exclusively Italian. North Beach, settled by Chileans in early Gold Rush days, and then by Irish and Germans, was predominantly Italian by the turn of the century. So was the new neighborhood forming in North Oakland along Telegraph Avenue.

Contrasted with Oscar Handlin's description of the immigrant as "the uprooted," Andrew Rolle has called Italians of California "the upraised." Although most Italian immigrants were city dwellers, some of the newcomers played a vital role in the development of Bay Area agriculture. They labored as agricultural and cannery workers and established truck farms, often on leased land at the edge of urban settlements. Before trolley lines promoted rapid development west of Twin Peaks and in the Outer Mission district, Italian farmers even produced substantial harvests within San Francisco itself. They also planted artichokes and other green vegetables along the San Mateo County coast, and established dairy farms in Marin and Sonoma counties. Italian vintners and fieldworkers were important to the growth of wineries in Napa and Sonoma counties, and in the Livermore and Santa Clara valleys. Italian immigrant families established fine restaurants and dominated the region's wholesale fruit, vegetable, and wine distribution network. They also were active at the other end of the food chain, organizing the scavenger companies that exist to this day in both San Francisco and Oakland.

Harvesting Grapes, Sonoma County, 1880s
California vintners have long produced wine from a variety of vines, primarily of European origin. One example is the zinfandel grape, whose lineage and name derivation are uncertain. Dry red zinfandel wine is a distinctive product of California and the Bay Area. (Wine Institute)

Temple Emanu-El, 1868
Temple Emanu-El on Sutter Street, forerunner of the present Byzantine-domed temple on Lake Street and Arguello Boulevard. Designed by an Englishman, William Patton, the architecture is a mixture of styles, including domes that some have called "Moorish," while others suggest that they symbolize the headpieces of the Torah, or resemble the bulbous cupolas observed on many central European Baroque-era churches and monasteries. (Southern Pacific)

Prejudice Against White Immigrants

Italians and other European immigrants experienced prejudice and discrimination at the hands of "native" Bay Area residents—who themselves had often arrived only a few years earlier. Sometimes anti-immigrant sentiment was combined with religious bigotry. Thus prominent Jewish businessmen in San Francisco established their own social club, the Concordia, in part because they were banned from many of the city's other men's clubs. Some leaders of the 1856 Vigilance Committee displayed a not-too-subtle anti-Irish bias, and anti-Catholicism was behind some of the furious competition between public and parochial schools in late 19th century San Francisco. By the beginning of the 20th century, the large influx of Italians and other southern Europeans was raising new nativist fears.

What is surprising, however, is not the existence of such prejudice, but that it was less vehement and had less impact than in most other American metropolitan regions. Overt job discrimination against European immigrants was rare in the Bay Area. Moreover, multinational working-class districts were the rule, although some exclusive ethnic neighborhoods did develop. While eastern employers often used national and religious differences and friction between immigrant groups to break unions and strikes, the powerful Bay Area labor movement was largely the creation of immigrants from many nations, who showed a remarkable ability to cooperate and maintain union solidarity.

The comparative lack of prejudice and discrimination was due in part to the very newness of the region. Within a few decades, hundreds of thousands of newcomers, both American and foreign-born, arrived in the Bay Area. Even at the end of the 19th century, almost everyone was a recent arrival, and rigid social structures had not had time to develop. Except for a few brief periods of severe depression, the economy was expanding and the success of one group did not necessarily have to come at the expense of another. It is also significant that a large portion of the Bay Area immigrants came west after first living in the east. They were not "fresh off the boat" and thus already had considerable American experience and knowledge of English. Consequently they were probably less willing than east-coast immigrants to work for very low wages and serve as strikebreakers. They may also have had less need to maintain very close-knit ethnic neighborhoods. A final and crucially important point is that Bay Area whites, both native-born and immigrant, shared a common target of prejudice: the Chinese. Historian Alexander Saxton has called them the white worker's "indispensable enemy."

The Chinese: A Common Target

The Bay Area's long heritage of anti-Asian discrimination goes back at least to 1852, the year of the first large-scale immigration of

Chinese to California. These immigrants came from the troubled region around the city of Canton. The Cantonese pioneers, like many others in California, hoped to get rich quick. But they soon faced racial discrimination, and were forced to look for economic activities that served white miners, instead of competing with them. Since there were few women in early Gold Rush California, many of the mostly male Chinese found a niche in what the 19th century considered ''women's work.'' They did laundry, cooking, and domestic service. Gangs of Chinese also worked otherwise-abandoned gold fields, and took low-paying jobs usually avoided by whites. By the time construction began on the transcontinental railroad, the immigration route from Canton and the tradition of cheap Chinese labor were well established. As we have seen, the Big Four and many other local employers took full advantage of that fact, profiting greatly from the prevailing racial prejudice.

Until the 1870s most California Chinese lived in the mountain counties where mining and railroad construction were centered. Even then, however, San Francisco was the unofficial capital of Chinese America. It was in San Francisco that wealthy Chinese merchants and labor contractors established stores, offices, and dormitories. San Francisco was headquarters for the regional associations, clan organizations, and tongs that were the institutional foundations of Chinese immigrant life. The Chinese community occupied old buildings near Portsmouth

Square that had been vacated by white businesses looking for more fashionable locations. The same was true along DuPont Street (Grant Avenue), where the Bay Area's oldest and most famous ethnic neighborhood developed. Other Bay Area communities also had Chinatowns, but none rivaled the size or importance of San Francisco's.

The completion of the transcontinental railroad in 1869 forced the Chinese out of the mountain counties and into new occupational fields. They became an important component of California's agricultural labor force, and often established small truck farms of their own. Chinese crewmen served on merchant ships, and the Asian immigrants also became a significant part of the urban workforce. The number of Bay Area Chinese increased steadily during the 1870s, and by 1880 Chinese comprised about 10 percent of all San Franciscans. This figure does not, however, adequately indicate the Chinese economic impact. Since the great majority of Asian immigrants were young, unattached men, they made up far more than 10 percent of the labor force.

Unfortunately the rapid growth in the Chinese population coincided with the major economic depression of the late 1870s. As unemployment increased, white workers were willing to take jobs traditionally reserved for Chinese. At the same time, companies that previously hired only whites were now tempted to employ cheaper Chinese labor. Direct economic competition between whites and Asians exacerbated American racial prejudice and poisoned the social and political atmos-

Denis Kearney Fanning Anti-Asian Sentiment
(Bancroft Library, UCB)

phere. The causes of the economic hard times were complex and poorly understood, but the Chinese made a perfect scapegoat.

The chief political agent of anti-Asian sentiment during the late 1870s was the Workingman's Party. Started by San Francisco labor leaders as a protest against economic conditions, the party's platform included rational reforms, and its organizational structure gave alienated workers a sense of participation in community affairs. Under the demagogic leadership of Denis Kearney, however, the reforms were largely forgotten and anti-Chinese rhetoric came to the fore. Kearney, an Irish immigrant like many of the workers who attended his sandlot meetings, linked racism, ethnic rivalry, and economic competition by using the simple slogan "The Chinese Must Go." While the party's main strength was in San Francisco, it had substantial support in many Bay Area communities. There was an active chapter in Oakland, and the Workingman's slate won Berkeley's first municipal election in 1878.

When prosperity finally returned in the 1880s, the Workingman's Party disintegrated and Denis Kearney became a conservative San Francisco businessman. But anti-Asian sentiment had been established as an important ingredient of California politics, and so it remained for another 60 years. Even passage of the federal Chinese Exclusion Law in 1882, the first case of significant immigration restriction in American history, did not lessen attempts at discrimination. The state Legislature tried to outlaw Chinese shrimp fishing in the bay, and San Francisco's Board of Supervisors attempted to ban Chinese laundries and rooming houses. The city's Board of Education excluded Chinese children from San Francisco public schools for nearly 15 years. When the courts finally ruled that such exclusion was unconstitutional, the city established a segregated public school for Chinese.

The federal exclusion law never fully stopped Chinese immigration. A few illegals continued to slip through, and the law allowed exemptions in certain cases. The government eventually established an interrogation center on Angel Island to investigate prospective Asian immigrants, and at least some Chinese immigration continued, both legal and illegal. Nevertheless, after 1882 the Chinese population gradually declined. Since most Chinese in California were single men intending to return home, there was only a small number of second-generation Chinese-Americans, and it took several decades for the Chinese population to recover to its 1880 level. San Francisco's Chinatown developed a siege mentality, as a place of refuge for a harassed people. Of the other Bay Area Chinatowns, only Oakland's survived the exclusion era. It relocated several times, occupying its present site east of Jack London Square after the 1906 earthquake.

The Japanese

Meanwhile Japanese had replaced Chinese as the most numerous Asian immigrant group, filling employers' demand for a new source of cheap, nonwhite labor. After the earthquake, the Japanese thus became the region's chief target of anti-Asian prejudice. The hostility was reinforced by the long international rivalry between the United States and Japan, and social conflict in California often coincided with major international incidents. In 1906, for example, the San Francisco Board of Education attempted to force all Japanese children into the city's segregated Chinese school. Japanese parents complained to Tokyo newspapers and to the Japanese government, and in Japan the matter was regarded as a national insult. President Theodore Roosevelt eventually forced the city to readmit Japanese children to regular public schools—the Chinese continued to be segregated—but the incident was one of many that left a bitter legacy on both sides of the Pacific. Later, California's attempt to deprive Japanese immigrants of their right to own agricultural property through an ''Alien Land Law'' had similar international repercussions.

Although substantial Japanese communities developed in San Francisco, Oakland, and Berkeley, southern California became the heartland of Japanese immigrant life. Job opportunities were restricted by the Bay Area's powerful labor movement with its strong anti-Asian tradition. Opportunities were also limited by the presence of other established immigrant groups, particularly the Chinese and Italians, who occupied economic niches that otherwise might have been available to Japanese. By contrast, southern California labor was weak, and the region was far less affected by 19th century immigration than the Bay Area. When Los Angeles and its neighbors began their remarkable metropolitan growth, the Japanese found opportunities in truck farming, wholesale and retail produce, and fishing. In the Bay Area such work was already being done by Italians and Chinese.

The New Migrations

After World War I, anti-immigrant sentiment grew throughout the nation. Congress banned further immigration from Japan, and also instituted quotas that sharply reduced migrations from southern and eastern Europe. This did not end immigration to California, however. Increasing numbers of Mexicans replaced earlier arrivals from Europe and Asia in the California labor market. Immigration from the Philippines, then an American territory exempted from the Asian Exclusion Law, also took up the slack.

After World War II, immigration restrictions were somewhat liberalized, and then drastically revised in 1965. As we shall see, the result was a great new migration from Asia, increased European immigration, and a continued flow of both legal and illegal arrivals from

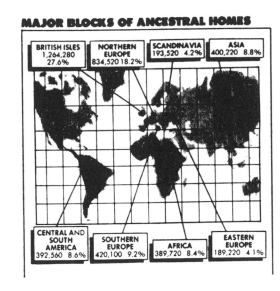

The Diverse Ethnic Roots of Bay Area Residents
(San Francisco Chronicle © 1984)

Latin America. According to the 1980 census, the percentage of "immigrant stock" people in San Francisco's population is almost as high today as it was a century ago. In short, the Bay Area has continued to play its traditional role as an immigrant metropolis.

□ □ □

11 Earthquake Era

Ruins of the Stanford University Library, 1906
Although most of downtown San Francisco was destroyed by fire, the city
suffered less direct damage from the earthquake than many other Bay Area
locations, including the Stanford campus, which sits almost on top of the San
Andreas fault. (Bancroft Library, UCB)

11

Earthquake Era

In 1905 a group of influential San Franciscans, led by former mayor James D. Phelan, commissioned Daniel Hudson Burnham to prepare a new physical plan for their city. Burnham was one of America's leading architects, and had already made similar plans for St. Louis and Washington, DC.

Local architect Willis Polk designed a wooden bungalow on Diamond Heights for Burnham. From this vantage point overlooking the city, the great man and his assistant came up with ideas that stunned many San Franciscans, proposing tree-lined boulevards to be carved through the existing street pattern, and advocating construction of great new public buildings, stadiums, and a new system of neighborhood

Burnham Civic Center Plan, 1906
(Environmental Design Library, UCB)

parks and playgrounds. The plan also envisioned extension of the Panhandle to Van Ness Avenue, a crescent-shaped civic center, and a vast expanse of permanent open space west of Twin Peaks that would make Golden Gate Park look small by comparison.

Burnham's boldness astonished even some of his sponsors, and most San Franciscans probably dismissed the plan as visionary in the extreme. Nevertheless the Board of Supervisors agreed to print several thousand copies of the document, which were awaiting public distribution when in the early morning of April 18, 1906 the Bay Area was rocked by the greatest natural disaster ever to hit a major American metropolitan region.

"The American Renaissance"

The San Francisco earthquake struck in the midst of an era that some architectural historians call "The American Renaissance," a time when impressive public and private buildings were constructed, often in neo-Renaissance style. (San Francisco's Ferry Building is a prime example.) More fundamentally, it was a time when American architects and planners, like the nation's Progressive political and social reformers, believed they could "civilize" the chaotic industrial cities that had evolved in the previous generation. Influential Americans wanted to improve the cities' appearance and quality of life, as well as their politics and social amenities, so that the new urban centers might live up to the impressive accomplishments of the century's industrial economy. People like Phelan and Burnham had an ideal image of the American city, based on the example of Europe's great urban centers, particularly Paris.

This was part of the message of the 1893 Chicago Exposition. The exposition grounds were a dream city that provided a tangible model of what American metropolises could become and, by implication, was an indictment of what they actually were. Among San Franciscans attending the 1893 Chicago fair was Michael deYoung, publisher of the *Chronicle*. He returned home convinced that San Francisco should hold its own exposition. The city was suffering the effects of the depression of the mid-'90s, and deYoung thought that a great fair would stimulate business and direct the attention of discontented workers away from the economic crisis. He won the support of other influential businessmen and politicians, the result being the 1894 Mid-Winter International Exposition in Golden Gate Park.

The fairgrounds were graced with impressive buildings and international exhibits, including the only present-day survivor, the Japanese Tea Garden. (The deYoung Museum and the California Academy of Sciences, however, are on sites once occupied by exposition buildings.) The exposition established Golden Gate Park as the city's chief recreation area, sealing the doom of private amusement grounds such as Woodward's Gardens in the Mission. The fair may have also convinced men like Phelan of the need for a physical and political regeneration of the city they dreamed might someday become the "Paris of the West."

Woodward's Gardens, 1893
Private amusement park on Mission Street, San Francisco. (Bancroft Library, UCB)

San Francisco's Competitors

By 1905, Phelan and his supporters saw in San Francisco's future both opportunities and dangers. The Spanish-American War resulted in American annexation of the Philippines, Guam, and Hawaii, making the United States a major Pacific power, a fact that was reinforced by construction of the Panama Canal. Prominent San Franciscans believed their city could profit tremendously from these international successes, becoming the financial, commercial, and political center of America's Pacific empire. But we have already noted how new urban rivals had begun to threaten San Francisco, which was no longer the west's only real city. Seattle, Portland, and even Oakland were growing more rapidly than the "Queen City of the West."

The most ominous rival was Los Angeles. In 1880 Los Angeles had less than a tenth as many people as San Francisco, but by 1905 it had over half the population of its northern rival. San Francisco's powerful labor movement had given the city the highest blue-collar wage rates in the nation, whereas Los Angeles was an "open-shop" city of struggling unions and comparatively low wages. The decentralized settlement pattern in Los Angeles produced spacious neighborhoods, which in comparison made San Francisco seem congested and unattractive. Burnham's beautification plan was thus seen as necessary to meet the growing urban competition, as well as to transform San Francisco into a city worthy of being America's great Pacific metropolis.

The Earthquake and Fire

The 1906 earthquake rudely interrupted the dreams of prominent San Franciscans. The initial shaking destroyed many brick buildings and caused severe damage where there was unstable fill, e.g., the South-of-Market area. But most of the city's structures, including the common wood-frame houses and the new concrete and steel highrise office buildings, stood up surprisingly well. Because the quake hit in the early morning, few people were on the streets, and, of a total population of 400,000, fewer than 500 San Franciscans were fatally injured.

The earthquake caused fires to start, however, and ruptured water lines needed to fight the flames. The uncontrolled fires joined in a great conflagration which destroyed about one-fourth of the settled portion of the city, before being stopped at Van Ness Avenue. Even this figure

After the Earthquake and Fire
Looking southeast across Nob Hill toward the still-standing but burned-out Fairmont Hotel and Flood mansion (now the Pacific Union Club). (San Francisco Archives)

does not tell the entire story. The flames ravaged the financial district, the downtown commercial center, much of the industrial sector, and the city's most densely populated residential neighborhoods north and south of Market. The economic and social core of the west's greatest metropolis was in ruins.

San Francisco was by no means the only community that suffered. The earthquake's epicenter was on the Bear Valley Ranch near Point Reyes. Several nearby western Marin towns, such as Bolinas and Point Reyes Station, were severely damaged, as was Santa Rosa, on unstable land 25 miles to the east. South of San Francisco, along the San Andreas Fault, buildings toppled on the Stanford campus and in the city of San Jose. The East Bay, on the other hand, got off lightly. A few old brick buildings collapsed and hundreds of chimneys fell, but Oakland, Berkeley, and Alameda remained fully functioning urban communities. They received thousands of San Francisco refugees and eagerly accommodated hundreds of San Francisco businesses forced to relocate. Downtown Oakland enjoyed a commercial boom, and the business district expanded rapidly northward along Broadway.

Within San Francisco, the massive refugee camps in Golden Gate Park soon emptied, and people crowded into residential districts that the fire had spared. Neighborhoods such as the Western Addition, Haight-Ashbury, and Inner Mission became densely populated. Vacant lots were quickly built on, and single-family houses were often transformed into flats. Fillmore and Mission streets became major commercial thoroughfares, taking up the slack from the destroyed downtown shopping area.

Reconstruction

As soon as the flames were out, San Franciscans began arguing about the city's reconstruction. Daniel Hudson Burnham returned to San Francisco, convinced that his plan was now feasible. While his ideas may originally have seemed impractical, the earthquake and fire had given planners a clean slate. The architect became chief consultant to the high-powered citizens' committee directing the reconstruction effort, and the committee included many of Burnham's ideas in its final recommendations.

Other San Franciscans, however, were not convinced that this was the time to experiment with elements of the Burnham plan. The *San Francisco Chronicle* spoke for many businessmen when it argued that Burnham's schemes would stall the process of reconstruction, forcing the city into conflicts over street redesign and property condemnation. Meanwhile, Los Angeles would boom, and relocated San Francisco firms would make their permanent homes in Oakland. The surest and simplest way to reestablish San Francisco's traditional urban and economic supremacy was to rebuild as quickly as possible on existing street and property lines. Ironically, the *Chronicle* seemed to be arguing that the earthquake and fire had made the Burnham plan all the more impractical.

The Graft Trials

The plan also got enmeshed in the complexities of San Francisco politics. Before the earthquake, Phelan and several other wealthy,

Burnham Athenaeum Plan, 1906
"The Athenaeum . . . would consist of courts, terraces and colonnaded shelters. . . . The central court would be the setting for the principal monument . . . a colossal figure symbolical of San Francisco." Daniel H. Burnham (Environmental Design Library, UCB)

reform-minded citizens had backed a secret investigation of the city's Union Labor Party administration. As expected, the probe turned up evidence of spectacular graft and corruption. A few weeks after the quake, the district attorney brought indictments against Mayor Eugene Schmitz, Boss Abe Ruef, and other Union Labor officials. Ruef, perhaps as a tactic to embarrass Phelan and his friends, suddenly became an avid supporter of Burnham's proposals, turning the plan into a political football. Burnham left the city in disgust.

In the end, very few of his ideas were ever implemented. Park Presidio Boulevard can be considered a small piece of Burnham's proposed system of parkways, and the city did build a civic center near the location recommended by the plan. But Burnham's document had remarkably little effect on the growth and development of San Francisco after 1906.

The graft trials dragged on for many months, with Ruef receiving a jail sentence but Schmitz's conviction being reversed on appeal. Many other Union Labor Party officeholders got immunity in return for testifying against their leaders. San Francisco juries, while willing to find politicians guilty of receiving payoffs, were reluctant to convict businessmen for giving bribes. Much to the reformers' dismay, the trials did not destroy working-class support for the Union Labor ticket, and in 1909 party candidate P. H. McCarthy won the mayoral election. A few years later Eugene Schmitz was elected to the Board of Supervisors.

Nevertheless, the trials did have an impact on state and local politics. The evidence of massive corruption strengthened the cause of reform, and California's energetic Progressive governor, Hiram Johnson, elected in 1910, got his first public exposure as a prosecutor in the San Francisco trials.

Oakland's Accomplishments

One of the reformers' chief targets was the Southern Pacific Railroad. The "Octopus" was finally cut down to size, in part because there were now other powerful economic forces whose interests conflicted with those of the railroad. In Oakland, for example, Mayor Frank Mott had substantial backing from local businesses when, in 1910, he forced the Southern Pacific to relinquish control over the city's waterfront. This allowed both the Western Pacific and the Santa Fe to lay tracks into Oakland. In return, Mott had to agree to drop a city suit against the SP, and give the railroad free use of waterfront terminals and tracks for 50 years. Nevertheless, Oakland controlled its own waterfront for the first time since Horace Carpentier's founding of the city.

Mott's triumph over the railroad was only one of Oakland's many substantial accomplishments during the earthquake era. Spurred by San Francisco refugees, as well as electric trolley construction and massive real estate development, the city's population doubled in the single decade 1900 to 1910, growing from 75,000 to 150,000. Not to be out-done by San Francisco, in 1905 Oakland commissioned its own beautification plan, prepared by Charles Mulford Robinson. Like Burn-ham, Robinson called for a massive expansion of public open space, in effect proposing what eventually became the East Bay Regional Park system. Within Oakland, he emphasized expansion of parkland around Lake Merritt and establishment of new neighborhood parks and play-grounds. Although much of Robinson's scheme was beyond Mott's reach, the mayor did persuade voters to approve bonds to expand open space around the lake, and to establish de Fremery and Bushrod parks. Other lasting monuments to the Mott years are the Oakland Auditorium, City Hall, and the massive Hotel Oakland, now a senior housing project. Each of these impressive structures symbolized Oakland's new image of itself as a major urban center.

Growth Elsewhere

Berkeley's growth was even more spectacular. During the first decade of the 20th century, the university town tripled its population, from 13,000 to 40,000, making it the fastest growing mid-size city in the nation. Berkeleyans lobbied to have the state capital moved from

Sacramento to Berkeley, and real estate promoters laid out the North-brea neighborhood with the proposed capitol in mind. Although this campaign failed, in the earthquake era Berkeley began a tradition of optimistic political and social experimentation. The city elected a socialist mayor, became the first California community to adopt residential zoning, and pioneered in developing modern police practices under Chief August Vollmer. Berkeley architects like Bernard Maybeck and Julia Morgan did much to develop distinctive Bay Area building styles, and other Berkeleyans experimented with what later generations would call "alternative lifestyles."

After the earthquake, southern Marin and northern San Mateo counties also grew, though not as rapidly as the East Bay, with its convenient ferry connections to San Francisco and its existing urban population base. Most surprising was the fact that, despite the destruction of 1906, San Francisco itself managed a modest population increase between 1900 and 1910. But clearly the city's growth lagged behind that of the Bay Area as a whole, and it was dramatically outstripped by Los Angeles.

In these circumstances, San Francisco leaders gave serious thought to some form of Bay Area regional government. They argued persuasively that the area's rapid development was causing regionwide problems that could be managed only by regional political agencies. Behind the argument also lay a conviction that San Francisco could maintain its traditional status as the west's leading city if it were the center of a unified regional metropolis.

In 1910 the city aggressively pushed for a borough form of government in the Bay Area, modeled after that of New York. Clearly, San Francisco would be the "Manhattan" of the proposed Bay Area metropolitan complex. San Mateo and Marin counties, which traditionally accepted San Francisco's regional leadership, supported the plan, but the East Bay, particularly Oakland, strongly objected. Oakland had no desire to be a west-coast Brooklyn, and led the successful opposition to the governmental consolidation proposal on the 1912 state ballot. (Opposition to San Francisco's imperial aspirations did not, however, prevent Oakland from making its own unsuccessful bid to annex Berkeley.)

Recovery and the 1915 Exposition

San Francisco quickly recovered from the earthquake and fire, most of downtown being rebuilt within four years. Business leaders waged a largely successful campaign to bring back into the fold firms that had moved out of the city immediately after the disaster. New industrial sites opened along the southern waterfront, and the brief boom along Mission and Fillmore streets ended when major stores returned to the rebuilt downtown shopping district. The phoenix had indeed risen from the ashes: if San Francisco was no longer the Queen City of the West, it had at least reestablished itself as the Bay Area's primary urban core.

The earthquake and fire had decisively changed the character of many of the city's districts. While the rubble was being cleared, new middle-class neighborhoods emerged in the Richmond and Sunset districts, attracting people from the Inner Mission and Western Addition. Immediately following the disaster, these latter neighborhoods had been heavily congested. They rapidly declined physically and in public esteem, as the middle-class population shifted to the Richmond and Sunset. New working-class housing appeared on Potrero Hill, accommodating people who previously had lived in the South-of-Market. The latter area was rebuilt with less housing and many more light industrial and wholesale facilities than had been the case before 1906. South-of-Market and the "Tenderloin" came to be home for increasing numbers of single workers, pensioners, and outcasts from the middle-class mainstream. The South-of-Market's inexpensive residential hotels also were refuges for seasonal workers—agricultural and cannery laborers during winter months, and coastal seamen when in port.

At the other end of the social scale, on Nob Hill, only the Flood mansion was rebuilt, becoming headquarters for the Pacific Union Club. Luxury hotels and apartments, as well as Grace Cathedral and Huntington Park, replaced the other burned-out Nob Hill mansions. San Francisco's elite neighborhoods moved further north and west, to Pacific Heights, Presidio Terrace, and Sea Cliff.

Recovery from the earthquake and fire was complete by 1915. San Francisco celebrated both its recovery and the completion of the Panama Canal with still another world's fair. The last extensive fill along the city's bay front created a magnificent fairgrounds, and provided the site of the future Marina district. The Panama Pacific International Exposition was the final great showcase of the American Renaissance with its optimistic view of the future, but the fair had opened a few months after World War I began in Europe. A new era had indeed dawned, but it certainly was not to fulfill the prewar generation's vision of peace, prosperity and progress.

Panama Pacific International Exposition, 1915
Of the structures put up for the fair, Bernard Maybeck's Palace of Fine Arts still stands (restored). (Bancroft Library, UCB)

12 Two Remarkable Women

Phoebe Apperson Hearst Holding Court, Circa 1910
Mrs. Hearst, in the Chinese robe, is entertaining a delegation of YWCA
women. (Bancroft Library, UCB)

12

Two
Remarkable
Women

T he evening after his beloved son's death in 1884 at the age of 15,
Leland Stanford dreamt that the boy came to him and said "Do
not say you have nothing to live for . . . live for humanity." The railroad magnate resolved to do that by donating a substantial portion of
his great fortune to higher education. While he may have considered a
gift to the University of California, the state Legislature had previously
refused to approve Stanford's appointment as a University regent and,
in any event, at the time, the Berkeley institution was hardly a promising educational venture.

Instead, Stanford established his own university in his son's
memory, locating it on the family's vast Palo Alto stock farm. Stanford
University opened in 1891, and Leland Stanford died just two years

later. For the next decade, Stanford's widow, Jane Lathrop Stanford, ruled the new university, seeing it through some supremely difficult years.

In that same period, another wealthy widow, Phoebe Apperson Hearst, played a major role in transforming the University of California from an unimpressive western college into a prestigious public university. Thus the Bay Area's present status as a major national center of higher education owes much to the efforts of two remarkable women.

The Beginnings of Collegiate Education

Collegiate education first came to the Bay Area in the 1850s. The Jesuits established Santa Clara University and St. Ignatius College (now the University of San Francisco). The Methodists founded the College of the Pacific in San Jose. It later moved to Stockton, and is now known as University of the Pacific. What was eventually to become Mills College in Oakland opened in 1852 as a women's seminary in Benicia. In 1862 the state established a two-year normal school in San Francisco, and in 1870 moved it to San Jose, where it ultimately evolved into what is now San Jose State University.

By 1868 many Californians were eager for the state to take advantage of the federal Land Grant College Act. In the Central Valley 200,000 acres of federal land were available to the state to support the establishment of a public university. The state could sell the land, using the revenues to operate the new institution. Speculators and investors pressured the politicians to form a university, and make the federal land available for private purchase. In 1868 the Legislature responded by establishing, as the new state university, the previously private College of California and its proposed Berkeley campus.

The University of California

At first, the University of California had two prototypes on which to model itself. One was the traditional liberal arts college such as the College of California had been. The other was the land-grant university concept of a people's college, emphasizing practical instruction in agriculture and mechanics. By the time the University had moved to its Berkeley campus in 1873, the new president, Daniel Coit Gilman, had presented still a third educational model: a research-oriented institution on the lines of the famous German universities.

Gilman's ideal proved a remarkable prediction of what the University was eventually to become, but in the 1870s the president's proposal was highly controversial. Conservatives condemned it as "godless education," while populists charged that it was inconsistent with the practical concept of the land-grant college. After two embattled years, Gilman was delighted to leave Berkeley and accept the presidency of Johns

Hopkins University. His departure left a leadership vacuum that was largely unfilled for two decades. During those years, a series of hapless presidents fared poorly, beset by interfering regents, rebellious faculty, and rowdy students. In Sacramento the University was treated as little more than a political football.

Stanford University

Given the University's unpromising start, it is understandable that Leland Stanford decided to establish his own college rather than contribute to the state university. Stanford, like many wealthy San Franciscans, had purchased a Peninsula estate, in his case located near *el Palo Alto,* the large, lone redwood tree that still stands near El Camino Real. "The Farm," as the Stanfords called their estate, was a favorite haunt of Leland Jr., and it was thus fitting that the grounds should become the site of a university established in the boy's memory. In 1891 classes began in a "quad" of buildings built in Romanesque and California mission styles, designed to symbolize the fact that the institution would not be a copy of a typical New England private college. Presence of the new university soon stimulated the development of the town of Palo Alto, located just east of the campus.

Leland Stanford undoubtedly assumed that his estate would provide an adequate endowment for the new institution, but after his death in 1893 it appeared that his various bequests and personal debts might amount to more than his assets. Moreover the federal government sued the Stanford estate for payment of railroad bonds owed by the Southern Pacific. As a result, probate lasted for more than five years, during which court orders prevented the spending of funds set aside for the university.

The will transferred ultimate control of the institution to Stanford's widow, Jane, who faced the apparently impossible task of maintaining a university without funds. Her husband's old partner and rival, Collis P. Huntington, advised her to "give up the circus." But Mrs. Stanford refused to admit defeat. The court allowed her to draw $10,000 a month from the estate for personal use. With that amount she paid off family debts, and supported herself and the university. President David Starr Jordan and the faculty took pay cuts, and the students accepted spartan living conditions. Mrs. Stanford sold her personal bonds, and even tried to peddle her jewels to support the university, but true to her husband's wishes, she refused to allow tuition. The institution was intended to be open to young people of all social and economic classes.

Mrs. Stanford's Control

Even after the university's assets were freed in 1898, Jane Stanford did not allow substantial faculty pay raises. Instead she began what

President Jordan wryly called "our great stone age," a massive building program to finish the physical plant as originally planned. Particularly important to her was construction of the University Chapel as a memorial to her son and husband.

Although Mrs. Stanford left day-to-day operations in the capable hands of Jordan, for more than a decade she maintained ultimate power over university affairs. For example, she pressured the president to fire brilliant sociology professor Edward A. Ross, an outspoken critic of big business and Asian immigration, and a stout defender of organized labor. In 1897, Mrs. Stanford wrote Jordan that "the fact that Professor Ross would speak before a gathering of Socialists" was grounds enough for dismissal. Jordan resisted for a time, but finally gave in, sacking Ross in 1900. Ross publicly blamed Mrs. Stanford and she was widely criticized for the dismissal. The incident gained national publicity, and did much to force American higher education to define the concepts of academic freedom and faculty tenure.

In 1903, Jane Stanford finally relinquished control of the university to a board of trustees, of which she remained a member. She died two years later, just months before the 1906 earthquake severely damaged many of the buildings she had worked so hard to see constructed and maintained. Included in the destruction was Mrs. Stanford's beloved chapel. President Jordan had the chapel ruin taken down stone-by-stone and entirely rebuilt, a fitting memorial to the strong-minded woman who refused to let the university die.

Jane L. Stanford
(Bancroft Library, UCB)

Mrs. Hearst and the University of California

While Jane Stanford was struggling to preserve one university, Phoebe Apperson Hearst was helping transform another. In 1862, at the age of 19, she eloped with George Hearst, a tough, nearly illiterate miner more than twice her age. He had come to California during the Gold Rush, and by 1862 already had made a fortune selling Comstock Lode silver claims. He was destined to make several more fortunes and eventually serve in the US Senate. Phoebe, an educated Missouri schoolteacher before her marriage, had little in common with her husband and lavished much of her affection on the couple's only son, William Randolph. She may have helped persuade George to allow young Willie to run the *San Francisco Examiner,* a newspaper the family bought to support George's political ambitions. Later she gave her son $7.5 million to build the Hearst publishing empire.

When her husband died in 1891, Phoebe Hearst was his sole heir at the age of 48, and one of the nation's wealthiest women. She also became one of the country's leading philanthropists, contributing to a number of educational ventures, including the University of California. Her first gift to the University was in 1896 when architect Bernard May-beck persuaded her to offer a $10,000 prize for the best design and plan for the institution's physical expansion. The competition committed the University to a policy of rapid growth, and attracted worldwide attention. A Frenchman, Emile Bernard, won the prize, and his designs, substantially scaled down and altered by University architect John Galen Howard, determined the shape of campus growth through the 1920s.

In 1897 Mrs. Hearst became the first woman regent and settled down in Pleasanton to make a career out of being "the busy mother of the university. . . ." She helped select Benjamin Ide Wheeler, an able scholar and administrator, as the institution's new president. She contributed money to hire bright young faculty members, support University archeological expeditions, and build new campus buildings such as the Hearst Memorial Mining Building. She influenced her son to build the Greek Theater, and began a tradition of close Hearst family identification with the University of California that has lasted to the present day. (Phoebe was Patricia Hearst's great-grandmother.)

1919 marked the end of a remarkable era for the Berkeley institution. In that year Benjamin Ide Wheeler retired as president, and Phoebe Hearst died at the age of 76. For 20 years they had played major roles in transforming the institution from an undistinguished western college into one of the nation's leading public universities. Enrollment more than tripled during the two decades, and faculty members such as anthropologist Alfred Kroeber and historian Herbert Bolton achieved international reputations. Mrs. Hearst's philanthropy had helped attract contributions from other prominent Californians, as well as stronger financial support from the Legislature. As the institution's prestige increased, wealthy families began sending their children to Berkeley. One of President Wheeler's few administrative defeats came when he attempted to outlaw fraternities, which he considered contrary to the public University's democratic purpose. The frats got support from affluent students, and from the influential parents and alumni who had become an important part of the institution's constituency.

A Large Educational Complex

By the time of Mrs. Stanford's death, in 1905, "the Farm" had also become a fashionable place to go to school, although Leland and Jane Stanford had envisioned their university as an egalitarian institution. In 1914 the trustees established tuition, a step that the Stanfords had firmly opposed. Eventually the universities at Palo Alto and Berkeley emerged at the top of a large Bay Area higher education complex, which today includes several private institutions, four units of the state college and university system, and more than 20 public community colleges. The whole system represents a vast regional commitment to mass collegiate education and intellectual opportunity, consistent with the egalitarian principles on which both UC and Stanford were founded. But the system's hierarchical arrangement, with Berkeley and Palo Alto having the bulk of public prestige and influence, also serves to maintain regional lines of class and power.

Women on Campus

UC and Stanford were also committed to coeducation at a time when many prestigious American universities were bastions of exclusive male privilege. Still, Jane Stanford worried that too many female students might somehow keep Stanford from developing as planned. So she decreed that the university should admit no more than 500 new women students per year. In 1933 the trustees loosened the restriction, but not until 1973 did the university finally obtain a court order allowing it to disregard Mrs. Stanford's instructions entirely.

Unlike Jane Stanford, Phoebe Hearst had no doubts that more women students were needed at Berkeley. Although the University was theoretically established as a coeducational institution in 1868, it was Mrs. Hearst's influence that persuaded UC to begin taking its female students seriously. She commissioned Bernard Maybeck to build a women's gymnasium (and for good measure also donated funds to expand the men's gym). Mrs. Hearst pressured the University to hire distinguished women teachers and researchers, and supported the founding of a women's faculty club. She also established scholarships for women students, and these grants inevitably came to be popularly known as "Phoebe's."

Phoebe Hearst eventually built a substantial home in Berkeley, spending some time there each year, keeping a particularly watchful eye on the progress and conduct of the "Phoebe" recipients. One of her protégées was Julia Morgan, a University graduate who became a distinguished architect, and who designed William Randolph Hearst's "Castle" at San Simeon.

Women in the Bay Area

Phoebe Hearst's and Jane Stanford's educational activities occurred in an era when Bay Area women had to assert their right to participate fully in public affairs. Earlier, in the mining period, entertainers such as Lotta Crabtree were well-known public figures, but feminine participation in political matters, such as Mary Ellen Pleasant's support of the pre-Civil War underground railroad, was rare in the Bay Area. Later in the 19th century, however, some middle- and upper-class women became active in social and moral reform efforts, such as the temperance movement. Women crusaders against "Demon Rum" played important parts in the campaigns to ban the sale of liquor in communities such as Palo Alto and Berkeley.

At the same time, thousands of Bay Area working-class women labored in low-paid industrial and domestic jobs. The region's canneries, for example, particularly depended on cheap, female labor. While Bay Area unions aggressively sought better wages and conditions for male workers, organized labor paid little attention to the plight of women in the workforce. During the early 20th century, the state Legislature instituted reforms that sought to control the worst abuses of women's labor, but not until World War II were women given access to well-paid, unionized, industrial jobs. (When the war ended, working-class women were once again directed to traditional "female" occupations.)

Nevertheless, the moral reform activities of the late 19th century naturally led some women into the suffrage campaign. California finally allowed women to vote in 1911, following more than two decades of organized suffrage activity. Today the Bay Area is again a center of feminist political activity. In 1982 the region's two largest cities—San Francisco and San Jose—had women mayors. Moreover women held a majority of the seats in the legislative bodies of the two cities.

Until recently, however, few women have had as much impact on the region's history as Jane Stanford and Phoebe Hearst. The universities they worked so hard to build are of crucial importance to the Bay Area's intellectual, social, and economic life. Berkeley and Stanford not only contribute greatly to the region's cultural activity, but also provide the education and credentials of much of the local corporate, professional, political, and bureaucratic leadership. Social ties originally made on campus become important lifelong bonds of friendship and contact, buttressing the region's (largely male) "establishment."

Finally, the two institutions' extraordinary record of scientific, technological, and medical research is the major reason why the Bay Area leads the nation in such fields as microelectronics, genetic engineering, and nuclear weapons development. Daniel Coit Gilman's dream of research-oriented American universities has come true with a vengeance, and no part of the country has been more affected by that fact than the Bay Area.

□ □ □

13 Great Constructions

Damming the Mokelumne, 1927

Steamshovels at work in a narrow canyon of the Mokelumne River about 38 miles northeast of Stockton, building EBMUD's Pardee Dam. Meanwhile the district was also laying an aqueduct across the San Joaquin Valley and Delta to bring 200 million gallons of water a day to the East Bay. (EBMUD)

13

Great
Constructions

In 1875 financier William Ralston suddenly became an advocate of municipal ownership of public utilities. Trying desperately to save his crumbling financial empire, Ralston offered to sell San Francisco the Spring Valley Water Company. The city refused the offer, and, as noted earlier, Ralston's economic house of cards collapsed. Since then, however, public versus private ownership of utilities has continued to be a matter of conflict, right up to the present. For example, in 1982 San Francisco voters had to decide whether to investigate the possibility of a municipal takeover of the privately owned Pacific Gas and Electric Company power facilities within the city. (They chose not to investigate, probably influenced by a vigorous PG and E campaign.)

Reaching Out for Water

As the first metropolitan region in the far west, the Bay Area pioneered in developing an "urban infrastructure," the basic public and private works essential to sustain city life. The Spring Valley Water Company was the far west's first integrated urban water system serving an entire city. Prior to Spring Valley's organization in 1858, San Franciscans had tapped a variety of streams and wells, and enterprising merchants even sold water shipped in barrels from Marin County. By the 1860s, however, Spring Valley had linked the entire city to such local sources as Lobos Creek, Lake Merced, Laguna Honda, and Pine Lake. In the 1870s, the company began developing a series of reservoirs in San Mateo County, and by the end of the 19th century Spring Valley had also tapped sources in southern Alameda County.

Spring Valley's expanding private water system allowed San Francisco to grow and prosper, but the company's operations were a source of constant controversy. Customers complained of high rates and poor service. Reformers often justifiably suspected that the company's monopoly franchise was maintained through graft and political influence. Many San Franciscans resented someone making a profit from providing a basic necessity of life such as water. And while up to 1900 Spring Valley had supplied more than enough water for current needs, many influential San Franciscans doubted the company's ability to keep up with the massive population and economic growth they foresaw in the near future.

The logical alternative was a publicly owned system to tap the great water resources of the Sierra Nevada. Even mad Emperor Norton had the vision to advocate such a system. In 1900 Mayor Phelan formally proposed damming the Tuolumne River at the Hetch Hetchy Valley, 150 miles east of San Francisco, to provide a water supply for the city. Federal authorities initially turned down the proposal on the grounds that Hetch Hetchy, part of the "Grand Canyon of Tuolumne," lay within the boundaries of Yosemite National Park. Phelan's successor, Union Labor Party Mayor Eugene Schmitz, advocated a plan to use the watershed of the American River's south fork. But this scheme, involving large financial kickbacks to Union Labor politicians, was killed by the postearthquake graft trials.

The city renewed its Hetch Hetchy application in late 1906. Los Angeles had initiated its Owens Valley project on the eastern side of the Sierra and, as usual, San Francisco was eager to keep up with its southern rival. President Theodore Roosevelt believed in the Progressive ideal of using the nation's natural resources for the general public good, rather than for the profit of selfish private interests. San Francisco's proposal—a publicly owned water system that would also provide hydroelectric power for a city that had just been destroyed by fire— seemed consistent with the President's concept of "the greatest good

Damming Hetch Hetchy, 1922
Looking toward what will become the dam's downstream face. The 350-ft. tower was used for elevating and pouring concrete. (San Francisco Archives)

for the greatest number." Opposition by self-interested corporations like Spring Valley Water and Pacific Gas and Electric probably reinforced Roosevelt's support.

The Damming of Hetch Hetchy

But there were other opponents of Hetch Hetchy besides large corporations. Famed naturalist John Muir had spent a major part of his life trying to protect Yosemite and similar wild places. To him conservation meant preserving such pristine beauty spots, not destroying them. In 1892 Muir had been one of the organizers of the Sierra Club, along with a group of Berkeley and San Francisco professionals. In 1906 he believed Yosemite had finally been saved, with the park boundaries extended to roughly their present location. But just when he thought victory was secure, San Francisco proposed to flood Hetch Hetchy, whose natural beauty was second only to Yosemite Valley itself. From his Martinez ranch, Muir thundered that damming Hetch Hetchy was like making the world's cathedrals into water tanks.

Muir and his preservationist allies forced a national debate on the proposal. The conflict even split the conservation movement. For example, Congressman William Kent of Marin County, a Sierra Club member who had donated Muir Woods to the federal government, sided with San Francisco. Mayor "Sunny Jim" Rolph strongly lobbied for the Hetch Hetchy project, and in 1913 Congress finally gave San Francisco the go-ahead. In retrospect, we should not be surprised that the city ultimately got permission to build its dam. What is surprising is that it won only after seven years of national controversy. For the first time, the American government weighed preservationist arguments and seriously considered *not* building a dam. Although Muir lost, his forceful defense of Hetch Hetchy defined the terms of countless conservation battles that have been fought since 1913.

East Bay MUD

San Francisco assumed that it was building a regional water system, one that would also serve the East Bay core cities of Oakland, Berkeley, and Alameda. But Oakland residents, in particular, suspected that this was another San Francisco scheme to deprive them of home rule, and the East Bay never bought into the Hetch Hetchy project. Much of the Peninsula, however, did take service from Hetch Hetchy, which today serves all of the urbanized parts of San Mateo County and a few portions of Alameda and Santa Clara counties. In fact, San Francisco itself uses less than half of the Hetch Hetchy water.

Their refusal to join San Francisco's project left the urbanized parts of the East Bay with a serious water shortage. During the 19th century, a series of private companies had supplied water to East Bay cities from such sources as Temescal and Chabot reservoirs. In 1918, however, the privately owned People's Water Company went bankrupt during a serious drought. Residents responded with strict conservation measures, and a newly formed company built additional storage capacity at San Pablo Reservoir, but this brought only short-term relief. Major industries refused to locate in the East Bay because of the lack of an assured water supply. The crisis finally convinced East Bay residents to adopt a proposal long advocated by Dr. George Pardee, a former Oakland mayor and California governor. He called for the area to construct its own independent public system tapping the Sierra watershed.

In 1923 the state Legislature authorized the establishment of the East Bay Municipal Utility District (EBMUD). Later that year a serious fire in North Berkeley again demonstrated the need for a reliable water system, and in 1924 East Bay voters overwhelmingly approved a bond issue to build a dam and aqueduct to bring water from the Mokelumne River, 100 miles to the east. While San Francisco was leisurely building its Hetch Hetchy project for anticipated future use, East Bay MUD constructed its system under the pressure of immediate needs. Thus in 1929 the first water from Pardee Reservoir on the Mokelumne reached the East Bay, more than two years before Tuolumne water reached San

Laying Pipes, 1922
Installing a 16-inch riveted and welded steel water line on Cragmont Avenue in Berkeley. (EBMUD)

Francisco. Indeed, for a short period in the early '30s, until the Hetch Hetchy system was completed, San Francisco actually purchased East Bay MUD water.

The rest of the Bay Area managed to survive for a number of years on local water resources. By 1940, however, eastern Contra Costa County began receiving supplies from the federal Central Valley Project. The invention of inexpensive gasoline and electric pumps had allowed the Santa Clara Valley to make extensive use of its groundwater after 1900. But serious overdraft of the subterranean resources caused the water table to drop and land to subside in San Jose and other parts of the valley. Eventually, the Santa Clara Valley Water District built a series of groundwater replenishment projects, but this did not solve the region's water problem. The valley now receives supplies from Hetch Hetchy, and from both the federal Central Valley and the State Water projects.

Southern Marin County also developed extensive local supplies on the Mount Tamalpais watershed. But during the 1976-77 drought, Marin was forced to import water from the state project, via a pipeline on the Richmond-San Rafael Bridge. Much of Solano County depends on water from the federal canals, while portions of Napa County buy supplemental supplies from the State Water Project. Most of the Bay Area, then, is linked to vast interconnected systems of public waterworks that mix local supplies with imports from the Sierra watershed.

Hydroelectric Power

Hetch Hetchy was built as a dual-purpose project, supplying both hydroelectric power and water. Hetch Hetchy and the Los Angeles Owens Valley system were the west's first major publicly financed water systems, and as such established precedents for the massive federal and state projects that came later in the 20th century. In each case, the sale of electricity offset much of the cost of dams and aqueducts.

The principle of hydroelectric power generation was well known in late 19th century California, but distance and technological limitations prevented such power from being put to much use. In California the major potential sources of hydropower were in the Sierra, while the greatest demand for electricity was in coastal cities. Not until the turn of the century did inventors perfect efficient, long-distance transmission technology, which opened the way to develop California's hydro potential. In 1900 a private company delivered to Oakland electricity generated on the Yuba River, more than 140 miles to the east. The success of this project encouraged San Francisco engineers to plan Hetch Hetchy as both a water and power system.

The development of hydroelectricity also stimulated the establishment of a unified regional private power utility. When all electricity was generated by individual local coal plants, it was reasonable for each community to have its separate power company, but when Sierra hydropower could be distributed on a regional basis, a single northern California electric system became practical. The Pacific Gas and Electric Company created such a system. After its founding in 1905, PG and E began buying out local firms and connecting them to the regional grid. Eventually, the company grew into the nation's largest private power utility, serving most of northern and central California.

PG and E naturally opposed establishment of municipally owned competitors and bitterly fought the Hetch Hetchy scheme. Although the company was unable to prevent construction of the project, it has successfully resisted the creation of a municipal power distribution system within San Francisco, despite the fact that Congress clearly intended such a system when Hetch Hetchy was authorized under terms of the Raker Act of 1913. In practice, however, San Francisco delivers Hetch Hetchy power only as far as Newark in southern Alameda County. Beyond that point the power is "wheeled" by PG and E, and San Franciscans continue buying electricity from the giant private utility. Palo Alto, Santa Clara, and Alameda, however, successfully operate municipally owned power systems which deliver electricity to customers at rates at least as low as PG and E's, and, in addition, return profits to the cities' treasuries.

Hydropower represented an important step towards California's energy independence. In the 19th century, industry and transportation were fueled principally by coal, and California had only small and inferior deposits. While some coal was mined on the northeastern slopes of Mt. Diablo at company towns such as Sommersville, the Diablo mines did not begin to meet the state's demand, and Californians depended on coal imported from as far away as Britain. In the 20th century, however, cheap hydropower generated by swift Sierra rivers became an attractive alternative to imported coal. The local coal mines were eventually driven out of business by new energy sources.

Petroleum: California's "Black Gold"

Even more important to the state's energy independence than hydroelectric power was the rapid development of California's petroleum industry after 1890. The lack of an economical process for refining heavy California crude had thwarted earlier attempts to establish the industry. In the 1890s, however, major advances in industrial technology made it possible for California's railroads and steamship companies to shift from coal to oil-burning engines. By the early 20th century, other industries also made the shift, including such electric utilities as PG and E. The resulting new demand caused a rush for the "black gold," and oilfields were opened in the San Joaquin Valley and southern California. Dependence on imported coal declined steadily and the Bay Area's once-prosperous whale oil industry was virtually destroyed. By the 1920s natural gas, which had initially been burned off as a bothersome byproduct of petroleum production, was also becoming an important energy source.

Few Californians seriously considered public ownership of the petroleum industry, except for the state's small but articulate band of socialists. The new west coast oilfields did, however, help break the national monopoly that John D. Rockefeller's Standard Oil Company had established in the early days when Pennsylvania produced almost all of the nation's petroleum. The discovery of California wells allowed new firms to enter the market.

Standard's Richmond Refinery, 1902
Early construction phase of Standard of California's Richmond refinery. (Chevron Corporation)

The Rockefeller interests were not long in coming west, however, buying out a local corporation, Pacific Coast Oil. The company was renamed Standard of California, and in 1900 its refinery moved from Alameda to the new town of Richmond, strategically located at the end of a pipeline from the San Joaquin oilfields. Since Richmond had also just been chosen as the terminus for the Santa Fe Railroad, in quick succession it received two major corporate residents. Standard's Richmond plant reinforced Contra Costa's industrial character, which had been established in the 19th century, when Bay Area powder companies producing explosives for western mines began operating along the Contra Costa County shoreline. As other oil companies began operating near Standard's facility, the county's waterfront emerged as the region's petroleum refining complex.

Transit: Electric Rail Lines

The new and cheaper energy sources helped to promote the development of electric railroad systems in the Bay Area. In 1891 a private company received a franchise to build an electric line from Oakland to Berkeley via Grove Street (renamed in 1983 Martin Luther King Jr. Way). The new transit system was an immediate success and stimulated construction of other electric lines throughout the region. Before the end of the century, efforts were already underway to consolidate the rapidly expanding electric rail network in the East Bay.

Chief consolidators were Francis "Borax" Smith, who had made a fortune mining Death Valley borax, and Frank Havens, a promoter with a particular talent for spending "Borax" Smith's money. The two formed a syndicate to develop thousands of acres of land in the Oakland, Piedmont, and Berkeley hills. Their transit empire was designed to serve the new neighborhoods they hoped to create, including the Claremont district with its luxurious Claremont Hotel. Smith and Havens bought up existing trolley lines and constructed new routes to interconnect the entire complex.

The result was the Key System, the Bay Area's most extensive electric rail network. At its height it stretched from Hayward to Richmond, and was connected to San Francisco by a ferry terminal located near the present Bay Bridge toll plaza. By 1910 a rush-hour commuter on the Key System could make it from Berkeley to downtown San Francisco in about 35 minutes, a time that today is difficult to equal by any means of transport. The Key System survived the financial collapse of the Smith-Havens empire, and continued as the East Bay's primary transportation utility until absorbed in 1959 by the publicly owned Alameda-Contra Costa Transit District (AC Transit).

The Key System gave Southern Pacific its first significant transbay service competition in 30 years, forcing SP to establish its own electric

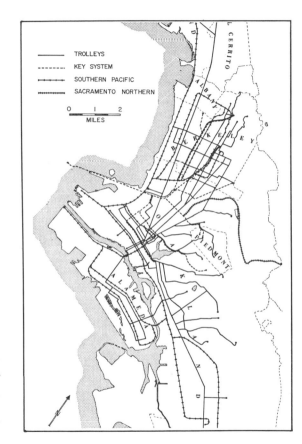

Traction Lines in the East Bay
Street railway and interurban lines at their greatest length. (Vance, *Geography* . . .)

rail system in the East Bay. In some communities, such as Berkeley, the two companies' trains ran virtually side-by-side. In 1913 still another electric line, the Antioch and Eastern, punched a tunnel through the Oakland hills and began service to the Sacramento Valley via a rail ferry. The line, later renamed the Sacramento Northern, provided regular service from Oakland to central Contra Costa County, thus opening communities like Lafayette and Walnut Creek to their initial suburban development. Within Oakland itself, the Sacramento Northern used Key System tracks to deliver customers to the latter's ferry terminal, with its access to San Francisco.

Except for Los Angeles, with its giant Pacific Electric, the East Bay's interurban rail network was the most extensive in California, and indeed one of the most extensive in the nation. This transit system maintained the East Bay's advantage over other Bay Area suburban regions. During the electric systems' heyday, between 1900 and 1930, the East Bay's population grew far more rapidly than that of the Bay Area as a whole.

Other parts of the region, however, were also affected by the new trolley systems. The steam rail line between Sausalito and San Rafael was electrified in 1903, and this was a major factor in the postearthquake growth of southern Marin. San Jose's electric lines eventually extended to Los Gatos and Palo Alto, and San Francisco's Market Street Railway reached south to San Mateo. The gap between Palo Alto and San Mateo was never filled, however, so the Peninsula remained dependent on Southern Pacific's relatively expensive steam line.

In San Francisco, electric rail construction increased dramatically after the earthquake and fire. Trollies replaced cable cars on many routes, while new streetcar lines stretched into the Sunset, Richmond, and Outer Mission districts, opening those regions for rapid development. Completion of the Twin Peaks tunnel in 1917 began the dramatic transformation of the West-of-Twin Peaks district from vegetable fields and eucalyptus forests into new urban neighborhoods. In that

Northwestern Pacific Electric Train
The electric rail lines in the North and East Bay promoted the growth of suburban communities, tied to San Francisco by ferries. (Southern Marin County, 1920s) (Waldemar Sievers, courtesy Harre W. Demoro)

area the Mason-McDuffie Company, already the developer of model neighborhoods in the East Bay, designed St. Francis Wood, the Bay Area's most ambitious attempt to realize the "city within a garden" ideal. In St. Francis Wood, Sherwood Forest, and Forest Hills, San Franciscans could, within the city limits, enjoy an almost suburban atmosphere. The transit lines emphasized service from neighborhoods to the downtown cores, and San Francisco's central business district, as well as that of Oakland, benefited from the electric rail construction.

The 1906 graft trials demonstrated that United Railways, San Francisco's major promoter of electric lines, was guilty of payoffs to Union Labor Party politicians. The revelation strengthened public opinion in favor of a city-operated streetcar system, and in 1911 Mayor Rolph supported the establishment of the Municipal Railway, the nation's first publicly owned urban transit line. Muni continued to compete against private systems until it absorbed its last rival, the Market Street Railway, after World War II.

American historians often refer to the early 20th century as the "Progressive Era," because of the serious attempts to reform government at all levels. In the Bay Area, however, the engineers and entrepreneurs probably had greater influence on public life than did the political reformers. The period's "great constructions," the water, energy, and transit systems, transformed economic and population patterns, laying the foundations for the 20th century metropolis to come.

□ □ □

14 Enter the Auto

A New Highway in San Mateo County, Early 1920s
No part of the Bay Area was more dramatically affected by the auto age than the Peninsula, with its direct highway access to San Francisco. (Bancroft Library, UCB)

14

Enter
the
Auto _____

When Hiram Johnson ran for governor in 1910, he campaigned
primarily by automobile as a way of symbolizing his
independence from the Southern Pacific "Octopus." Whether he realized it or not, Johnson's campaign was a harbinger of the automobile
age that was about to dawn in California. Two years earlier, in 1908,
Henry Ford had initiated the mass-produced Model T, a development
that soon made near-universal car ownership possible for average
American families. In 1909, the state Legislature authorized the sale of
bonds to begin California's first integrated network of paved roads.
Thus by the time of Johnson's campaign, the automobile was on the
verge of becoming a major factor in the life of California and the Bay
Area.

The Bay Area's first horseless carriages had appeared in the late 1890s. By the turn of the century, the *San Francisco Examiner* was already predicting that the new contraptions would eventually make the horse obsolete. Precisely such concerns prompted San Francisco livery stable owners to try to have autos banned in Golden Gate Park. Car owners responded to such attempts by forming the California State Automobile Association. The organization not only lobbied against auto restrictions, but also campaigned for public funds to build paved roads and highways, thus taking up a fight begun earlier by bicycle enthusiasts.

Building Highways

The local effort was part of a nationwide campaign on behalf of road construction. One specific aim was to build a transcontinental motor route, the Lincoln Highway, from New York to San Francisco. In 1911 and 1915 the California Legislature had approved state highway bond issues, and in 1916 Congress approved the first federal appropriation for motor roads. The transcontinental project was officially declared open in 1915, in time for the Panama Pacific International Exposition, although the route was actually still unfinished.

In California, auto enthusiasts' most important victory came in 1923 when the Legislature passed the gasoline tax. This levy on each gallon of gas sold was to be used solely for building and maintaining streets and roads. With this source available, the highway program no longer had to depend on individual bond issues or annual legislative appropriations, but instead had its own "self-generating" financial support. Without quite realizing it, California had provided for a substantial continuing public subsidy to the automobile, a source of support that private rail, trolley, and ferry companies did not enjoy.

The Bay Area's most active early highway construction took place in San Mateo County. In contrast to the East Bay, San Francisco, and even Marin, San Mateo County was not well served by the regional trollies and ferries, but still depended heavily on the Southern Pacific's relatively expensive steam rail service down the Peninsula. Consequently, San Mateo's population and economic growth lagged behind that of the region. The county remained primarily a place of estates, farms, and ranches. But the automobile would change all that.

San Mateo County invested local funds in Skyline Boulevard along the ridge of the coastal mountains, and Highway 1 along the sea. It eagerly promoted construction of "El Camino Real," which became a major statewide project of auto enthusiasts, tourist promoters, and land developers. In theory the road followed the "King's Highway" that had linked California's 21 Spanish missions. In fact, in colonial times the "highway" was little more than an interconnected network of local trails, but the concept of El Camino Real appealed to an early 20th century population eager to adopt a romantic view of the state's Hispanic past. The highway was promoted in much the same manner as the housing tracts featuring Mission Revival architecture, or the "Old Spanish Days" celebrations in many California communities.

The Peninsula section of El Camino was one of the earliest portions constructed. By the beginning of World War I, the highway had been paved from San Francisco to Gilroy, and its existence encouraged the rapid development of San Mateo County communities. Old estates were sold and subdivided. Developers built modest stucco bungalows in the flatlands, and more elaborate homes on the lower hills. During the 1920s the county's population more than doubled, and El Camino developed into a classic automobile-created commercial strip, extending for more than 30 miles. Traffic along the highway became so heavy that another major north-south route was needed, and by 1931 the newly constructed Bayshore Highway stretched from San Francisco to Palo Alto. The road was a 100-foot-wide, three-lane, accident-prone speedway that richly deserved its popular epithet, "Bloody Bayshore."

In addition to the Peninsula, other portions of the Bay Area were also dramatically affected by the auto. North of the Golden Gate, US 101 became the "Redwood Highway," another major tourist and development effort built around a road. Automobile suburbs grew in southern Marin, linked to San Francisco by the Sausalito auto ferry. In the East Bay, San Pablo Avenue became a part of US 40, which eventually crossed Carquinez Strait and proceeded to Sacramento and beyond. In San Francisco, the city built major new arterials, including Park Presidio, Sloat, and Marina boulevards.

Auto-Age Residences

One indication of the auto's effect on Bay Area life was the fact that almost all residences built after World War I included garages. Before the war, urban neighborhoods had always been planned with stores and shopping districts within walking distance of most homes, but now that was no longer necessary. In new developments, for example in the Berkeley hills or Oakland's Montclair district, only centralized shopping areas were provided, two or three miles distant from some of the homes. The corner store was no longer needed, as parents could shop by automobile. Of course, the children had to walk, so schools were still located in close proximity to most homes.

The automobile created a particular problem for San Francisco builders. Being a product of the Gold Rush, and the ferryboat and cable car era, the city had a compact, dense settlement pattern. The city's confinement to the tip of a peninsula helped reinforce its density.

Nevertheless after World War I most San Franciscans, like most other Californians, aspired to a single-family home and a car. Builders met this demand by designing a unique two-story wooden row house. The bottom story was devoted to a garage, storage, and perhaps a spare room. The living quarters were on the second story, often divided into a five-room floor plan. Each house had a small, rectangular backyard, and perhaps a patch of greenery in the front. The builder might also add another story to the basic plan, to produce a duplex. The fronts of the houses were decorated with stucco to conform to whatever architectural appearance was desired.

After World War I, such homes appeared by the thousands in newly opened regions of San Francisco's Richmond, Sunset, Outer Mission, and Marina districts. Although the elaborately decorated "Victorian" is often considered the typical San Francisco house, the stucco-faced row house with its built-in first-story garage is actually far more common. It allowed San Francisco to build a large stock of single-family dwellings and conform to California's typical high rate of automobile ownership, while still retaining the city's traditional dense settlement pattern. In the 1950s builders such as Henry Doelger were constructing the last rows of such houses along the western edge of the Sunset district. Doelger and his fellow contractors were thus conquering the city's last uncovered sand dunes, completing a process begun a century earlier along the shores of Yerba Buena Cove.

Ferries, Tubes, and Bridges

San Francisco Bay proved to be the new auto age's greatest challenge. We have seen how all the major regional transit corridors had to cross the bay, except the route along the Peninsula. The traditional transportation system responded to growing automobile use by establishing car ferries at key bay crossings. As early as 1912, however, auto drivers were forced to endure long delays waiting for the ferry ride between Oakland and San Francisco. Although service expanded greatly in the 1920s, the car ferries simply could not keep up with demand. At the end of summer holiday weekends, motorists might wait as long as four hours to catch the Sausalito-San Francisco ferry. Automobile ferry service from the new three-mile-long Berkeley pier to San Francisco began in 1929, but this did not prevent massive delays for motorists on such occasions as the annual Cal-Stanford "Big Game."

In short, the automobile forced the building of bridges across the bay. Although bridges had been discussed by everyone from Emperor Norton to the Southern Pacific, the only major span built before World War I was the Dumbarton railroad crossing of southern San Francisco Bay. In 1926, however, a private firm constructed an auto toll bridge at Antioch, and the following year similar efforts produced San Mateo and Carquinez bridges, as well as the Dumbarton auto bridge. Also opened in the mid-'20s was the Oakland-Alameda tube under the Estuary. The

Carquinez project was particularly impressive, as it crossed one of the region's deepest and most treacherous channels.

A bridge to span the Golden Gate was the idea that fired public imagination the most. In 1919 San Francisco City Engineer M. M. O'Shaughnessy persuaded a noted Chicago bridge designer, Joseph Strauss, to study the possibility of a Golden Gate span. Strauss became a strong advocate, lobbying on behalf of the project for the next decade. In 1928 the state Legislature authorized the Golden Gate Bridge and Highway District, which eventually included San Francisco, Marin, Sonoma, Napa, and Del Norte counties, plus parts of Mendocino County. University of California geologist Andrew Lawson assured the public that a bridge could be built to withstand a 1906-magnitude earthquake. Strauss allayed some of the conservationist opposition by agreeing to design an arch that would preserve Fort Point. Eventually, voters approved bonds to finance the project, and in 1937 the new bridge was completed and opened for business. In addition to the bridge itself,

Placing the Center Span of Carquinez Railroad Bridge, 1929
(Southern Pacific)

Strauss designed the Marin bridge approach, including the Waldo Tunnel, and San Francisco's Doyle Drive on-ramp. These were, in effect, the Bay Area's first limited-access freeways.

As dramatic as was the Golden Gate Bridge, its importance to the regional transportation network was dwarfed by the Bay Bridge. Since completion of the transcontinental railroad in 1869, the Oakland-San Francisco corridor had been the Bay Area's major transit route, linking the two primary components of the region's urban core. Nineteenth-century residents had often talked about an Oakland-San Francisco bridge, but little came of the talk until the automobile age. Even then, the project seemed stymied by military objections to a central bay crossing. In 1928, however, a joint federal-state commission, including soon-to-be President Herbert Hoover, agreed to an Emeryville-to-Rincon Hill route via Yerba Buena Island. In 1933 the Roosevelt administration appropriated federal public works funds for the project, and in 1936 the Bay Area's single most important arterial went into operation.

Completion of the Golden Gate and Bay bridges caused the rapid demise of what had once been the world's most extensive ferry system. The Sausalito-San Francisco and Oakland-San Francisco runs were by far the region's chief ferry routes, and patronage declined precipitously after the bridges' construction. World War II gas rationing and labor demands temporarily promoted a ferryboat renewal, but after the war ferries declined again, almost disappearing from the bay after completion of the Richmond-San Rafael and Martinez-Benicia bridges. Passenger service to Southern Pacific's Oakland depot continued for a while, and in the 1970s the Golden Gate Bridge District renewed ferry service between San Francisco and Marin. But today's financially troubled Golden Gate system is only a pale shadow of the huge ferry network that once crisscrossed the bay. The bridges also brought about other changes, including the rapid shift of regional freight hauling from small bay and delta craft to trucks, and the replacement of north coast

lumber boats by diesel monsters on US 101 and the Golden Gate Bridge.

Rail Service Declines

In much the same manner, the new transbay automobile links contributed to a decline of the regional rail passenger system. In southern Marin, the Northwestern Pacific ended rail passenger service,

Building the Bay Bridge, Early 1930s
The Bay Bridge between San Francisco and Oakland is actually two distinct bridges that join at Yerba Buena Island. On the Oakland side (*left*) is a truss and cantilever bridge. On the San Francisco side (*right*) is a suspension bridge. Seen plying the waters of the bay is one of the many ferries that the bridge made obsolete. (Pacific Aerial Surveys)

Greyhound buses replacing the electric trains. Highway construction on the Peninsula caused several lines to close, including Market Street railway service to San Mateo, the electric lines out of San Jose, and the Ocean Shore rail route down the San Mateo County coast. Similarly, completion of the Broadway (Caldecott) Tunnel through the Oakland-Berkeley hills resulted in termination of Sacramento Northern passenger service to Contra Costa County and beyond. The Bay Bridge was originally built to accommodate trains on its lower deck. The Southern Pacific, however, ended its East Bay electric rail service in 1941, whereas the Key System continued to run trains across the bridge until the late 1950s. On all other lines except the transbay runs, the Key System rapidly shifted to buses. Formation of the publicly owned AC Transit District in 1959 brought the final demise of what had once been the Bay Area's most extensive electric rail system.

Some critics have charged that the rapid decline of the urban rail systems between the 1930s and the 1950s was due to the influence of National City Lines, a corporate conglomerate that purchased many urban transit companies throughout the country, including the Key System. The charge is that National City purposely destroyed the rail networks in order to benefit General Motors and other automobile-oriented businesses that controlled the conglomerate's corporate policies. This may be true, but it does not explain the equally rapid decline in rail service in the many transit systems not controlled by National

City. In San Francisco, for example, after 1956 the city-owned Muni kept only those streetcar lines that operated through tunnels unsuitable for auto traffic. Otherwise, all electric rail routes were shifted to bus or trolley coach service. Muni also maintained a small remnant of the city's once-extensive cable car network, but only because of popular sentiment and the tourist trade.

It seems apparent that by the 1930s the private rail and ferry transit systems could no longer compete against the convenience, mobility, and social status of the automobile, especially when the latter benefited from massive subsidies of public funds for streets, highways, and bridges. Far from receiving subsidies, the private transit companies had to pay taxes on rights-of-way, repair streets used by trains, and suffer schedule delays caused by increased auto traffic. [In the 1970s, as gasoline prices skyrocketed, local public transit activity and patronage made a remarkable recovery. Except for Southern Pacific's Peninsula service, however, none of the systems was operated privately, and all, including the new Bay Area Rapid Transit (BART) and Muni trains, and the Golden Gate Bridge District's ferries, received large local, state, and federal subsidies.]

By the 1930s, then, the auto was already victorious in the Bay Area. Even some of the Depression's most desperate victims, the "Okies" and "Arkies" from the Dust Bowl, were completely dependent on cars to migrate to California and to obtain jobs once they were here.

Automobile sales, service, and repairs were big business in the Bay Area, and the East Bay was the location for major auto manufacturing facilities: a Ford factory in Richmond and a GM plant in East Oakland. Indeed, Oakland called herself "the Detroit of the West." Yet the effects of the Depression and World War II limited the impact of the auto on the region. Only after 1945 did the full implications of the automobile age become apparent in the Bay Area.

□ □ □

15 Boom and Bust

Waterfront Strike Scenes, 1934-1936

Inset: Strikers' demonstration, 1934. *Large photo:* Striking longshoremen on picket duty, keeping warm on a cool evening, 1936. Note the white caps that were once a typical part of a longshoreman's attire. (San Francisco Archives, 1934; Otto Hagel/Maritime Council, ILWU, 1936)

15

Boom
and
Bust _____

It was July 3, 1934, and striking longshoremen and other maritime
workers had kept west coast ports closed for nearly two months.
Shipowners, supported by influential business leaders in the region,
decided it was high time to get cargoes moving. They sent truckloads of
strikebreakers through the picket lines on the San Francisco waterfront,
and the strikers fought back. Soon the police intervened to protect the
strikebreakers, and the "Battle of Rincon Hill" was on.

Hostilities were suspended on July 4 so the combatants could celebrate Independence Day, but on July 5 the conflict resumed. By night-
fall two strike supporters were dead, victims of police bullets. Ten days
later, in response to the killings, San Francisco unions called a general

strike, virtually shutting down the city and profoundly affecting Oakland and several other Bay Area communities. The walkout lasted four days, ending primarily because of disagreements among the various unions. Nevertheless, labor had made its point. After a lapse of more than a decade, trade unions were again ready to play a major role in Bay Area economic and political life.

The War Against Labor

In the years before World War I, the region's union organizers had faced more determined and united opposition than ever before. Major employers, many of them frightened by having to compete against the Los Angeles "open-shop" economy, organized a substantial effort to break union power around the bay. In 1916 San Francisco business strongly supported a "Preparedness Day Parade" to celebrate conservative, patriotic sentiment. In the midst of the procession, a bomb was dropped on the marchers, killing 10 people.

The next day San Francisco police arrested four labor radicals and charged them with the crime. Two of the accused, Tom Mooney and Warren K. Billings, were soon convicted. Mooney was sentenced to die, Billings to life in prison. Subsequently it became clear that the convictions were the result of a crude frame-up that included fraud, perjury, and tainted evidence. The governor commuted Mooney's death sentence, but the two men remained in prison for more than 20 years before finally being freed in 1939 by Governor Culbert Olson.

World War I and the Twenties

After America entered World War I, labor and capital largely suspended their conflict. During the war years moderate unions gained members and power, but antisyndicalist laws were used to jail radical opponents of the war effort. After the armistice, business used the increasingly conservative political climate to break unions. By the early '20s, the once-proud Bay Area labor movement was a shadow of its former self, and San Francisco became almost as much an "open-shop" city as Los Angeles. The waterfront unions were particularly hard hit. Longshoremen could work only if they had a "bluebook," showing membership in a company-sponsored association. Malcontents who attempted to form independent maritime unions were simply fired.

Nevertheless, Bay Area workers benefited from the general prosperity of the 1920s. The region's population and economy grew rapidly in the midst of a statewide boom. California farms, often controlled from San Francisco offices, expanded their markets, contributing to the growth of Bay Area canning, processing, and shipping. A. P. Giannini's

Bank of Italy (later named the Bank of America) spread its branches throughout California, but the institution's headquarters remained in San Francisco, further solidifying the city's role as a national banking center. In the East Bay, steel and autos led a general industrial expansion. Building tradesmen had plenty of work as new homes went up in San Francisco's Richmond, Sunset, West Portal, and Outer Mission districts, and in the new automobile suburbs of the Peninsula, East Bay, and southern Marin. The business expansion was symbolized by new highrise office buildings in downtown San Francisco and Oakland, and the region's first highrise apartment houses also appeared in those cities.

Pleasure-seekers were uninhibited by Prohibition, despite efforts by crimebusters such as Alameda County District Attorney Earl Warren to break up illegal liquor operations. Big-time college football arrived on the scene, particularly with the 1920-25 "Wonder Teams" at Berkeley. Both UC and Stanford built massive stadiums, while minor-league professional baseball thrived in San Francisco and Oakland. Movies also offered inexpensive entertainment in scores of neighborhood and downtown theaters. Before World War I, the Bay Area, particularly Niles Canyon, had been a major center of motion picture production. In the 1920s, production was centralized in southern California, but the Bay Area participated in the national enthusiasm for the silver screen.

Business, working with Republican administrations in Washington and Sacramento, had thus produced a consumer-oriented boom that was best symbolized by the rapid increase in auto ownership. As Herbert Hoover put it, the nation had reached a "permanent plateau of prosperity." In such an atmosphere, labor unions seemed almost archaic.

The Great Depression

In 1929 the "permanent plateau" collapsed, the Great Depression began, and the consumer-oriented boom went bust. As a result, social conflict and tension reappeared on the surface of Bay Area life. Radical spokesmen began to get a hearing, and many workers once more supported aggressive union organizing campaigns. Under the terms of President Franklin Roosevelt's National Recovery Act, employers could no longer prevent industrial workers from organizing and bargaining collectively. Bosses were prohibited from firing employees who formed or joined unions. In this situation, there were dramatic strides in reestablishing labor power, particularly in the maritime trades. The 1934 Waterfront Strike was the culmination of this process, and in the end federal mediators negotiated a settlement that was a significant union victory.

There were other major maritime strikes in 1936 and 1948, and after World War II longshoremen leader Harry Bridges faced possible deportation because of his alleged communist ties. Nevertheless, the

1934 maritime workers' victory marked a sharp reversal of the labor losses of the 1920s. Other local unions, affiliates of both the AFL and new CIO, were quick to take advantage of that fact and assert labor power.

Washington's role in reaching the 1934 settlement was part of a growing trend toward greater federal influence in Bay Area (and US) life. The scope of the economic disaster was so great that only the federal government could respond effectively. By 1933, local relief efforts in San Francisco and several other Bay Area communities had been exhausted, and authorities turned to Washington for immediate help. While Herbert Hoover had acted more vigorously in combating economic hard times than any previous President, he resisted direct federal assistance to the unemployed. When Franklin Roosevelt became President in 1933 he had no such compunctions—indeed he probably had no choice. He opened financial pipelines from Washington to local communities in the Bay Area and elsewhere that are still open. Thus began the tradition of the "welfare state" in America.

The New Deal

Roosevelt was enough of a traditionalist not to give "something for nothing," and wherever possible federal relief came in the form of jobs. The most massive federal jobs program, the Works Progress Administration, was responsible for building scores of Bay Area parks, post offices, playgrounds, schools, and other public facilities. WPA workers built San Francisco's Aquatic Park, Oakland's Lake Merritt seawall, and Berkeley's Rose Garden. They also worked to create Treasure Island, man-made site of the 1939 Golden Gate International Exposition. WPA operated a federal theater in Oakland, and a federal writers' project in several Bay Area communities. WPA artists painted the murals that still grace the interior of San Francisco's Coit Tower. Another well-known Depression program, the Civilian Conservation Corps, established a work camp in Wildcat Canyon behind Richmond, El Cerrito, and Berkeley. The "CCC boys" built many of the original public facilities in the newly formed East Bay Regional Park system. Throughout the Bay Area, they cleared ridgetop fire trails and constructed campgrounds and picnic sites.

These direct federal jobs programs were important to the Bay Area, but public works projects contracted to local private employers had an even greater impact on the regional economy. Federal funds helped build the Bay Bridge, Broadway (Caldecott) Tunnel, and scores of other road and highway projects. In the early 1930s, the government contracted with a consortium of western companies, including four Bay Area firms, to build giant Boulder Dam, now called Hoover Dam, on the Colorado River. The "Six Companies," as the consortium was called, was led by Henry J. Kaiser, an East Bay contractor who had built local roads during the 1920s. Also included was the W. A. Bechtel Company of San Francisco.

The transformation of Kaiser and Bechtel from essentially local concerns into national and international corporate empires started with their participation in the Boulder Dam project. The two companies, along with their consortium partners, developed a talent for winning government contracts that was to stand them in good stead for decades to come. The ties they established between Bay Area business and Washington, DC, were best symbolized in the early 1980s by the presence of two former Bechtel executives in Ronald Reagan's cabinet.

Federal money pumped into the Bay Area economy by the Roosevelt administration helped thousands of families through the Depression. It also contributed to the survival of Bay Area businesses, as well as the capitalist system itself. The New Deal programs encouraged a substantial shift of voters to the Democratic Party, though most often this was reflected in national rather than local election results. Still, the New Deal did not end the Depression. In 1939, 10 years after the stock-market crash, and seven years after Roosevelt took office, the local and national economies had not returned to their pre-Depression levels. Only with World War II, and massive federal defense expenditures that made the Depression programs seem puny by comparison, did the Bay Area economy fully recover.

Effects of Hard Times

The widespread poverty of the 1930s was reflected even in the physical appearance of many neighborhoods. In San Francisco, for example, city officials found it impossible to enforce health and safety codes in working-class and poor areas. To do so would have forced thousands of people out of their homes, as many property owners were unable to afford repairs and maintenance. Districts such as the South-of-Market and Western Addition thus suffered increasing deterioration. Much the same thing happened in West Oakland and in older neighborhoods in other Bay Area communities.

Rural poverty was omnipresent throughout the region. "Hoovervilles"—impoverished collections of makeshift shacks and shanties—grew up on the outskirts of many farming communities. During the spring and summer, ethnically diverse armies of migrant workers, including "Okies," Filipinos, and Mexicans, visited Bay Area agricultural districts looking for work. Federal protection of the right to collective bargaining did not extend to farm laborers, but union organizers, including Communist Party activists, urged agricultural workers to strike for better wages and working conditions. Farmworker walkouts occurred in Half Moon Bay, Decoto, and San Jose. The strikers won no long-term victories, and in some communities, such as Vacaville, union leaders were assaulted by violent "patriotic" mobs.

The Vine and the Fair

Golden Gate International Exposition, 1939-40
Entrance to the section of the fair called Court of the Pacific. (Bancroft Library, UCB)

At least one Bay Area industry began its recovery during the 1930s. Prohibition had nearly destroyed the region's extensive wine industry. Vintners could produce only limited quantities for home use and sacramental purposes, and most vines were harvested for the raisin

or table-grape markets. Of course, some local wine found its way into speakeasies, and many of the region's most respectable restaurants surreptitiously served local zinfandel or burgundy in coffee cups. Repeal of Prohibition in 1933 began the recovery of the wine industry, but only after World War II did Bay Area wineries prosper.

Despite the Depression, the region's talent for self-promotion did not falter. By the mid-1930s, San Francisco businessmen had convinced the area to sponsor still another international exposition, the third such event in the Bay Area in 45 years. The fairgrounds on Treasure Island, like those of the exposition of 1915, were designed to be a magical city within a city, a place whose architecture and exhibits symbolized the belief in a confident, prosperous future for California and the Pacific Basin.

Entertainment at the 1939-1940 fair included the symphony and opera, a "swing" version of the Mikado with a black cast, and Sally Rand's "Nude Ranch." But the fun and frolic, and certainly the optimistic visions of the future, were hampered by the knowledge that, as in 1915, the Bay Area had opened its world's fair at almost the same time that war began in Europe. Even more disastrous and devastating than World War I, this coming world conflict would change the Bay Area as much as any event since the Gold Rush.

□ □ □

16 World War II Revolution

Shift Change in the Richmond Shipyards
During World War II, Kaiser yards at Richmond became the world's largest shipbuilding complex, employing more than 100,000 workers. (Bancroft Library, UCB).

16

World
War II
Revolution

On the evening of August 16, 1945, the end of World War II was celebrated by rioting in San Francisco. Mobs of drunken young men roamed Market Street, some of them fighting, looting, and raping along the way. Not until early the next morning were city and military police able to restore order. The riot was in part a twisted emotional expression of gratitude for peace and victory, but it also was a violent release of social tensions built up by the massive, largely unplanned expansion of the Bay Area economy during the war years. The military conflict had caused great demographic and social transformations that challenged the region's traditional ways of life and threatened to overwhelm local institutions. Like the Gold Rush a century earlier,

World War II was a watershed in Bay Area history, ushering in revolutionary changes that dramatically affected the region's subsequent development.

The "Relocation" of Japanese Residents

Although the war set off the largest sustained population boom in Bay Area history, the immediate effect of the conflict was to displace many residents. While some left to serve in the armed forces, others of Japanese descent had to spend most of the war years sequestered in concentration camps. President Roosevelt's Executive Order 9066 required all people of Japanese origin living on the west coast—adults and children, native-born and Japanese aliens—to be transported to camps located primarily in the Great Basin. In the Bay Area, relocation authorities established a temporary center at Tanforan Race Track in San Bruno, from which internees were shipped to permanent camps. At Tanforan whole families were forced to live in stalls designed for a single horse. In some cases, the straw and excrement of the former equine occupants were still present when the new tenants arrived.

Subsequent investigation has concluded the relocation to be wholly unjustified. No evidence was ever found of either disloyalty or fifth-column activities, the principal alleged reasons for the relocation put forth at the time. Neither German- nor Italian-Americans suffered the same fate as the American-born Nisei. Indeed, most German and Italian aliens were not even interned, though their lives were somewhat restricted.

The Japanese relocation was actually prompted in large part by the west coast's long-established prejudice against Asians. Some interpreted the attack on Pearl Harbor as a validation of many vicious stereotypes that had been a part of Bay Area life since the anti-Chinese movement of the 19th century. In the fearful atmosphere following the attack, the few brave public statements that questioned the relocation were voices in the wilderness. The extreme measures actually taken were supported by most local and state politicians, including Democratic Governor Culbert Olson and Republican Attorney General Earl Warren.

The War Effort and the Massive Influx

But if the immediate effect of the war was an exodus of many Bay area residents, the longer-term result was a massive influx of newcomers. More than a million servicemen and women passed through the region on their way to Pacific war zones. Additional tens of thousands were stationed at a vast complex of old and new local military installations. The entire bay became a quasi-military base. Even Treasure

Island, the glittering site of the 1939-40 world fair, was transformed into a naval station. Still more important to the war effort was the region's industrial and commercial output. The Bay Area supplied the military with a tremendous variety of goods and services, and the billions of federal dollars funneled into the local economy produced a boom of unparalleled proportions.

The shipbuilding industry was the most dramatically affected. The Bay Area had long been a center for ship construction and repair, including several major private yards, as well as the government installation at Mare Island. In 1941 the navy also began a rapid expansion of facilities at Hunters Point in San Francisco. Even more spectacular was the creation of "instant" shipyards by Kaiser and Bechtel.

At Richmond, Henry J. Kaiser built the world's largest shipbuilding center, four separate plants devoted primarily to constructing prefabricated "Liberty ships." At the height of their operation, the Richmond yards employed more than 100,000 people, who kept the plants operating seven days a week, 24 hours a day. Temporary wartime housing was slapped up near the Richmond waterfront, and ferries brought workers from San Francisco. The Key System operated special trains, bought from the old New York elevated lines, along San Pablo Avenue to bring additional workers to the Richmond yards. By the end of the war Kaiser had built more than 1,000 ships at Richmond, including one Liberty ship assembled in just four days.

Bechtel's shipyard at Sausalito in Marin County was small in comparison with the Kaiser facility, but still employed over 22,000 workers at the height of operations. The company created an entirely new community, Marin City, to house several thousand workers and their families. But most of Bechtel's Marinship employees commuted from San Francisco by car, bus, or special ferries. In addition to the new yards, existing private plants experienced tremendous growth, including Todd and Moore in the East Bay, and Bethlehem and Western Pipe on the San Francisco side of the bay. In 1944 the Bay Area was the world's largest shipbuilding center.

The labor demands of the shipyards were prodigious. By 1944 the industry employed more than 250,000 workers, at a time when over 10 million Americans were in the armed forces and other Bay Area economic activities were booming. Hundreds of thousands of new workers were recruited from outside the region, swelling the population of places like greater Vallejo (which jumped from 30,000 in 1940 to about 100,000 in 1943). Before the war, Mare Island Naval Shipyard had employed less than 5,000 men; by 1944 the workforce numbered more than 40,000.

In addition to the Kaiser yards, Richmond was also the site of a Ford assembly plant and a Standard Oil refinery, both of which expanded greatly after Pearl Harbor. In 1940, Richmond's population was a little under 24,000; by 1943 the number was over 100,000. More than 25,000 units of new housing were built in Richmond, primarily by governmental agencies. Schools operated in double or triple sessions, with 60 or more students to a classroom. Hospitals, jails, and recreation facilities were overwhelmed. Streets and roads deteriorated rapidly, and raw sewage was discharged on marshes and tidelands. While Vallejo and Richmond were extraordinary cases, almost every Bay Area community suffered overcrowding, housing shortages, and overtaxing of public facilities.

The new workers included former "Okies" and "Arkies" from rural California, retired people and teenagers, and thousands of women recruited by "Rosie the Riveter" campaigns. Initially, shipyard unions, led by the Boilermakers, resisted the presence of women in the work-

Mural of Shipyard Workers
(San Francisco Arts Commission, Rincon Annex Post Office Murals, by Anton Refregier, 1941, 1945-49)

force, but the labor organizations soon backed down because of military necessity and strong demands by women for access to high-paid industrial jobs. Sexism was alive and well in the yards, but it did not prevent women from making a massive contribution to the war effort. After the fighting stopped, however, government agencies and private employers made tremendous efforts to persuade women to leave the industrial workforce. Servicemen were returning to the civilian economy, so it was "back to the kitchen" for thousands of skilled and semiskilled women workers.

The Migration of Blacks

The most dramatic demographic change the war brought about was the large-scale migration of blacks to the Bay Area. While blacks had been a part of regional society since even before William Leidesdorf's arrival in Yerba Buena in the mid-1840s, their numbers had never been large. Small numbers of blacks came to California during the Gold Rush. While the state Constitution of 1849 abolished slavery, it also prohibited Afro-Americans from voting, holding public office, or even testifying in court against whites. Not until the 1870s were these restrictions lifted. Also in the 1870s, and after two decades of segregated education, communities like San Francisco, Oakland, and Vallejo finally allowed blacks to attend integrated schools.

San Francisco's Palace Hotel initially hired blacks for most service occupations, but ended this practice around the turn of the century, possibly because of pressure from white workers. After the arrival of the transcontinental railroad in 1869, the presence of workers in rail occupations that had become traditionally black—such as Pullman porters—made West Oakland a center of black settlement. By the early 20th century, the East Bay had a larger Afro-American population than San Francisco, but in Oakland and South Berkeley, as in other Bay Area communities, blacks lived in multiracial, working-class neighborhoods, rather than all-black ghettos.

As late as 1940, however, the Bay Area's black population was still only about 20,000, a minuscule portion of the region's total of 1.5 million. Once the war began, the numbers grew rapidly. Kaiser and other local employers actively recruited blacks, particularly from the western rim of the southern US—Louisiana, Texas, Oklahoma, and Arkansas. The recruitment was successful, and by the end of 1942 a major black migration was under way. The Bay Area's overall black population more than tripled during the war years. San Francisco's grew fourfold, and the growth in Richmond and Vallejo was more than tenfold.

Most of the region's black neighborhoods now in existence trace their origins to the war years. For example, Hunters Point, Marin City, and many of the black districts of Richmond and Vallejo, got their start as wartime public housing projects. Relocation had removed Japanese-

Americans from San Francisco's Western Addition, and new black residents moved in. Since racial discrimination in housing was chronic throughout the region, blacks who were unable to find accommodation in public projects crowded into the working-class neighborhoods where Afro-Americans traditionally had been welcome, particularly in the Oakland and South Berkeley flatlands. Not until the postwar white suburban exodus, however, did these neighborhoods become virtually all black.

Federal defense contracts prohibited racial discrimination in employment. Nevertheless some—but by no means all—Bay Area unions resisted black economic equality. Although the Longshoremen were in the forefront of civil rights activity, the Boilermakers would not allow blacks to attain full union membership. Since the Boilermakers had a "closed-shop" contract in the shipyards, employers required black workers to pay dues to that union, even though blacks were deprived of equal membership rights. Afro-American workers protested against this situation and in 1943 even staged a brief strike at Bechtel's Marinship facility. Eventually, in 1945, the state Supreme Court found the practice unconstitutional, and adjudged both union and management guilty of racial discrimination.

But the court decision came when work in the yards was already rapidly declining. After "V-J Day," Marinship and Kaiser closed, and activity at other yards was drastically reduced. Between 1945 and 1947,

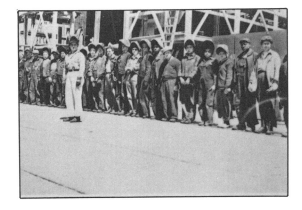

Marinship Workers, 1943
(*Marin-er,* August 21, 1943. Courtesy of Sausalito Historical Society)

employers laid off literally hundreds of thousands of Bay Area shipyard workers. Blacks, often the last hired, were likely to be the first fired. Many of the recent arrivals from the south had little education, training, or experience in urban life. Workers were no longer in short supply, and government nondiscrimination policies no longer applied. The postwar decline of the shipbuilding industry was an economic disaster from which the region's black population has never fully recovered. Even the civil rights protests, antidiscrimination laws, and antipoverty programs of the 1960s did not afford economic opportunities comparable to the wartime boom.

The presence of a large, new black population in the region during World War II resulted in much social tension, and at least one full-scale race riot (in Vallejo). Black sailors, serving in segregated laborers' units, refused to load ammunition at Mare Island, producing one of the most publicized racial incidents of the war. The refusal came after a massive explosion at the Port Chicago munitions depot had killed more than 200 black sailors as well as their white officers and other personnel. Nevertheless, a Treasure Island court martial found 50 of the Mare Island men guilty of mutiny and sentenced them to long prison terms. Vocal protests from the NAACP and others got the sentences commuted in 1946, and played a major role in convincing Washington to end formal segregation in the armed forces.

Multinational, Multiracial Migration

In addition to blacks, the wartime emergency allowed Chinese to obtain lucrative, unionized industrial and clerical jobs for the first time in Bay Area history. The shipyards also recruited workers from Nicaragua and El Salvador, thus laying the foundation for contemporary San Francisco's substantial Central American population. Thousands of Mexican nationals arrived in the region to work at agricultural and railroad jobs, under terms of the formal US-Mexican Bracero Program of 1942. In addition to these "official" legal migrants, thousands of other Mexicans came to work in the fields and canneries of local agricultural regions, such as Santa Clara Valley. Like the Gold Rush before it, World War II produced a massive, multinational and multiracial migration that transformed the Bay Area socially and demographically.

The University and the Atomic Bomb

While hundreds of thousands of war workers labored in Bay Area factories, a few University of California professors were involved in a wartime project that would ultimately influence the course of world history. Back in the late 1920s, the University recruited two young professors, Ernest O. Lawrence and J. Robert Oppenheimer, who were to be instrumental in establishing Berkeley as one of the primary centers of research in nuclear physics. In the 1930s Lawrence developed a cyclotron that allowed scientists to "split" the atom. He was strongly supported by University President Robert Gordon Sproul, who allowed the young researcher to establish an independent laboratory, and won approval for him to become a full professor at the young age of 29. Lawrence more than repaid the University with publicity and prestige, earning a Nobel Prize in 1939. Initially Oppenheimer was not nearly as well known to the general public, but by the end of the '30s he had become one of the nation's leading theoretical physicists.

When President Roosevelt established the Manhattan Project in 1942 to develop nuclear weapons, it was inevitable that Berkeley would play a major role in the effort. Lawrence's Radiation Laboratory was greatly expanded and moved to a hill behind the University campus. Oppenheimer became director of the Los Alamos laboratory in New Mexico, where the first atom bombs were produced in 1945. Although the two labs were owned and paid for by the federal government, they were operated by the University, under contract. In 1952 a third laboratory was established at Livermore, primarily to enable another Berkeley professor, Edward Teller, to continue his work on the hydrogen bomb.

The University continues to operate all three institutions. The Berkeley lab no longer does classified research, but Livermore and Los

Alamos remain the nation's major nuclear weapons laboratories. In a sense, the remarkable wartime accomplishments of the Berkeley scientists marked the realization of President Daniel Coit Gilman's 1872 dream that his new university would become a world center of scientific research. Gilman believed that this would occur through free and open inquiry, contributing to peace and progress. It is a commentary on our age that, instead of Gilman's idyll, one of the world's great public institutions of higher education devotes significant intellectual resources to the production of secret weapons that could destroy civilization as we know it. That is another legacy of the World War II revolution.

□ □ □

El Camino

Homestead Road

Stevens Creek Boulevard

El Camino

Homestead Road

Stevens Creek Boulevard

17 The Great Sprawl

Suburban Growth in Santa Clara County
Air views of an area near Santa Clara in 1950 and 1970. Note the virtual disappearance of the orchards and cropland in 20 years. (California Tomorrow, *Cry California*)

17

The
Great
Sprawl _____

In 1970 Karl Belser, who had recently retired as planning director of Santa Clara County, wrote an article for the conservation journal *Cry California*. Its title was "The Making of Slurban America." He dealt with the way "uncontrolled growth" had transformed a pleasant agricultural region into the Bay Area's largest population center. The place was the Santa Clara Valley and the time was the 1950s and 1960s, while Belser was planning director. In effect, the article was an acknowledgment of professional and political failure. Belser believed that the valley's growth during that period had been guided by anything but sound planning principles. Instead, in his own words, "the behavior of all elements of the community during the time from 1950 to 1965 can best be described as pandemonium."

Santa Clara Valley Orchard
Orchards like this gave way to rapid postwar suburban expansion. (Santa Clara County Department of Planning and Development)

Santa Clara Valley's postwar growth is a dramatic example of a state and national trend that profoundly affected the Bay Area. Between 1940 and 1970 the nine-county population nearly tripled, whereas after 1945 the population of the major central cities, San Francisco and Oakland, actually declined. Of the smaller core cities, only Alameda showed substantial growth. Berkeley held its own, but Richmond declined. Thus, virtually the entire postwar population growth of the region occurred in the suburban periphery. By 1970 only about one-quarter of all Bay Area residents lived in the old core cities.

"The Valley of Heart's Delight"

The part of the region most affected by this spectacular suburban growth was Santa Clara County, the place that once called itself "The Valley of Heart's Delight." As we have seen, the county had been the Bay Area's granary during the 1850s and '60s. Later in the 19th century, during the Central Valley's wheat boom, Santa Clara farmers began to experiment with fruit and vegetable crops. The climate was ideal for such products, the land being composed of rich alluvial soil, and the underground water resource easily tapped for irrigation. Often it was European and Asian immigrant farmers who first experimented with the new crops, and their efforts helped to create one of the nation's richest local agricultural economies. Prunes, peaches, pears, walnuts, apricots, cherries, grapes, and a great variety of vegetables thrived in the Santa Clara Valley sunshine. After the turn of the century, development of inexpensive gasoline and electric pumps promoted a steady expansion of irrigated agriculture.

The old Spanish pueblo of San Jose was the county seat, as well as the chief commercial and population center for the South Bay region. By 1940 about 50,000 people lived in the city, whose chief industry was canning, packing, and processing the products of the surrounding farms. Farther north, Stanford University helped support a smaller population clustered around Palo Alto. The rest of the valley was primarily rural, with a few small towns dotting the landscape. Each spring, thousands of Bay Area residents drove down the Bayshore and El Camino to view the remarkable floral display of the blossoming Santa Clara Valley orchards.

Economic activity picked up dramatically during World War II. Stanford pioneered in wartime electronic research, and the Joshua Hendy Company in Sunnyvale as well as the naval air station at Moffett Field expanded rapidly. During the war, thousands of newcomers arrived or passed through the region, and once hostilities ceased, many decided to stay. When wartime building restrictions ended, a construction boom began and growth itself became a major industry. The area's economic base substantially expanded in the early 1950s, when

Lockheed and Westinghouse decided to build major plants in Sunnyvale. By this time, Santa Clara Valley communities were competing to attract more housing, shopping centers, and factories. According to Belser, the county's business and political leaders were quite frank about their goal of making San Jose "the Los Angeles of the north."

The postwar boom came at a difficult time for some valley farmers. Many of the orchards had been started 50 or 60 years earlier, and it was time for the expensive process of replanting. Moreover years of intensive irrigation had overdrawn underground aquifers, causing land subsidence in some parts of the valley and a steady increase in pumping costs everywhere. Farmers suddenly found themselves with suburban neighbors, including children who were not above stealing a few ripe plums, teenagers who enjoyed joyriding and necking in the orchards, and parents who complained about the noise of farm machinery and the smell of fertilizers and pesticides. To make matters worse, the farmers found their land being taxed on the basis of its potential value for housing and industry, rather than its actual value as agricultural property. In these circumstances, it is not surprising that farm families were willing to sell their holdings to developers who could offer premium prices.

Belser persuaded the county government to make a belated try at saving the orchards through agricultural zoning. Preservation of farmland and orchards was opposed by the publisher of the *San Jose*

Mercury, who reportedly commented that trees don't buy newspapers. Moreover, the county's jurisdiction was limited to unincorporated lands, and the cities, led by San Jose, rapidly annexed new areas to bring them under municipal and pro-growth control. In 1967 the state Legislature passed the Williamson Act, allowing land placed in a 10-year agricultural preserve to be taxed on the basis of farm use rather than urban potential, but by this time most of the 100,000 acres of orchards that once flourished in northern Santa Clara County were gone. In a hungry world, some of the nation's finest agricultural land was taken out of production, perhaps forever.

By 1980 Santa Clara was the Bay Area's most populous county, with 1.3 million people, nearly 10 times its 1940 population. San Jose, the nation's fastest-growing large city, with 630,000 residents, seemed likely to pass San Francisco as the Bay Area's largest population center by 1990. "The Valley of Heart's Delight" had become "Silicon Valley," the core of the nation's most promising "high tech" industrial development. Rapid growth had adverse effects, as Santa Clara County suffered from a rising crime rate, serious traffic congestion, air pollution, and the specter of future water shortages. At least some local residents would certainly have agreed with Karl Belser's assessment: the postwar boom had caused "the flagrant ruination of the Santa Clara Valley."

Santa Clara Valley, 1950s to 1960s
Suburban encroachment on Santa Clara Valley orchards. (Santa Clara County Department of Planning and Development)

Other Parts of the Region

The South Bay was by no means the only part of the region to experience suburban growth. Rapid development of the Sausalito-to-San Rafael corridor allowed Marin County's population to grow fourfold between 1940 and 1970, though the county experienced almost no additional growth in the following decade (1970-1980). Sonoma County's population tripled during the 1940 to 1970 period, and then grew by another third between 1970 and 1980, the growth being concentrated along the Highway 101 route. The number of Contra Costa residents increased by more than six times between 1940 and 1980, most of the growth occurring in a string of suburbs stretching along Highway 24, from Orinda to Concord. Walnut Creek, once a stable agricultural community, saw its population explode from 10,000 to 40,000 during the 1960s alone. In the 1970s rapid growth also occurred along the Interstate 80 corridor in northern Contra Costa County. The community of Hercules, once an industrial company town, expanded from 250 to 6,000 residents, thus growing faster than any other California city.

Southern Alameda County also felt the effects of the suburban boom. The 1950s saw the virtual end of commercial agriculture in San Leandro and Hayward, and in 1956 the incorporation of Fremont brought five older communities and nearly 20,000 acres of farmland into a single political unit. During the 1960s the new city's population

more than doubled, to over 100,000, and in the 1970s completion of
BART stimulated further growth. Agricultural lands gave way not only
to housing, but also to heavy industry. In the 1950s, General Motors
moved its assembly plant from Oakland to Fremont, while Ford made a
similar move from Richmond to Milpitas. In the Livermore Valley, a
very different kind of industrial development—establishment of a
nuclear weapons laboratory—also resulted in rapid population growth.

Immediately south of San Francisco, in Westlake and parts of
Pacifica, contractors like Henry Doelger built seemingly endless blocks
of detached, enlarged, suburban versions of San Francisco row houses.
It was Westlake that inspired Malvina Reynolds' popular song "Little
Boxes." Along the bay side of the Peninsula, expansion of San
Francisco's airport was a major stimulus for the rapid growth of a series
of communities from South San Francisco to Redwood City. In addition, completion of the Bayshore Freeway in the early 1950s facilitated
the commute of thousands of Peninsula residents to San Francisco. San
Mateo County's population grew fivefold between 1940 and 1970,
though, like Marin, San Mateo experienced almost no additional growth
in the following decade.

Social Segregation

In the Bay Area and elsewhere, unremitting suburban growth reinforced patterns of social and economic separation. By 1970 the great

bulk of the region's white middle class lived in suburban communities, while the majority of poor and minority residents were concentrated in old central city neighborhoods. This pattern even applied to the Santa Clara Valley. The area's most affluent residents lived in pleasant west-valley towns like Los Altos Hills and Los Gatos. Much of the Chicano population was concentrated in parts of San Jose and on the valley's east side. The prewar stream of Mexican immigrants who had entered the valley to work in the fields and canneries had become a flood during the labor-short war years. San Jose emerged as the informal capital of a disconnected strip of Chicano settlement stretching through the remaining agricultural communities of southern Alameda County north to Oakland's Fruitvale district. By the 1950s the east San Jose *barrio* had taken on the unofficial name of *Sal Si Puedes,* "get out if you can."

During the boom years of the 1960s and early 1970s, a portion of the Mexican-American population did in fact get out, joining the move to middle- and working-class suburban neighborhoods. But the rapid decline of employment opportunities in local fields and canneries left other Hispanics trapped in poverty. A 1973 Rand Corporation study identified the growing economic and social gap between the white and Chicano populations as the Santa Clara Valley's number one problem.

Blacks found it even more difficult to break into the suburban mainstream. In the early 1950s a San Francisco dentist became Mill Valley's first black homeowner, but only after considerable protest by many white neighbors. Where substantial suburban black populations did exist, e.g., in Marin City and East Palo Alto, they tended to comprise isolated, largely minority communities. The Eichler Company was almost unique among developers in its attempts to produce racially integrated suburban neighborhoods in the late 1950s and early 1960s. The state's fair housing law, sponsored by Berkeley Assemblyman Byron Rumford, was repealed by a popular initiative in 1964. Although the courts eventually held the initiative unconstitutional, covert housing discrimination continued as a chronic problem.

By 1980, however, the situation had improved in many areas. Tara Hills and Hercules in Contra Costa County included well-integrated tracts with Asians, Latinos, blacks, and whites living side-by-side in new suburban homes. Of course, these houses were only available to middle-income people, and incidents of cross burnings and Ku Klux Klan activity in the area showed that the bay region's long heritage of racism was not dead.

Public Subsidy for Sprawl: Housing and the Freeways

Until quite recently, the suburban boom was supported by substantial public expenditures, as local communities invested heavily in new schools, parks, streets, and water and sewage systems. While suburban development did increase local government revenues, often expenditures grew even more rapidly. In the Santa Clara Valley, for example, Karl Belser pointed out that the increase in total public debt outstripped even the snowballing population growth. In the early 1970s Palo Alto's city government concluded that it was cheaper for the municipality to buy a large tract of hillside land than to pay the public costs associated with private development. Toward the decade's end, the 1978 passage of state Proposition 13 sharply reduced the property tax revenues available to local governments, compounding the difficulty of finding public funds to support suburban growth.

Federal and state governments also did their share to subsidize the postwar development of the suburbs. Middle-class families found it far easier to get low-interest FHA, VA, or Cal-Vet loans to purchase new suburban tract homes, than to obtain similar loans to buy or remodel old housing in racially mixed urban neighborhoods. The problem was compounded by the practice of "red-lining," whereby private banks and savings institutions restricted mortgage funds available for minority neighborhoods. By far the greatest federal and state contribution to sprawl was in highway construction. The postwar suburban boom represented a major triumph of the automobile in Bay Area life. Prewar depression and wartime rationing had delayed the car's full impact, but after 1945 the newly dominant suburban lifestyle was heavily dependent on the auto, without which the suburbs could not exist.

In 1947 the state Legislature approved a plan for massive freeway development. Washington fully cooperated, particularly after the initiation of the federal interstate system in the mid-1950s. By 1980 a freeway network circled the bay, providing links with every major suburban community. Perhaps the age was best symbolized by Eichler-built homes in Palo Alto and San Rafael. The garage was virtually the only part of an Eichler house visible from the street. Equally symbolic were the vast parking lots surrounding suburban shopping malls. Such commercial centers typically devoted more ground space to parking than to retail sales.

Ironically, the Bay Area's very first postwar shopping mall did not appear in the suburbs, but in the Stonestown development near San Francisco's Lake Merced. But Stonestown was followed by dozens of other such centers that were located outside of the old urban cores. The malls became economic and social centers of the new suburban communities, virtually destroying the old downtown shopping areas in cities like Richmond and San Jose, and seriously threatening other central business districts, including Oakland's.

Freeway Revolt . . . Open Space . . . Slow Growth

Perhaps the most dramatic evidence of the automobile's influence is the character of the first popular protest against the nature of the Bay

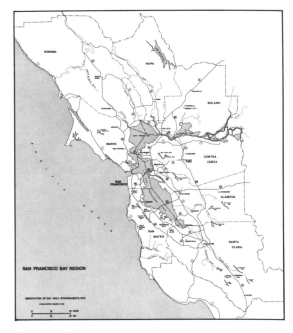

Bay Area Freeways
(Association of Bay Area Governments)

Area's postwar boom: it was a "freeway revolt." By the early 1960s many San Franciscans were appalled at what massive highway construction was doing to their compact city. After the Embarcadero Freeway was begun, effectively walling off San Francisco's central waterfront from the rest of town, the Board of Supervisors refused to approve further plans for freeway construction in the affluent northern and western portions of the city. (Freeway building did continue in the industrial and working-class districts on the southeast side of town.) San Francisco's battles against highway construction set a precedent for similar struggles in many other Bay Area communities.

Also in the early '60s, conservationists began major efforts to preserve important open space areas from development. Establishment of the Point Reyes National Seashore in 1962, and the Golden Gate National Recreation Area 10 years later, not only preserved a vast expanse of valuable coastline, but also set a precedent for national parks in highly populated metropolitan regions. During the 1960s and 1970s the East Bay Regional Park System expanded dramatically, becoming an example for a similar regional preserve in the Peninsula hills. In 1968, Napa County effectively used zoning to prevent the transformation of valuable vineyard property into suburban tracts. Significantly, both Marin and Napa counties turned down freeway proposals that would have encouraged suburban development in regions devoted to open space and agriculture. In 1972 the Association of Bay Area Governments approved a plan calling for the preservation of over 3 million acres of Bay Area open space. A decade later a regional conservation organization, People for Open Space, called for action to protect the area's remaining 2 million acres of agricultural land.

By the early 1970s, "no growth" or "slow growth" sentiment had reached the suburbs themselves. In the previous 20 years, for example, Livermore had grown from under 5,000 to more than 38,000 people. In 1972 a group of citizens proposed a moratorium on further residential building, until the city found solutions to problems of overcrowded schools and overburdened water and sewer systems. In a single weekend, the group gathered three times the number of signatures necessary to put the moratorium measure on the ballot. In the April election, the initiative passed by a wide margin.

Petaluma established a limit of 500 new housing units per year, while southern Marin County voters turned down proposals to expand their water system, on grounds that the plans would open the way for further population growth. San Mateo County zoned much of its coastal region for agriculture and open space, and allowed only limited development on San Bruno Mountain south of San Francisco. Even San Jose, the region's ultimate "Sun Belt" metropolis, passed ordinances designed to slow runaway growth and preserve open space in the southern part of the city. San Jose also made plans to revitalize its downtown core, and the Santa Clara County Transit District approved a

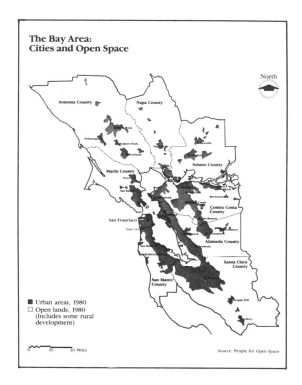

Cities and Open Space
(People for Open Space)

proposal for a $320 million electric rail system, linking San Jose with the north county "high-tech" industrial complex.

In short, by the early 1980s the postwar, automobile-oriented suburban boom had sparked a regional reaction that put developers very much on the defensive. One such builder claimed he lost $2.5 million when he was unable to get permits to develop a piece of San Mateo County marshland. In frustration, he moved to Texas and reported that in Houston projects were okayed in a matter of days that would take months or years to win approval in the Bay Area.

Directions for the Future?

In 1979, Massachusetts Institute of Technology city planning professor Bernard Frieden contended that the Bay Area's inflated housing prices, rated the highest in the nation, were primarily due to the region's attempt to preserve open space and limit growth. In his book *The Environmental Protection Hustle,* Frieden supported his thesis with a series of anecdotes and case histories. But he did not attempt to assess the impact of other factors that certainly affect housing prices, such as real estate speculation, high interest rates, costs of material and labor, demographic change, and the effects of the region's big expansions in office space and "high-tech" industry.

Frieden did, however, make at least one valid point: new or pro-spective homeowners and renters are seldom represented in community debates that rage among developers, conservationists, residents, politi-cians, and city planners. During the postwar years, builders presumably gave many people what they wanted: low-density suburban housing where families could pursue an ideal of western living best expressed in the pages of Menlo Park's *Sunset* magazine. But the 1970s brought ris-ing energy and transportation costs, increased environmental awareness and concern, and dramatic changes in lifestyles and household size. Given these factors, what kind of housing will the environment support and people need and want in the 1980s and 1990s? Are conservation-ists right in thinking the region now needs more dense, city-centered development? Will the rate of regional population growth continue to decline as in the 1970s? While we ponder these questions, suburban tracts continue to go up on the regional periphery—in communities like Santa Rosa, Fairfield, Benicia, and Antioch. The Great Sprawl may have been slowed, but it has not been stopped.

□□□

18 Regional Governance

The Berkeley Dump in the 1960s
Bay-fill scenes like this promoted the emergence of a citizens' movement that led to the creation of the San Francisco Bay Conservation and Development Commission. (Rondal Partridge)

18

Regional Governance _____

In 1960 Berkeley's general plan provided for the filling of more than 2,000 acres of San Francisco Bay. An area extending two miles off the city's present shoreline would be developed for housing, industry, a community college campus, and an airport. This prospect provoked citizen opposition led by three East Bay women—Esther Gulick, Sylvia McLaughlin, and Kay Kerr. They founded an organization eventually named Save San Francisco Bay Association, and in 1961 persuaded the Berkeley City Council to amend the plan, eliminating all but a small fraction of the proposed bay fill.

Although the city council decision was a major victory for the save-the-bay crusaders, they realized that several other Bay Area communities also had fill plans at least as ambitious as Berkeley's. Richmond, for example, intended to extend its shoreline beyond Brooks

Island, leveling the island's hills in the process. Emeryville and Alameda also planned substantial fill, and the Port of Oakland proposed to extinguish a two-square-mile area of open water near the Bay Bridge toll plaza, as well as a significant portion of San Leandro Bay. San Francisco had ambitious plans for fill in the Candlestick Park area, and San Rafael contemplated developing 3,000 acres of bay tidelands. San Mateo County's master plan called for filling 23 square miles of bay and shorelands, including the area now occupied by Foster City. The developers of Redwood Shores planned a residential community in an area previously used for salt ponds, and West Bay Associates, a combination of Crocker and Rockefeller interests, proposed to bulldoze a portion of San Bruno Mountain for bay fill material. The Save San Francisco Bay Association leaders recognized the difficulty of lobbying effectively in each of these separate political entities. Thus they proposed to control regional bay fill by asking the state Legislature to establish an agency to protect the bay and to plan for the uses of its shoreline. In short, the save-the-bay crusaders had concluded that the Bay Area needed a new arm of regional government.

Early Attempts at Regional Governance

The first serious proposal for an overall regional government in the Bay Area, the "Greater San Francisco Movement," was put forth in

1910. As previously noted, San Francisco business and political leaders called for a borough system, similar to that recently established in New York. Separate boroughs would retain limited government functions within the larger supercity. The system was to encompass San Francisco, Colma, and South San Francisco; much of southern Marin, including Sausalito, Mill Valley, and San Rafael; and the urbanized section of the East Bay, including Richmond, Berkeley, Alameda, and Oakland. San Franciscans hoped the new governmental structure would be in place by the time of the 1915 Panama Pacific Exposition, but in 1912 the plan went down to defeat in a statewide initiative. Alameda County voters were strongly opposed, rejecting the initiative by more than a two-to-one margin.

During the 1920s, San Francisco's prestigious Commonwealth Club supported a Regional Plan Association, but the organization accomplished little before its demise in 1928. In the 1920s and 1930s, three single-purpose multicounty agencies were established under state enabling legislation: the East Bay Municipal Utility District (1923), the Golden Gate Bridge and Highway District (1928), and the East Bay Regional Park District (1934). Other attempts at effective regional planning during the Depression and World War II, however, had little success.

Near the end of World War II, Bay Area business gained a regional voice with formation of the Bay Area Council. Initially established in

1944 as a postwar planning forum for both public and private interests, it soon emerged as a business-dominated private organization. The council's policy positions generally represent the point of view of the region's largest and best-established corporations, e.g., Bank of America, Southern Pacific, PG and E, and Chevron. While big business has thus had an effective regional forum and lobbying organization for 40 years, Bay Area labor continues to be divided into separate county building trades and labor councils.

"Progress Demands That the Bay Area Be De-Balkanized"
(Bob Bastian © San Francisco Chronicle)

A Council of Governments (ABAG)

In the 1950s there was a growing awareness of the need for a regional forum of local government officials, and in 1961 a majority of the Bay Area's cities and counties established a voluntary council of governments, called the Association of Bay Area Governments (ABAG). This move was undoubtedly hastened by state legislative and business-community efforts in 1959-1961 to create a "Golden Gate Authority" with power to take over the money-making toll bridges, and to acquire or build seaports and airports. The proposal was narrowly defeated in 1961, but the proposal's real and implied threat to local governmental interests, and its demonstration that local officials were poorly organized to influence policies affecting the region, nudged along the formation of ABAG. Operations of the latter began in 1961 with a budget of $17,000 and a membership of six counties and 56 cities. A decade later, ABAG had a $1.3 million budget and a membership of eight counties and 82 cities. The association's professional staff wrote important reports on matters such as regional open space, housing, transportation, economic development, and population growth. In 1970 the organization produced the Bay Area's first comprehensive regional plan.

ABAG had no legal authority over its member governments, but wielded considerable influence through competent staff work and its ability to reach consensus. Thus, in 1975, ABAG opposition to "Las Positas," an ambitious "new town" development proposed for the Livermore Valley, was a major factor in persuading the Alameda County Board of Supervisors to reject the project. ABAG gained additional clout through its role as reviewer of certain categories of federal grant requests made by local governments. Washington also chose ABAG as the local agency to prepare the Bay Area's comprehensive plan to meet federal clean air standards.

Nevertheless, ABAG is what its name implies: a voluntary association of local governments. If a member government disagrees strongly with ABAG policy, it can simply drop out of the organization, as Sonoma County did in 1972. Much of the association's budget is based on dues paid voluntarily by member agencies, and after passage of Proposition 13 in 1978, local governments cut back their ABAG contributions. These local austerity measures coincided with reductions in federal and state grants to ABAG, forcing serious budget and staff cuts. For all its good work, ABAG has not been able to operate as an effective regional planning agency or regional government.

Postwar Efforts at Regional Governance

The concept of a multipurpose governing body for the Bay Area was resurrected in 1967 by the efforts of San Francisco Senator J.

Eugene McAteer and Contra Costa Assemblyman John Knox, who cosponsored a joint legislative committee on Bay Area regional organization. The work of the joint committee resulted in a 1969 Knox bill to establish a regional government. ABAG also accepted the regional government idea, and Marin Assemblyman William Bagley introduced a 1969 bill embodying its version of the concept. Knox sponsored several variations of the concept in subsequent years—1970, 1971, 1972, 1973, and 1975. Most passed the Assembly but were defeated in the Senate.

While the proposals differed in specifics, all gave the regional body only limited powers and assumed the continued existence of local and county governments. Nevertheless, the Bagley and Knox bills failed, defeated by opposition from development interests, local governments, and local politicians, as well as by conflicts between various jurisdictions within the region. The deceptively simple question of whether the board of the new agency would be appointed or elected divided even strong supporters of the general concept of regional government. Finally, there was opposition from elsewhere in the state, due to fears of a precedent being established that might someday apply outside the Bay Area.

Lacking a consensus on an overall regional agency, the Legislature has instead established or provided for a number of additional single-purpose bodies in the bay region. In a sense, this has been a continuation of the trend started before World War II with the East Bay

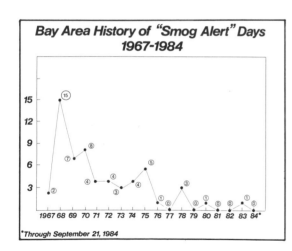

Bay Area History of "Smog Alert" Days 1967-1984

*Through September 21, 1984

Smog Alert Days, 1967-1984
Despite continued population growth, air quality controls have reduced smog alerts to a minimum. (Bay Area Air Quality Management District)

Municipal Utility and Regional Park districts and the Golden Gate Bridge District. But since the war, the new regional agencies have had jurisdiction over all or most of the region rather than just a portion of it.

In 1949, the state thus established a water quality board for the Bay Area as a whole, as part of a statewide system of such boards. After construction of the Eastshore approach to the Bay Bridge in the 1930s routed bridge users along the Emeryville waterfront, local residents became painfully aware of the fact that raw sewage was flowing directly into the bay. The highway passed near sewage outlets, and at low tide the stench was overpowering. Backed by increasingly tough federal and state standards and progressively generous federal and state construction grants, the water quality board succeeded in forcing and cajoling Bay Area communities and agencies to build effective sewage treatment plants. As a result, bay waters are probably cleaner today than at any time since the 1920s, although occasional sewage-plant failures and the presence of new industrial and agricultural waste products still create serious problems.

In 1955 the Legislature created the Bay Area Air Pollution Control District (now called the Air Quality Management District). The "smog board" first banned open-dump garbage burning and then concentrated on reducing pollution from stationary sources. Eventually, federal and state agencies enacted and enforced automobile emission standards, and rising fuel prices contributed to the effort by encouraging residents to drive smaller, more efficient cars. Again the results have been impressive: a significant regionwide reduction in most forms of air pollution in spite of continued population and economic growth. Nevertheless, smog remains a serious problem in certain parts of the area, particularly the Santa Clara and Livermore valleys.

Initially, the San Francisco Bay Area Rapid Transit District, established in 1957, was supposed to plan and build a rail transit system for the area's five "core" counties (Alameda, Contra Costa, Marin, San Francisco, and San Mateo). By the time voters approved the $800 million BART bond issue in 1962, however, Marin and San Mateo had dropped out of the district. BART, in effect, became one of several Bay Area public transit systems competing for federal and state subsidies. As a result, the Legislature formed the Metropolitan Transportation Commission in 1970 to serve as an overall regional planning agency. MTC gained substantial power because of its role in allocating subsidies to various local transit systems.

The Save-the-Bay Movement

In the 1960s, when the save-the-bay crusaders called on the Legislature to create an agency to control bay fill, they were simply asking the state to approve another single-purpose regional governance body for the Bay Area. The first official action to control bay fill had come nearly a century earlier, in 1869, when the state harbor commission banned further filling beyond a bulkhead constructed along the central San Francisco waterfront. But elsewhere state actions actually encouraged the filling of bay marsh and tidelands. All such property originally belonged to the state, but by 1960 about a quarter of the total had been sold to private parties, who usually filled the area for urban or agricultural purposes, or diked it off for oyster beds and salt ponds. Another quarter of the marsh and tidelands had been granted to cities and counties, which often leased it to private parties who again diked or filled it. By 1960 only about half the bay shoreline was still in state hands, and at mean high tide San Francisco Bay was about 25 percent smaller than it had been in 1850.

Over the years, local politicians and private developers had come to view the bay shore as a logical place for profitable urban expansion. Thus the Save San Francisco Bay Association faced powerful opponents, including most local governments, and private owners of tidelands, such as the Santa Fe Railroad. But the women who organized the association were not without resources. Many were Berkeley faculty wives—Kay Kerr's husband Clark was the UC president—and they were able to gain important academic support. In 1963 the University's Institute of Governmental Studies published Mel Scott's persuasive monograph,

The Future of San Francisco Bay, arguing for regional control of bay fill and development.

The campaign was waged at a time of growing environmental and social consciousness. Influenced by association fliers that portrayed the issue as a choice between "a bay or a river," public opinion increasingly sided with the save-the-bay effort. The association won the support of disc jockey Don Sherwood, probably the most popular local entertainer of his day. Each morning on KSFO, tens of thousands of Bay Area commuters heard Sherwood's impassioned commentaries on the issue. The save-the-bay effort scored another coup when it persuaded state Senator J. Eugene McAteer, San Francisco's most powerful politician and an influential force in the Legislature, to join Alameda County Assemblyman Nicholas Petris in sponsoring the association's bill in Sacramento. Thousands of Bay Area citizens wrote letters in support of the bill and joined save-the-bay lobbying excursions to Sacramento.

In 1965 the Legislature passed the McAteer-Petris Act establishing the Bay Conservation and Development Commission. The commission was charged with preparing a plan for the permanent protection and development of the bay and its shore and submitting the document for legislative approval within four years. In the interim, BCDC had the power to approve or deny all permits for new bay fill. In 1969 the Legislature approved the bay plan, thus continuing the commission's existence with strong powers. The plan allowed fill for only limited pur-

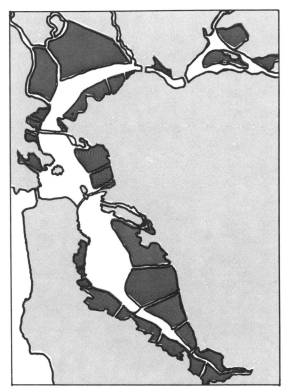

"Bay As a River"
This somewhat stylized map shows how the bay would look if there were no public controls and all the areas susceptible to filling were in fact filled. (Carolyn Sue Hughes, based on Army Corps of Engineers, San Francisco Bay Model)

poses, and gave BCDC significant authority to encourage public access to the bay shore. Although certain projects such as Emeryville's Watergate were "grandfathered in" and thus allowed to proceed, BCDC essentially stopped substantial fill for residential and commercial purposes not directly tied to water-related uses. By the mid-1970s, the commission was requiring some developers to remove old piers and fill, so that the net annual result was a small increase in the size of the bay.

BCDC's most politically difficult decision came in 1971 when it rejected the multimillion-dollar Ferry Port Plaza and United States Steel projects on the San Francisco waterfront. In 1969 the city had regained control of its port after more than a century of state control, and the new port commission considered large-scale real estate development as crucial to the waterfront's economic viability. The two projects were strongly backed by San Francisco Mayor Joseph Alioto and much of the city's business, labor, and political establishment. But the US Steel building's proposed height (500 feet) and location (just south of the Ferry Building) violated the city's master plan and provoked substantial environmental and aesthetic opposition. BCDC found itself in the middle of this controversy because both proposals involved bay fill and loss of open water. After due consideration, the commission found the projects contrary to the bay plan's requirements on several counts, and thus killed both proposals. Although Alioto and the port commission protested mightily, BCDC's decision stood, and the projects were not built.

Other Bay Area regional agencies have also made politically difficult decisions. For example, the Metropolitan Transportation Commission's requirement that local transit systems earn one-third of their revenues from the fare box has forced unpopular rate increases for Bay Area buses, trains, and ferries. In the mid-1970s, the water quality board temporarily banned new sewer hookups in portions of San Francisco to force the city to embark on a massive expansion of its wastewater treatment system.

The Dow Chemical Controversy

The most highly charged political decision by a regional agency involved the Air Quality Management District. Environmentalists had often criticized it, but in 1976 the district refused to issue a permit to Dow Chemical Company for a giant petrochemical plant on the Solano County shore of Suisun Bay. The proposed $500 million complex was to be located in an area that was already booming due to the presence of Travis Air Force Base, an Exxon refinery at Benicia, and a new Anheuser-Busch brewery in Fairfield. Solano County political and business leaders strongly backed the project, but the plan was opposed by environmentalists, concerned about air and water pollution and the loss of agricultural and marsh lands. Some trade unionists, critical of Dow's labor and safety practices, also opposed the project. The air quality board denied Dow a permit on grounds that the company had failed to demonstrate that the plant would not violate air emission standards. At the same time, the state attorney general's office questioned the adequacy of Solano County's environmental impact report on the project, warning that the county might violate state law if it removed the proposed Dow site from the Williamson Act agricultural preserve.

In January 1977 Dow abandoned the project, blaming "bureaucratic red tape" and the multiple permit process. Prominent politicians and business leaders cited the Dow experience as a prime example of California's "antibusiness climate." In fact, however, state and local authorities had agreed to joint hearings to deal with the several different permit decisions simultaneously. Moreover, much of the bureaucratic duplication was due to Dow's choice of treating the project as 13 separate units rather than a single plant. At the hands of the air quality district, at least, Dow received reasonably quick and efficient treatment: the district issued a prompt, though negative, decision.

Strengths and Weaknesses of the Single-Purpose Approach

The Dow case, like BCDC's decision on the US Steel project, increased the prestige of the regional bodies, at least among environmentalists and reformers. The single-purpose agencies had proved they could make tough decisions and stand up to powerful corporate and political interests. Indeed, Assemblyman John Knox found that much of the local opposition to an overall regional government came from those who feared it might weaken the environmental protection now afforded by agencies such as BCDC.

Nevertheless, the Bay Area's practice of achieving regional governance by establishing single-purpose agencies raises some potential problems. Separate boards and districts can make uncoordinated and even conflicting decisions. The power wielded by most of the agencies tends to be negative: boards can *deny* permits and *prevent* projects but have little abiiity to *initiate* positive plans. Most important, the single-purpose agencies usually operate with little or no public attention—indeed, many Bay Area residents are unaware of the agencies' existence. The most extreme example of invisibility was the Bay Area Sewage Services Agency, founded in 1971 and abolished in 1978, having made no apparent impression on the public consciousness. News media virtually ignore the agencies' decisions, except in the most controversial cases, and many of the agency governing boards are appointed rather than elected.

This situation of invisibility makes these powerful regional bodies susceptible to control by the very interests they are supposed to regulate. The fact that BCDC or the Air Quality Management District have shown heroic independence in the past is no guarantee that they will continue to do so in the future. Perhaps that is why the founders of the Save San Francisco Bay Association conceived of their organization as a permanent force—a continuing advocate for the bay and watchdog of BCDC. The save-the-bay crusaders realized that even the best of governmental agencies cannot be trusted if they operate without regular public scrutiny.

□ □ □

19 Protest Decade

Free Speech Movement Demonstration, 1964
Students and onlookers throng Sproul Plaza and surrounding Berkeley campus area to hear protest speakers. (Bancroft Library, UCB)

19

Protest
Decade

During the early 1960s UC Berkeley students, following the examples of previous generations of activists, began setting up card tables at the campus entrance at Bancroft Way and Telegraph Avenue. The tables were used to publicize and advocate various political causes, activities prohibited since the 1930s on the campus proper. Because the corner was presumed to be property of the city of Berkeley, the tables were not considered in violation of University rules. But during the summer of 1964, the situation changed when administrators belatedly discovered that the area in question was indeed University property. When students returned to school in September, they learned that the sidewalk card tables were no longer allowed. Student political groups, from radical to conservative, protested and formed a united front to call for "free speech" on campus. Some students also set up tables in Sproul Plaza, which they knew would subject them to disciplinary action. This resulted in a growing series of mass protests, culminating on December 2, 1964 in a nonviolent sit-in at Sproul Hall, the campus administrative building. Hundreds of the sit-inners were arrested and, in reaction, protest leaders called a student strike.

Thus began the Free Speech Movement, first of the great rebellions that engulfed American colleges and universities during the 1960s. But if FSM, as the Berkeley protest was called, was the beginning of a national and even international movement, it was also the result of a local trend of political activism that had been growing since the late 1950s.

Postwar Politics

For a decade after World War II, politics in the Bay Area, and in most of the nation, had been moderate-to-conservative. Republican, business-oriented interests supported by the Knowland family's *Oakland Tribune* had turned back a liberal-trade union attempt to win control of Oakland politics after a serious labor-management confrontation in 1947. In San Francisco, federal prosecutors almost succeeded in deporting labor leader Harry Bridges to his native Australia on grounds that he was a communist alien. The period's anticommunist crusade was also felt elsewhere in the region. In 1949 the University of California Regents imposed a loyalty oath on campus employees and eventually dismissed several professors and staff members who refused to sign the pledge. Although the courts later reinstated the fired University personnel, Bay Area cities, including San Bruno, Burlingame, Oakland, Richmond, and Berkeley, established similar anticommunist oaths for municipal employees. The Legislature followed suit with a similar requirement for all state workers and public school teachers.

By the end of the '50s, however, the politics of anticommunism were coming under increasing attack. The political mood shifted in 1958 as a state "right-to-work" initiative failed and Democrat Edmund G. "Pat" Brown won election as governor. On college campuses, many members of a new generation of students, raised in the affluence of the postwar economic boom, expected reality to square with the ideals of American democracy. In the southern United States the civil rights movement focused attention on the nation's shortcomings, and validated mass protest tactics as a way of righting social wrongs.

Beginnings of Campus Activism

The great majority of students were, of course, not political activists, and the biggest "demonstration" at Berkeley in the latter half of the 1950s was a "panty raid." But in 1957 a new leftist student political party called SLATE appeared on campus. Three years later scores of students were among the crowd protesting a meeting of the US House Committee on Un-American Activities at San Francisco's City Hall. When protesters refused to disperse, city police turned on the fire hoses and washed them down the building's great marble stairs.

Between 1961 and 1963, there were large Bay Area protests against job discrimination. Targets included San Francisco automobile dealers, hotels, and restaurants, as well as regional supermarket and gas station chains. The presidential election of John Kennedy strengthened local liberals, and after 1960 they won significant victories. In Berkeley, for example, after years of organizing, a coalition of white and black liberal Democrats won majorities on both the city council and school board, taking over from Republican forces that had controlled city politics for 50 years. In 1964 the school board's liberal majority began a process of school integration that by 1968 led to the establishment of two-way busing of all elementary students.

The University of California administration, led by President Clark Kerr, attempted to adjust to the new political climate by liberalizing campus rules. But the effort had not gone far enough by 1964 to prevent the confrontations that led to the Free Speech Movement. In early 1965, after the Academic Senate supported many of the FSM demands, Kerr and the regents gave in, allowing new rules that put few restrictions on campus political activity.

Broadening the Protest Movement

FSM had won most of its original demands, but by 1965 the issues had broadened. During the mass meetings, student leader Mario Savio, recently returned from civil rights activity in the south, portrayed the University's policies and procedures as symptoms of deeper problems in an increasingly bureaucratic and impersonal society. Many in the first generation of students with access to mass higher education felt themselves on an academic assemblyline. During the FSM student strike, demonstrators wore IBM cards decorated with the slogan: "I am a UC student. Do not fold, spindle, or mutilate."

The settlement of the free-speech controversy coincided with a shift in focus of national black protest from the southern United States to the north and west. Proposition 14, overturning the state's fair housing law, was passed during the same autumn that FSM fought its battles in Berkeley. In the following summer, the Watts upheaval in Los Angeles dramatically demonstrated that California was not immune either to racism or to the violent reactions of racial minorities. In 1966 and 1967 there were similar though much smaller riots in San

Berkeley Campus Protest Speaker, 1969
(Third World Liberation Front Strike, photo by Dick Corten, Bancroft Library, UCB)

Francisco's Hunters Point (1966), and East Oakland (1967). Huey Newton and Bobby Seale organized the Black Panther Party in Oakland in 1966, and for the remainder of the decade that organization was a focal point of both militant protest and violent police reaction. The Delano farmworkers' strike, which began in 1965, and the publicity given to its Chicano labor leader Cesar Chavez, helped produce a new era of Latino consciousness and militancy. By the time of the Native American occupation of Alcatraz in 1969, demands for ethnic studies programs had produced major disruptions on several Bay Area campuses, including a student-faculty strike at San Francisco State University.

Finally, and most important, 1965 was the year Lyndon Johnson sent combat troops to Vietnam. In the early 1960s, student leftists had increasingly criticized American foreign policy toward Cuba and protested the 1964 intervention in the Dominican Republic. Vietnam was portrayed as the culmination of "the Establishment's" policies of international empire-building and domestic racism. The moral fervor of the campus crusade was reinforced by the male students' knowledge that they faced a military draft if they were so unlucky as to lose their deferments. Some may have harbored a sense of guilt—and of injustice—that the war was being fought by nonstudents who were less fortunate than they. In any event, Vietnam divided American society as few issues have done since the abolition of slavery. Understandably the war

was the prime issue on campus during the latter part of the Protest
Decade.

"Lifestyle" Revolt

Along with increased political activism came a cultural revolt—or
in 1960s terminology, a "lifestyle" revolt. Some members of minority
groups claimed to reject white, middle-class values, in favor of an ethnic
or third-world identity. Many young, affluent whites seemed to rebel
against the suburban way of life their parents had worked so hard to be
able to enjoy. Youths who had grown up in secure, "healthy" environ-
ments moved to slum-like conditions in San Francisco's Haight-
Ashbury district and experimented with hallucinogenic drugs. Children
who had received expensive lessons in classical music turned instead to
hard-driving "acid rock."

The Bay Area had, of course, long been a home to "counter-
cultural" activity. In the 19th century, nonconformist writers and
artists had formed the Bohemian Club, now ironically transformed into
a bastion of the regional and national establishment. In the early 20th
century, people like George Sterling and Jack London were part of a
writers' and artists' colony in Carmel. By the 1920s a bluff overlooking
the Berkeley campus was sometimes called "Nut Hill" because of the
eccentric behavior of some of its residents. The 1930s produced more

political than cultural radicalism, but after World War II San Francisco's North Beach area became a center for the "Beat Generation." The beats were hardly a unified "movement," but collectively they did represent an artistic and literary revolt against mainstream American culture in the Eisenhower era.

As such, the beats may have paved the way for the broad youth rebellion that exploded in the mid-1960s. It was a phenomenon that swept much of the western world, but the Bay Area was one of its unofficial capitals. Most Bay Area young people did not fully participate in what the mass media called the "hippie" lifestyle, but enough did so to affect and disturb society at large. If the 1967 "Summer of Love" in San Francisco and Berkeley quickly turned sour, and if the pop-gurus and drug experiments failed to produce answers to "great mysteries," aspects of the lifestyle revolt of the '60s struck responsive chords among many people who were neither young, hip, nor rebellious. Mainstream American culture seemed to leave little room for the ecstatic, and for the virtues of simple, youthful idealism. These were some of the qualities the "new consciousness" promised, though it did not always deliver.

Blending of the Rebellions

By the late 1960s there was a blending of the lifestyle and political rebellions, particularly in South Berkeley neighborhoods where students, street people, and black activists shared more or less adjoining turfs. "Communes," living groups committed both to radical political causes and new social and cultural experiments, cropped up throughout the area.

The south-campus section of Berkeley witnessed the region's greatest confrontation of the '60s, the 1969 battle for control of "Peoples Park." The "park" was in fact an unimpressive vacant block owned and recently cleared by the University but claimed by the activist Telegraph Avenue community. Through a series of University administrative decisions and activist responses, Peoples Park came to symbolize the conflict between the established order and the "counterculture." In a battle that cost one onlooker his life, the combined power of city and University police, county deputy sheriffs, state highway patrolmen, and combat units of the California National Guard finally restored "law and order" to Peoples Park and the campus community. The episode ended with a big, peaceful march by demonstrators who carried flowers and laid sod along the street.

Bayonets in Berkeley, 1969
Part of the Peoples Park controversy. (Lonnie Wilson, *Oakland Tribune*)

End of the Protest Decade

The 1970 American invasion of Cambodia, followed by the deaths of student demonstrators at Kent State University in Ohio and Jackson

State College in Mississippi, sparked the Bay Area's last great street demonstrations of the protest era. After that, "the movement" seemed to unravel. While some of its participants continued various forms of progressive political engagement, others had become tired, confused, and disillusioned. Some found comfortable niches in mainstream society; others were burned out by drugs and violence. Conventional politicians increasingly took up the antiwar campaign, the termination of the draft removed a major concern of many young men, and, finally, American combat troops were withdrawn from Vietnam. Government harassment, provocation, and infiltration of radical organizations also took a toll. Some at the fringes of the movement seemed to lose contact with political and moral reality: thus in 1974 the "Symbionese Liberation Army" assassinated Oakland School Superintendent Marcus Foster and kidnapped Patricia Hearst in Berkeley.

During the 1960s, movement leaders had consciously tried to avoid the sterile, ideological debates that had plagued earlier generations of American radicals. At the heart of the "New Left," then, was not a well-defined ideology or program, but a strong sense of moral indignation. By the 1970s, it was obvious that such an emotional crusade could not be maintained indefinitely. The fact that few bridgeheads had been established to organized labor or other potential allies further weakened the staying power of the New Left. The movement never became institutionalized; indeed its essential spirit was anti-institutional.

The great exception to this generalization was in Berkeley. There, using the massive voting strength of students and south-campus residents, the New Left successfully entered electoral politics. The election of Ron Dellums to Congress in 1970, and of three "April Coalition" candidates to the city council in 1971, established the left as a major force in Berkeley politics. A moderate-to-conservative organization was formed in response, and for more than a decade the city's elections have been contested by two local political parties, both predominantly Democratic in national partisan affiliation. In addition to Berkeley's unique political configuration, the emergence of powerful black politicians in several Bay Area communities, particularly Willie Brown in San Francisco and Lionel Wilson in Oakland, is also in part a reflection of the social and demographic changes of the 1960s.

It is, however, the ultimate irony of the Protest Decade that the major political figures it produced were not part of the movement, but of the conservative "backlash." During his 1966 campaign for governor, Ronald Reagan found he received an enthusiastic response from statewide audiences when he attacked the Berkeley demonstrators. After assuming office, Reagan endorsed if he did not indeed engineer the dismissal of liberal UC President Clark Kerr, and for the remainder of his eight-year incumbency, the governor made political capital by attacking Berkeley students and faculty. In San Francisco, S. I. Hayakawa was catapulted into the limelight and eventually the United

States Senate by his colorful and highly publicized opposition to student protests and faculty strikes at San Francisco State University.

Influence of the Sixties

In the end, the lifestyle revolt of the 1960s may have had far more continuing influence on the society at large than did the political protests. During the 1970s much of the counterculture's music, drugs, and vocabulary, as well as hair and clothing styles, entered the mainstream. Indeed, many aspects of the counterculture became immensely profitable. Bill Graham transformed the Haight-Ashbury's tradition of free rock concerts into a major commercial enterprise. Werner Erhard, among others, institutionalized the quest for spiritual truth and personal fulfillment and turned it into a profitable business venture, called est. Marijuana became a significant, if not legitimate, part of California's great agribusiness economy. By the 1970s, the revolt against the "plastic" quality of American culture had spawned hundreds of excellent (and expensive) new Bay Area restaurants and shops. Hot tubs replaced swimming pools as regional status symbols.

On a more substantial level, the 1960s produced significant changes in attitudes toward sex and marriage. The 1980 census showed that among major American metropolitan areas, San Francisco-Oakland led the way in characteristics indicating a "lifestyle revolution." Compared to other regions, Bay Area cities had the highest percentages of unmarried adults, divorced people, and one-person households. Conversely, San Francisco-Oakland had the lowest percentage of households consisting of families. In emphasizing personal freedom and liberation from oppression, the 1960s paved the way for the powerful gay and women's movements that had been building gradually for years and emerged publicly in the Bay Area during the 1970s. By the same token, the politics of the 1960s contributed to the Bay Area's important record of environmental protection and conservation activism in the 10 years that followed.

Today, Berkeley's Sproul Plaza, site of so many great confrontations during the 1960s and 1970s, is a prime tourist attraction. Along Telegraph Avenue, the street merchants who once advocated counterculture trade and barter now accept credit cards. On the plaza itself at midday there are usually dozens of card tables advocating various political causes, and the University administration is trying to reach an agreement with its neighbors on the fate of still-undeveloped Peoples Park. But in the classrooms and laboratories, the University continues to function pretty much as it did from the beginning. The Protest Decade shook great national institutions at Berkeley and elsewhere, but did not break or even alter them very much. For better or worse, despite significant changes in many aspects of American life, the center held. But because of that, some valid questions about the nature of American institutions and culture raised during the 1960s remain unanswered. Those questions will undoubtedly be asked again by another generation during another Protest Decade.

□ □ □

20 Silicon Valley

What the Microchip Begat
The "Valley of Heart's Delight" of earlier years has become "Silicon Valley" in the high-tech era. (Hewlett-Packard, and Santa Clara County Department of Planning and Development)

20

Silicon
Valley

I n 1980 the late Frederick Terman said "I understand how these things work, but I still don't believe it . . . I simply disbelieve that anyone can put 5,000 transistors on a little silicon wafer one-half inch square." What Terman referred to was the microelectronics revolution that has turned the South Bay into the nation's new high-technology industrial center. In the 1970s Silicon Valley, stretching from Belmont (some 20 miles south of San Francisco) to San Jose, generated an estimated 20 percent of all high-technology industrial jobs in the United States, and was the nation's ninth largest manufacturing region. It also was the Bay Area's greatest economic success story, completely outstripping the older industrial center in the East Bay. By 1980 Silicon Valley accounted for nearly 70 percent of the dollar value of durable goods produced in the entire nine-county region.

"The Godfather of Silicon Valley"

In the mid-1970s *Fortune* noted two major reasons why Silicon Valley developed where it did: the presence of plenty of vacant land, and the influence of Frederick Terman, godfather of the South Bay's remarkable industrial expansion. Son of a well-known Stanford professor who had developed the famous Stanford-Binet intelligence test, young Frederick had earned a PhD at the Massachusetts Institute of Technology, returning to Stanford in 1925 to begin a long career teaching electrical engineering. By that time the university already had ties with the Peninsula's infant electronics industry. Stanford president David Starr Jordan had been one of the original investors in the Federal Telegraph Company based in Palo Alto, and in 1912 one of the firm's employees, Lee de Forest, perfected the vacuum tube for use as a sound amplifier. Another Federal Telegraph worker, Charles Litton, went on to establish a Redwood City enterprise that grew into the giant Litton Industries. In 1927 Stanford scientist Russell Varian assisted Philo Farnsworth of San Francisco in achieving a prototype form of television transmission.

Despite the presence of these pioneering men and firms, in the 1920s the heart of the US electronics industry was still on the Atlantic Coast. Terman realized that most of his best graduate students had to leave California to get top jobs in their chosen profession. This bothered him, and he determined to use his personal influence and university ties to promote the growth of the local electronics industry. Thus Terman persuaded William Hewlett and David Packard, both former students, to start Hewlett-Packard Company in a Palo Alto garage. Another pioneer firm in Silicon Valley, Varian Associates, was established by Russell and Sigurd Varian, both former Stanford research assistants who invented the klystron tube, a major contribution to the development of airborne radar and microwave technology.

During World War II, Terman led a government research project at Harvard. When he returned to Stanford in 1946 as dean of the College of Engineering, he brought a keen appreciation of the role federal defense dollars were destined to play in the future of the electronics industry. He used his considerable reputation to attract federal funds to Stanford and to neighboring private firms.

As a university administrator, Terman was also a strong promoter of the Stanford Industrial Park concept. Leland Stanford's will prevented the university from selling any of its vast landholdings, but there was no prohibition against leasing. In the late 1940s the university began signing long-term leases with industrial firms wishing to build plants on Stanford property. (The giant Stanford Shopping Center is also located on leased university land.) The new industrial development not only earned Stanford much-needed revenue, but also reinforced the growing informal partnership between Stanford and its corporate neighbors. Hewlett-Packard and Varian were among the park's earliest tenants, building campus-like facilities that set a precedent for Silicon Valley industrial architecture. By the late 1970s the valley had more than 50 private industrial park developments, most of them patterned on the Stanford complex.

The Military-Industrial-Intellectual Complex

Although local firms accounted for much of the South Bay's post-World War II growth in electronics, the region also attracted large national companies. After the war, IBM and General Electric established major research facilities in San Jose, and Lockheed and Westinghouse located giant defense plants in Sunnyvale. As American weaponry became increasingly sophisticated and reliant on complex electronic systems, it made sense for major defense contractors to be located near large universities and private research centers, like Stanford Research Institute in Menlo Park. Whereas 19th and early 20th century industrial development needed to locate close to markets, resources, and transportation routes, the new high-tech enterprises stimulated by defense dollars put a premium on easy access to appropriate brainpower and technical skills.

Although the markets of Silicon Valley firms eventually broadened to include important civilian commercial and industrial fields, the postwar beginnings of the region's high-tech economy depended heavily on defense-related expenditures. Thus the presence of Lockheed and Westinghouse in the valley was particularly important, as they funneled millions of additional defense dollars into the region in the form of lucrative subcontracts. In the 1960s the establishment of the National Aeronautics and Space Administration's Ames Laboratory at Moffett Field, and the Atomic Energy Commission's decision to support construction of the Stanford Linear Accelerator, poured additional federal funds into the valley's expanding economy. Of course, similar expenditures affected other parts of the Bay Area, particularly Alameda County, which was the home of the Lawrence Berkeley and Livermore laboratories, funded by the federal government and operated by the University of California. Nowhere, however, was the influence of the new military-industrial-intellectual complex greater than in Silicon Valley.

Development of Microelectronics

In 1956 another Stanford faculty member, William Shockley, established Shockley Transistor Company on the Peninsula. Although now primarily known for his controversial ideas on the biological basis of intelligence, Shockley received a Nobel Prize for his work in developing transistors. His firm attracted bright young engineers and scientists. Within two years, eight of them had left Shockley to form Fairchild Semiconductor, backed by the Fairchild Camera and Instruments Company. This established a precedent for Silicon Valley companies behaving in amoeba-like fashion, regularly splitting and spinning off new enterprises. By 1980, Fairchild Semiconductor itself had spun off at least 40 other firms, begun by ambitious engineers and executives wanting to go into business for themselves.

Much of the capital that funded this process of corporate procreation was generated in the Bay Area, although some of it also came from eastern and international sources. The region produced a group of ambitious "venture capitalists" who hoped to profit from the rapid rate of technological development. In addition to helping finance microelectronics, Bay Area banks and investment houses also successfully gathered funds for new ventures in laser technology, robotics, and genetic engineering. Much of the research on which these endeavors were based had occurred at UC Berkeley, Stanford, and the UC Medical Center in San Francisco. Consequently the universities were forced to frame new policies to deal with potential conflicts of interest, and threats to free scientific inquiry. Nowhere in the world did there appear to be as yeasty a combination of scientific expertise, private capital, government funds, university facilities, and personal ambition as in the Bay Area. The region thus became a center of technological revolution.

Declining defense contracts in the late 1960s caused a temporary economic downturn in the Peninsula electronics industry, but boom times returned in the 1970s. The rapid development of the microchip, electronic games, personal computers, and other nondefense, consumer products, led *Fortune* to observe that "Santa Clara County can be said to mass-produce millionaires." San Jose was the nation's fastest growing big city during the 1970s, and Santa Clara County gained 220,000 people during that decade. It accounted for nearly half the total population increase of the entire nine-county Bay Area. The valley's burgeoning population included some of the world's finest scientists and engineers. Thus by 1980, 15 percent of all the people in California with doctorates lived in Silicon Valley.

Labor and Management, Silicon Valley Style

The valley's elite labor force was not only extremely skilled but also very mobile, as ambitious people with highly marketable skills sought better positions and opportunities. Thus the microelectronics industry's annual job turnover rate was an astonishing 23 percent. Such mobility and competition produced high incomes. In 1982 valley firms were offering annual salaries of nearly $30,000 for new university graduates with only a bachelor's degree in electrical engineering. The strong bargaining position of such employees made a rigid, authoritarian work environment impossible. Company presidents often brainstormed alongside young, long-haired PhDs. Like their employees, top executives often dressed in jeans and sport shirts, jogged and played volleyball during lunch periods, and attended Friday afternoon beer busts sponsored by the firm.

In spite of their casual workstyle, however, the valley's employers often held strongly traditional capitalist views. As pioneers in new industrial fields, they had little tolerance for offering government assistance to the hard-pressed old "smokestack" industries of the east and midwest. Such assistance was condemned as a subsidy to prop up enterprises that were no longer efficient and competitive. But their criticism of public help for private enterprise also conveniently ignored the great role of federal research and defense dollars in the creation of much of the high-tech industry itself. Moreover, when severe recession weakened the microchip market in 1982, some Silicon Valley firms were not above calling for government help to combat Japanese competition.

Most valley employers also strongly opposed unionization of their workforce. As might be expected, unions have made little headway among well-paid scientists and engineers. But valley production workers, many of them Hispanic and Asian women, earn far less than the highly educated elite, and less even than the traditionally unionized blue-collar workers in many of the older Bay Area industries. Silicon

Valley should be a bright new frontier for the labor movement, but by the early 1980s the microelectronics industry was still largely unorganized, casting a cloud over labor's future in the Bay Area.

Departure of Production Facilities

One difficulty union organizers confronted was that much of Silicon Valley's actual production work could take place almost anywhere, even in places quite remote from the valley. The basic product—the microchip—was so small and light that transportation and shipping costs were insignificant. Accordingly, many firms were locating production plants outside the valley in places where labor and other costs were low. By the late 1970s less than half of Hewlett-Packard's employees worked in Santa Clara County, and the company was planning new plants in Rohnert Park near Santa Rosa, and in Roseville in the Sacramento Valley. Other firms planned moves to Sun Belt cities in the southwest, or even to Asia and Latin America. Atari, for example, closed a large valley production plant in the spring of 1983, eliminating 1,700 local jobs. The plant was to be replaced by Asian production facilities. Significantly, a union organizing campaign was under way when Atari made its decision to move.

Other factors also contributed to the uncertainty of Silicon Valley's future. Despite the fact that microelectronics was supposed to be a "clean" industry, Santa Clara County had the Bay Area's worst air quality. Local automobiles and wind drift from other parts of the region were responsible for most of the smog, but fumes from solvents used in producing chips were also a significant factor. Equally serious was the fact that chemicals from at least one valley electronics plant have been detected in well-water serving residential neighborhoods. In any event, the region's general environmental decline has adversely affected recruitment of scarce, skilled labor, since one of Silicon Valley's chief attractions has been its natural beauty and the possibilities for outdoor living.

The valley has been especially hard hit by the Bay Area's regional housing crunch. We have seen how new construction failed to keep pace with increased housing demand in the 1970s. Although the birth rate went down, the number of young adults entering the housing market grew rapidly. Consequently many communities, in Silicon Valley and elsewhere, faced extreme shortages of reasonably priced housing, ironically at a time when they were also closing public schools for lack of students. Tract homes that had sold for $25,000 in 1970 were worth five times that figure in 1980. In contrast to employers in other regions, Bay Area firms seeking top talent had to offer very high salaries to offset the effect of local housing costs. Even Stanford and UC Berkeley were forced to provide university-subsidized home loans to attract first-rate young professors. Of course, the very high salaries offered by high-technology firms to scientists and executives had helped to create the runaway housing prices in the first place.

High housing costs affected Silicon Valley's elite labor force of scientists, engineers, and executives, but caused far greater hardship among the much lower-paid production workers. Middle-class whites seeking reasonably priced homes moved into previously black and Chicano neighborhoods in East Palo Alto and San Jose. This drastically raised housing prices in those areas, making it difficult for employers to find low-income workers among those who were able to live in the local area. One electronics executive quipped, "It's a little hard to hire millionaires to work in production."

Future of Silicon Valley

Even if production facilities continue to leave Silicon Valley, research, development, and management are likely to stay. These functions depend on highly trained brainpower, which is still concentrated in Silicon Valley in particular, and in the Bay Area generally. The region's vast pool of scientific and technological talent facilitates recruitment, training, and regular movement of skilled employees from company to company. This helps the electronics industry keep itself sharp and creative. In short, there is compelling logic in maintaining a close-knit complex of offices and laboratories near the Bay Area's universities and research institutions. Consequently Silicon Valley—like San Francisco and much of the rest of the Bay Area before it—may become primarily a headquarters and service center, rather than a place of actual production. But as industrial jobs disappear, new employment opportunities will have to be created for a large part of the valley's workforce. New technologies already have displaced thousands of Bay Area workers in traditional industrial fields. It would be ironic if thousands of additional people, primarily nonwhite women working in industries at the forefront of the new technologies, were added to the ranks of the structurally unemployed.

In 1980 Dean William Kays of Stanford commented that our generation is 50 years into an Electronics Revolution that may ultimately be as important as the Industrial Revolution. When we were only 50 years into the Industrial Revolution, few seers could have predicted the vast social and cultural upheavals that were to result from the new methods of production. If Kays is correct, Silicon Valley's scientists and engineers may be in the first stages of creating not only a new technology, but a new social and cultural reality.

□ □ □

21 A Tale of Two Central Cities

"Manhattanization," Before and After

By 1983, highrises blocked the views of or actually replaced most structures pictured in the 1958 photograph, hiding the configuration of San Francisco's famous hills. (1958 photographer unknown, photo property of Stewart H. Bloom. Stewart H. Bloom, 1983 photographer)

21

A Tale of
Two Central
Cities _____

In the early 1960s geographer James Vance categorized the Bay Area's three leading cities by referring to the transportation technologies that had contributed most to their initial urban development. San Francisco began as a city where walking, sailboats, and horsecars provided the principal transportation, and even today retains a compact, dense development pattern. Oakland was heavily influenced by rail construction, and is laid out along principal north-south thoroughfares that once were major steam or trolley lines. San Jose is the ultimate automobile city, a great decentralized mass of suburban housing tracts and shopping malls.

In the 1960s San Jose's auto-influenced pattern seemed like the wave of the future, and Vance noted that even then, more Bay Area automobile trips were made each day between different suburban locations than between the suburbs and the old urban cores. Since then San Jose has grown to exceed Oakland's population, and may well exceed San Francisco's by 1990. Yet even as this growth has continued, rising energy and transportation costs, environmental concerns, and major cultural and demographic changes, pose serious questions about the viability of the postwar suburban ideal. Moreover the old cities, San Francisco and Oakland, have not exactly dried up or become obsolete. They retain a vital role in the region's life and even show signs of substantial new growth.

Downtown-Centered Development

Downtown San Francisco regarded the suburbs' postwar growth as just one more challenge to its regional urban leadership. Since Benicia's establishment in 1847, the bay city had successfully fought off a series of urban rivals, and after World War II San Francisco was not giving up without a fight. Downtown business and civic leaders, organized into groups like the Bay Area Council, envisioned an expansion of downtown's traditional function as a major corporate office and headquarters location for western America. In addition, the United States victory over Japan promised vast new commercial opportunities in the

Pacific Basin. San Francisco offered itself as a center for business decisionmaking and capital formation in this new globe-girdling westward thrust of American economic influence. Manhattan was the conscious model for downtown's proposed postwar development. In the late 1940s New York was still seen as an example to be emulated, rather than to be avoided.

San Francisco also assumed it would continue as the Bay Area's major cultural and entertainment center. Though people might live in the suburbs, they would still come to the city to enjoy and enlighten themselves—and in the process do a bit of shopping, eating, and drinking. Finally, the city was ready to exploit its vast potential as a tourist and convention center.

Thus, with the advantage of hindsight, we can see how San Francisco's strategy for postwar development was clear. Political scientist Frederick Wirt, complaining in the 1970s how the city's maze of conflicting interest groups prevented public policy decisions from being made and carried out, may have had trouble seeing the forest for the trees. Wirt's thesis may seem supportable in dealing with day-to-day, issue-by-issue decisions. But the long-term policies that favor downtown office construction, support cultural and entertainment activities, and promote the growth of the convention and tourist industries, have been consistently and effectively pursued for more than three decades.

The results were impressive. Beginning with the construction of the Zellerbach Building in the late 1950s, San Francisco experienced by far the greatest highrise boom in its history. During the 1970s alone, the city added 16 million square feet of new office space, and by 1982 another 20 million were under construction or planned. Great towers such as the Bank of America and Transamerica buildings dramatically changed San Francisco's appearance. The massive, multiblock Embarcadero Center Project added 18,000 new jobs to the city's workforce, and produced $10 million in new tax revenues annually.

The building boom was concentrated in the financial district, but by 1980 new highrises were also appearing south of Market Street. Developers were transforming old industrial and warehouse buildings along the northern waterfront and at the base of Potrero Hill into fashionable offices and showrooms. Farther south, Southern Pacific was planning a huge office and residential development on the filled tidelands of old Mission Bay. In 1981, in spite of substantial construction elsewhere in the Bay Area, San Francisco's office vacancy rate was only 1 percent, although the city's office rents were among the highest in the United States.

Additional Development

City government also gave substantial financial backing to cultural and athletic enterprises. For a city of 700,000 people, San Francisco supports an impressive complex of public museums, as well as major opera, symphony, ballet, and dramatic repertory companies. In 1958 Mayor George Christopher persuaded the New York Giants to move to San Francisco on the promise that the city would build a new municipally financed stadium at Candlestick Point. The Giants and Forty-Niners are important to the city's economy and self-image. In 1982 the Board of Supervisors approved a study for a still newer, domed stadium near the downtown center.

Finally, city agencies like the Convention and Tourist Bureau aggressively promoted San Francisco's image as "America's Favorite City." In the 1970s the pace of new hotel construction rivaled even the highrise office-building boom. Tourist facilities were concentrated near Union Square, and along a strip of northern waterfront stretching from Pier 39 and Fisherman's Wharf to Aquatic Park. William Matson Roth's transformation of the old Ghirardelli Chocolate factory into a complex of shops and restaurants in the 1960s pioneered similar rehabilitation efforts throughout the nation. By 1980 tourism had become the city's biggest business.

Unlike the office boom, which added largely unorganized white-collar and clerical employees to the city's workforce, tourism produced new jobs in unionized occupations. The Hotel and Restaurant Workers became the city's largest labor organization, far outstripping the declining industrial and waterfront unions. Another area of labor strength was public employment, but this sector suffered from the effects of

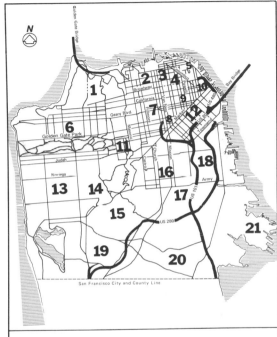

1. Presidio	12. South-of-Market
2. Marina/Pacific Heights	13. Sunset
3. Russian Hill	14. Forest Hill
4. Chinatown	15. Diamond Heights
5. North Beach	16. Mission
6. Richmond	17. Bernal Heights
7. Western Addition	18. Potrero
8. Civic Center	19. Ingleside
9. Union Square/Nob Hill	20. Visitation Valley
10. Financial	21. Hunters Point
11. Haight-Ashbury	

San Francisco's Principal Districts
(Carolyn Sue Hughes)

Proposition 13, as declining local government revenues caused layoffs and reduced union bargaining power. Moreover government employee strikes in the mid-1970s generated substantial public resistance. The tourist industry thus became central to the well-being of San Francisco's labor movement, and labor strongly backed city construction and operation of large convention facilities, first at Brooks Hall, and later the long-delayed Moscone Center. Rapid expansion of the airport also helped promote the convention and tourist industry.

Tourism, along with the office boom and the thriving cultural and entertainment complex, contributed to the growth of the downtown commercial establishment. Despite development of giant suburban malls—e.g., Hillsdale in San Mateo, Sun Valley in Concord, and Hilltop in Richmond—San Francisco's Union Square continued to be the Bay Area's largest and most profitable shopping center. Macy's Union Square store was the region's biggest retail outlet in dollar terms, and the addition of elite establishments like Saks Fifth Avenue and Neiman-Marcus reinforced Union Square's status as one of the nation's most prestigious shopping areas.

Transit Links

San Francisco's economic viability had always depended on transportation links to the rest of the Bay Area. Downtown survival during the postwar era depended on suburban residents having easy access to the city's offices and commercial facilities. Much of this access was by automobile, and by the time of the freeway revolts of the 1950s and 1960s, highway links with the Peninsula had already largely been completed. But the resistance to freeways effectively crushed dreams of a second auto crossing to the East Bay. Removal of the old Key System tracks and establishment of one-way auto decks increased the Bay Bridge's auto-carrying capacity in the 1960s. But by the 1970s, BART was, in effect, a necessary substitute for the automobile bridge that was never built.

Although BART was originally planned in the 1950s to include Marin and San Mateo counties, only the three-county East Bay-San Francisco routes were constructed. The system does not operate primarily as an urban subway linking various neighborhoods, but as a commuter railroad bringing East Bay residents to San Francisco. Of course, BART also provides valuable service within San Francisco, as well as within and between several East Bay communities. Moreover, unlike the proposed second Bay Bridge, the system brings riders directly into downtown Oakland. But BART's major beneficiary is downtown San Francisco, and the bulk of the system's passengers ride the transbay commute routes.

BART's commuter service is effectively complemented by AC Transit's excellent bus system, which is available throughout most of the urban East Bay. The 1970s also saw rapid expansion of the Golden Gate Bridge District's bus and ferry service from Marin to the city. In addition, the state of California began subsidizing Southern Pacific's rail passenger line up the Peninsula, and San Mateo County's samTrans began bus service from the county to downtown San Francisco. Within the city, these lines linked up with San Francisco's extensive Muni system. With such improved service available from the various transit systems, by 1980 the Bay Area had the third-highest per capita rate of public transit use of any major metropolitan region in the nation.

The transit lines were heavily subsidized, barely making one-third of operating revenues from the fare box. But they have effectively countered some of the influence of the publicly subsidized system of auto transportation, and thus have helped to maintain a viable urban core. Bay Area suburban communities remain wedded to the auto, whereas downtown San Francisco is absolutely dependent on tax-supported public transit systems.

Oakland's Development

While San Francisco worked hard to maintain its traditional urban supremacy in the region, Oakland continued its historic role as San

Containership Entering Port
(Oakland Port Commission)

Francisco's chief rival. Even though San Jose is the area's second-largest city, it has not challenged San Francisco's role as the primary urban core. Indeed, San Jose's growth followed a pattern that is the antithesis of traditional core-city development. Oakland, on the other hand, is an old central city itself. Almost by reflex action, Oakland has steadily resisted San Francisco's assumption of natural supremacy.

Oakland's greatest postwar success came in the development of its port. As we have seen, in 1910 Oakland won control over its waterfront from the Southern Pacific. The area was put under the jurisdiction of a nearly autonomous city port commission in the 1920s, and in the '30s the commission got pilot fees and other procedures removed that had discriminated against Oakland. During World War II and the Korean War, the military made substantial improvements in Oakland's port facilities.

Thus by the end of the 1950s, the city's waterfront was in a position to take advantage of its strategic location on the "continental side" of the bay, and its proximity to both the Southern Pacific and Western Pacific railroad terminals. The port commission invested heavily in the untried technology of containerization. The Longshoremen's Union agreed to the introduction of the new labor-saving devices, in return for liberal retirement and retraining benefits. By 1970, the commission's gamble had paid off handsomely. Oakland was the Bay Area's leading shipping terminal and one of the world's largest container ports.

Gantry Cranes Handling Containerized Cargo
(Oakland Port Commission)

Meanwhile, for more than a century, San Francisco's port had remained under state control, a throwback to the days when much of California's commerce had passed through the city's waterfront. By the time San Francisco won back control of its port in 1969, Oakland's supremacy, based on geographical advantage and managerial skill, was already established. San Francisco built its own container facilities on the southern waterfront, and by the early 1980s the West Bay port was making a modest comeback. But the once-great role shipping had played in the city's economy had all but disappeared. The Pacific Far East Line failed under the ownership of former Mayor Joseph Alioto's family, and the Matson and American President lines moved their terminals to Oakland.

While San Francisco debated the fate of its obsolete northern waterfront's finger piers, Oakland argued about the distribution of its substantial port revenues. The Oakland commissioners believed that the port should continue to reinvest its profits in port-controlled facilities, including the Oakland airport. But critics contended that the commission's surplus should go to the city's general fund, to help offset budget deficits caused by Proposition 13 and cutbacks in federal programs. Meanwhile, other Bay Area ports, particularly those of Richmond and Redwood City, were planning substantial expansion.

Another significant Oakland achievement was joint construction with Alameda County of the Coliseum complex, a new stadium and arena superior to comparable San Francisco facilities. The Golden State Warriors moved across the bay to Oakland, and during the 1970s the Oakland A's and Raiders had greater financial and athletic success than the San Francisco Giants and Forty-Niners. The accomplishments of Oakland's athletic teams, which included World Series and Super Bowl victories, attracted national attention and reinforced civic leaders' claims to Oakland's "Major League" status. The apparent loss of the Raiders to Los Angeles in 1982 was a blow to civic pride, as well as to Coliseum finances. Oakland took the unprecedented legal step of attempting to use its power of eminent domain to return the team to the East Bay.

In addition to promoting professional athletics, Oakland, like San Francisco, increased its public support for "high prestige" cultural activities, such as the Oakland symphony and ballet companies. The city also built a magnificent new museum near Lake Merritt, and the orchestra association raised the money to restore the art deco-style Paramount Theater as a symphony hall and performing arts center.

Plans for Downtown Oakland

Unlike San Francisco, however, Oakland has long had trouble with the prosperity of its downtown core. During the 1950s and 1960s, the city's central district steadily lost business to suburban shopping centers.

Deterioration of the Key System in the immediate postwar years, and disruptions caused by BART construction in the 1960s, dealt downtown Oakland additional blows. Construction of the Kaiser Center, headquarters of Henry J. Kaiser's giant industrial empire, brought new office workers into Oakland, but the building's location along Lake Merritt actually pulled business activity away from the old downtown area on lower Broadway.

In 1967 Oakland announced the City Center Redevelopment Project, an ambitious effort to revitalize the old downtown core. The Redevelopment Agency used federal funds to condemn, purchase, and clear space for a giant retail commercial center which would be sold to private investors at bargain prices. Extension of the Grove-Shafter Freeway and the location of a major BART station were to provide access to the project, initially designed as a kind of downtown version of a suburban shopping mall. Ironically, the City Center project destroyed most of the Washington Street Mall, an earlier attempt at commercial revitalization completed just four years before the new project was launched. But City Center has not yet been able to attract the major retail outlets necessary to get the project moving. Although two office buildings have been built, most of the land remains a giant vacant lot, contributing to downtown blight rather than alleviating it.

In 1982, City Center was reborn. Officials announced that the shopping mall scheme was scrapped in favor of a large highrise office complex. Adjoining the area, the city was constructing a new convention center, and private investors were building a modern hotel, again on land cleared by the city. Nearby, on other redevelopment land, Asian investors were putting up the Trans Pacific Centre, then envisioned as the first stage of a four-block highrise project that might eventually include a 78-story tower—tallest building in the west. The city was also assisting private developers in revitalizing "Victorian Row," two blocks of 19th century commercial buildings that were planned to become a Ghirardelli Square-like complex. These various publicly subsidized projects were only part of the new construction planned for downtown Oakland. Kaiser Center intended to add more towers to its complex, and private investors planned several other highrise buildings.

In effect, Oakland was attempting to cash in on San Francisco's vast office boom. If corporations preferred expensive office space in San Francisco for high-level executives, perhaps firms would locate lower-level clerical staff and computer operators in less expensive Oakland facilities. As the Bay Area lost blue-collar workers—both the GM and Ford assembly plants closed in 1982—Oakland hoped to get its share of the "new collar" labor force of the high-tech age. But as has traditionally been the case, San Francisco rather than Oakland would remain the principal site of the private-sector decisionmakers.

By the end of 1982, even this new scenario remained in doubt. In the midst of a severe recession, San Francisco's office vacancy rate climbed to 10 percent, and suburban builders were putting up new "office parks" in places like Concord, Walnut Creek, Dublin, San Ramon, and Pleasanton. There was a serious question how much demand there really was for Bay Area office space, and this raised doubts about at least some of Oakland's planned highrise projects. Meanwhile, downtown Oakland was still suspended between the deterioration of its immediate past and the unfulfilled dreams of its hoped-for future.

Demographic Changes

Both San Francisco and Oakland underwent dramatic demographic changes in the postwar years. By 1971 San Francisco's black population was large enough to prompt federal district Judge Stanley Weigel to order the city to begin a controversial busing program to achieve school desegregation. Oakland School Superintendent Marcus Foster commented that busing would be of little use in his city, because there were not enough remaining white students to go around. By 1980 nearly half of Oakland's population was black, and other minorities comprised another 15 percent of the total. In that same year, Oakland had a black mayor, city manager, community college chancellor, school superintendent, and editor of the daily newspaper. In no other large western city had blacks gained so much civic power so quickly. The new black leadership had no wish to be in charge of a destitute municipality, and Mayor Lionel Wilson worked closely with white businessmen on measures to encourage economic development. Because of this, black business leaders complained that Wilson was not allowing them to participate in the city's anticipated downtown renaissance.

During the 1970s, the region's fastest-growing ethnic groups were Asians and Hispanics. San Francisco's Chinese population burst out of the traditional borders of Chinatown into North Beach and Russian Hill. Chinese and other Asians also became important components of the Richmond and Sunset district population. The Inner Mission was home for several Latin American groups, and Southeast Asian refugees settled in both Oakland and San Francisco. East Oakland was an important center of Chicano population, and the bay region as a whole, particularly Daly City, attracted growing numbers of Filipinos. By the end of the 1970s, immigrants had caused a dramatic rise in the inner-city school populations at a time when suburban school district enrollments were declining significantly. By 1982 San Francisco was the fastest-growing large urban school system in the United States, and Oakland's enrollment was also increasing.

Also during the seventies, San Francisco and Oakland had an influx of single young whites, attracted by the region's tolerant and cosmopolitan lifestyles, its universities and colleges, and the jobs

Bay Area's Great Ethnic Diversity

By Gary E. Swan

Oakland reported most integrated city

By Kathy O'Toole
Tribune Staff Writer

Ethnic Diversity and Racial Integration
Children and parents of many ethnic and racial backgrounds are seen enjoying Steinhart Aquarium's whale and the circular swings in Golden Gate Park. (The clippings are from the *San Francisco Chronicle* and the *Oakland Tribune;* photos by Janet Isadore-Barreca.)

created by new downtown development. Included was a large gay population, especially concentrated in San Francisco's Castro district. The presence of an openly gay community in the region caused some cultural and social conflict. One San Jose fundamentalist minister recommended capital punishment for homosexuals, and San Jose voters turned down a local "gay rights" ordinance.

The gay community made major contributions to the region, not the least of which was economic. Often well-educated and well-trained, homosexuals became an important part of the region's pool of skilled office, professional, and service workers. Like most middle-class single people, they had a great deal of disposable income, and were thus important consumers and investors. Establishment of gay Democratic clubs institutionalized homosexual political power in San Francisco, and helped win the election of Harvey Milk to the San Francisco Board of Supervisors in the mid-1970s. In 1978 fellow-supervisor Dan White murdered Milk and Mayor George Moscone, and White's relatively light sentence for the crime provoked a large protest demonstration at City Hall. Even in "tolerant" San Francisco, gay liberation proved to be a painful process of social change.

The Housing Crunch

In the 1950s and 1960s, as both San Francisco's and Oakland's populations fell, the cities engaged in massive "slum clearing" redevelopment projects. Some of the results were impressive, e.g., Oakland's Acorn Project, but in all, the efforts probably destroyed more moderate-priced housing than they produced. By the 1970s, the growing numbers of young adults in the population confronted both cities with increased demands for housing. Still more recently—in the early 1980s—the overall population seemed to be rising in both San Francisco and Oakland for the first time in over 30 years. Yet high interest rates greatly limited construction of housing to meet the new demand.

Middle-class citizens moved into San Francisco's older neighborhoods, repairing and rebuilding dilapidated homes. While this greatly improved the housing stock in parts of the Western Addition, Haight-Ashbury, and Inner Mission, it also forced low-income residents out of the neighborhoods, and perhaps out of the city entirely. During the 1970s, the black population actually declined in both San Francisco and Berkeley, perhaps due to increased housing costs caused by this process of "gentrification."

Destruction of residential units to make way for office and tourist projects compounded the housing problem. Old residential hotels, often the last refuges for retired people and low-paid seasonal workers, were particularly threatened by the highrise boom. Both San Francisco and Berkeley passed rent-control and condominium-conversion ordinances in an attempt to limit escalating housing costs. Oakland voters twice considered rent-control proposals that resembled the strict Berkeley law, but rejected them. As a result, neighborhoods situated close to

Oakland's downtown, especially the city's Chinatown, may experience huge rent increases if the highrise boom proceeds as planned. In San Francisco, Mayor Dianne Feinstein's administration began requiring office-building developers to contribute funds to help finance housing construction or rehabilitation, as a condition of receiving city permits for new highrise buildings.

Debate Over Downtown Development

The intense pressure on the housing supply symbolized for some San Francisco and Oakland residents the folly of the downtown-centered development policies their cities were pursuing. In San Francisco, especially, critics condemned decisions that seemed to favor tourism, developers, and suburban commuters, rather than the interests of the city's own residents and neighborhoods. The critics claimed the downtown development overtaxed the transit systems and cost more in public services than it could produce in new city revenues. In the early 1970s, Mayor Joseph Alioto fought proposals to limit highrise development, but his successor, George Moscone, seemed sympathetic to the critics' anti-highrise contentions. For a brief time the city switched to district elections for the Board of Supervisors, and it appeared that neighborhood interests might force a change in development strategy.

After Moscone's assassination in 1978, however, citywide elections were reinstated, and Mayor Feinstein again favored the traditional downtown development emphasis. Establishment of district elections in Oakland in 1982 did not prevent Mayor Wilson from continuing to pursue similar downtown development strategies in his city.

Reformers often attacked Feinstein and Wilson for having allegedly "sold out" to big business. Undoubtedly the downtown developers in San Francisco and Oakland often represent powerful vested interests with vast resources at their command, but the actions of mayors Feinstein and Wilson hardly seem surprising in the light of history. They are simply following policies aimed at maintaining their cities' traditional roles in the regional metropolis, and this means attracting more downtown business. But if such policies have the effect of harming the cities' fabric, of destroying neighborhoods and forcing poor people out of the urban core, then we will need a *new* vision of the appropriate roles for the old central cities in the regional metropolis. If San Jose represents the area's "future," San Francisco and Oakland represent its vital past. A decent society should preserve the best of the old, while moving cautiously toward the new.

□ □ □

View of the Bay Area
(Pacific Aerial Surveys)

22

Afterword ————————————————————

In April of 1983, San Francisco voters, by a four-to-one margin, turned down an attempt to recall Mayor Dianne Feinstein. Almost as controversial as the recall itself was the coverage the event received on the popular CBS television show, "Sixty Minutes." In an apparent effort to understand San Francisco politics, the program began with an interview of "Sister Boom Boom," a transvestite who had previously run unsuccessfully for the Board of Supervisors, listing his occupation as "Nun of the Above."

Many local residents complained that such media treatment turned a serious city matter into a national joke. But the Bay Area may have contributed to this process of "trivialization" by refusing to take its history seriously. Despite the efforts of some excellent local historians, the dominant popular vision of the Bay Area's past is a romantic pageant led by kindly friars and colorful forty-niners. If the region's history is viewed as little more than light-weight comic opera, it is hardly surprising that regional politics are sometimes treated as amusing trivia.

Of course, there is nothing trivial about the problems facing the nation's fifth largest metropolitan region. By the year 2000, at least another million residents will be living in the area—an increase roughly equal to the present populations of San Francisco and Oakland combined. While the growth *rate* will be slower than that of earlier·decades, the sheer number of new residents will put great demands on the regional economy and environment. The area will have to produce new jobs, housing, and social services, as well as add to the transportation, water, and power systems, without further polluting the air and water and destroying the region's natural beauty. The population will become even more ethnically and culturally diverse. And, unless present trends are reversed, the economic gap between rich and poor and white and nonwhite will widen.

These essays were written on the assumption that a knowledge of the region's history can help citizens better understand and cope with the effects of rapid change in the present and future. Such change is, of course, nothing new for the Bay Area. Since 1848, there probably has never been a time when a majority of the people living in the region were actually born here. Each new generation has seen the coming of still newer migrations, creating new mosaics of culture and tradition. The resulting mix of heritages has been rich and creative, but has not promoted the recognition of a common Bay Area past. Nevertheless, as James Houston has observed about California as a whole, while the *people* may not share a common history, the *place* definitely does. In the Bay Area, for example, all residents, old and new, are affected by settlement patterns begun by the Spaniards, and by transportation routes established by early rail and ferry systems.

The regional history of the place binds the Bay Area population together, creating a series of shared social and economic conditions, and common experiences and lessons. The Bay Area's past is therefore a great resource that should be cultivated and treasured, rather than ignored and debased. This book will have accomplished its primary purpose if it helps readers appreciate the value of such a regional historical perspective.

□ □ □

Sources and
Further Readings

Writing history is always a process of collaboration between the historian and the sources. That is particularly true with a synthesis or summary history such as this, which relies primarily on the published works of other historians and scholars. Not only did I depend on such sources for factual information, but also I shamelessly borrowed ideas and perspectives from a variety of previously published books and articles. What follows, then, is a discussion of my major collaborators, without whom the writing of this book would have been impossible.

This treatment of sources is arranged in the order of the chapters, so the reader can readily identify the primary works relied on for coverage of specific subjects or periods. (In many cases only partial titles are used in this essay. A complete bibliography follows, giving full titles, publishers, and dates.) With a few exceptions, I have not included the substantial number of individual community histories that exist for the region. These often have been written by dedicated amateur historians whose principal incentive is personal pleasure and interest in the subject. Often scorned by academics, these authors have in fact made significant contributions in research, preservation, and presentation of local history. Their works are not listed here because of a lack of space and because in most cases their community-centered material does not lend itself to this book's regional perspective.

As noted in Chapter 1, the book-length accounts of Bay Area regional history are Mel Scott's *The San Francisco Bay Area* (1959), James E. Vance Jr.'s *Geography and Urban Evolution in the San Francisco Bay Area* (1964), and Lawrence Kinnaird's *History of the Greater San Francisco Bay Region* (1966). (Scott's book, long out of print, is being reissued with a new final chapter.) A good listing of materials on specific Bay Area communities is found in Margaret M. Rocq, ed., *California Local History* (1970). John Reps' *Cities of the American West* (1979) is a monumental work on the establishment of western cities. Gerald D. Nash, *The American West in the Twentieth Century* (1973), discusses western cities. For recent trends in American urban historiography see Kathleen Neils Conzen, "Community Studies, Urban History and American Local History" in Michael Kammen, ed., *The Past Before Us* (1980), Stephen Thernstrom and Richard Sennett, eds., *Nineteenth Century Cities* (1969), and Sam Bass Warner, Jr., *The Urban Wilderness* (1972).

Harold Gilliam has done some of the most important and entertaining writing on the Bay Area environment, including *San Francisco Bay* (1957), *For Better or For Worse: The Ecology of an Urban Area* (1972), and *Weather of the San Francisco Bay Region* (1962). The latter is part of a University of California Press series that also includes Arthur C. Smith's *Introduction to the Natural History of the San Francisco Bay Region* (1959), and Arthur David Howard's *Evolution of the Landscape of the San Francisco Bay Region* (1962). Also see California Division of Mines and Geology, *Geologic Guidebook of the San Francisco Bay*

Counties (1957), and Robert Iacopi, *Earthquake Country* (1971). For a state-wide perspective see Elna Bakker, *An Island Called California* (1971), Michael W. Donley, et al., *Atlas of California* (1979), Warren A. Beck and Ynez D. Haase, *Historical Atlas of California* (1974), David Hornbeck, *California Patterns: A Geographical and Historical Atlas* (1983), and Crane S. Miller and Richard S. Hyslop, *California, The Geography of Diversity* (1983).

Basic sources for California Indian cultures are Alfred Louis Kroeber, *Handbook of the Indians of California* (1925), and Robert F. Heizer, ed., *California* (1978). The latter is a volume in the Smithsonian Institution's *Handbook of North American Indians*. Heizer wrote, along with Albert Elsasser, an excellent general survey, *The Natural World of the California Indians* (1980), and edited, with M. A. Whipple, *The California Indians* (1971). Finally, Heizer also edited *The Costanoan Indians* (1974). Malcolm Margolin's *The Ohlone Way* (1978) is an informative and entertaining account of Bay Area Indian culture. Sherburne F. Cook, *The Conflict Between the California Indian and White Civilization* (1943), covers the drastic decline in Native American population. James Rawls also discusses the white-Indian conflict in *Indians of California* (1984).

Theodore E. Treutlein deals with the initial Spanish contact in *San Francisco Bay: Discovery and Colonization, 1769-1776* (1968). Herbert E. Bolton, *Outpost of Empire* (1931), and Harlan Hague, *The Road to California* (1978), cover the Anza expedition. Bolton also defined the institutional purposes of the mission in *Wider Horizons of American History* (1939). Maynard J. Geiger's *The Life and Times of Fray Junipero Serra, O.F.M.* (1959), and Robert R. Archibald's *An Economic History of the California Missions* (1978), contain much information about missions in the Bay Area. For critical analyses of the missions' impact on the Indians and of Indian resistance see Sherburne F. Cook, *The Conflict Between the California Indian and White Civilization*, and George H.

Phillips, "Breakdown of the Spanish Mission System," in David Weber, ed., *New Spain's Far Northern Frontier* (1979).

Richard Henry Dana, *Two Years Before The Mast* (1840), includes a contemporary description of the hide and tallow trade. Another account by an American in the Bay Area during Mexican rule is William Heath Davis, *Seventy-Five Years in California* (1929). Cecil Alan Hutchinson, *Frontier Settlement in Mexican California* (1969), covers some of the major social and political conflicts of the Mexican era. Madie Brown Emparan, *The Vallejos of California* (1968), gives a sympathetic picture of Mariano Vallejo, as does Don Mariano's own "Historical and Personal Memoirs Relating to Alta California" (1875). Neal Harlow, *California Conquered* (1982), gives an iconoclastic view of the events surrounding the American takeover, while Ferol Egan, *Fremont, Explorer for a Restless Nation* (1977), gives a somewhat more favorable account of the role of John C. Fremont.

Basic interpretations of the development of Gold Rush San Francisco are Roger W. Lotchin's *San Francisco, 1846-1856* (1974), and Gunther Barth's *Instant Cities* (1975). For broader perspectives on Gold Rush California see John Caughey, *Gold is the Cornerstone* (1948), and J. S. Holliday, *The World Rushed In* (1981). Rodman W. Paul, *Mining Frontiers of the Far West, 1848-1880* (1963), covers the spread of the mining industry out of California. The politics of the era are discussed in William Henry Ellison's *A Self-Governing Dominion* (1950). "Vigilante" rule is discussed in John Caughey's *Their Majesties, the Mob* (1960), George R. Stewart's *Committee of Vigilance* (1964), and also in Doyce B. Nunis, Jr., ed., *The San Francisco Vigilance Committee of 1856* (1971).

Peter R. Decker, *Fortunes and Failures: White Collar Mobility in Nineteenth Century San Francisco* (1978), and Richard H. Peterson, *The Bonanza Kings: The*

Social Origins and Business Behavior of Western Mining Entrepreneurs (1977), use the techniques of "the new history" to investigate emerging business elites. David Sievert Lavender, *Nothing Seemed Impossible: William C. Ralston and Early San Francisco* (1975), and George D. Lyman, *Ralston's Ring: California Plunders the Comstock Lode* (1937), give contrasting interpretations of Ralston's career and influence.

Prime sources for a discussion of California land conflicts are William W. Robinson's *Land in California* (1948), William Henry Ellison's *A Self-Governing Dominion* (1950), and the many articles of Paul W. Gates, especially "The California Land Act of 1851," *California Historical Quarterly* (December 1971). Information on the Peralta grant is included in Beth Bagwell, *Oakland, Story of a City* (1982), and the establishment of Golden Gate Park is covered in Raymond H. Clary, *The Making of Golden Gate Park* (1980). Effects of the land conflicts on Spanish-speaking Californians are analyzed in Leonard Pitt's *The Decline of the Californios* (1966). The Bay Area could profit from studies such as Richard Griswold del Castillo's *The Los Angeles Barrio, 1850-1890* (1979), and Albert Camarillo's *Chicanos in a Changing Society* (1979). Mariano Vallejo's experiences are chronicled in Madie Brown Emparan's *The Vallejos of California* and Don Mariano's memoirs.

A good general source for Bay Area maritime history is John Haskell Kemble's *San Francisco Bay* (1957). Also see William Martin Camp, *San Francisco: Port of Gold* (1947), Felix Riesenberg, Jr., *Golden Gate: the Story of San Francisco Harbor* (1940), Richard H. Dillon, *Embarcadero* (1959), and Neill Compton Wilson, *Here is the Golden Gate* (1962). The struggle to organize maritime workers is covered in Ira B. Cross's monumental *A History of the Labor Movement in California* (1935), and David Selvin's popular survey *The Sky Full of Storm* (1966). Particular studies of the seamen's union are Hyman

G. Weintraub's *Andrew Furuseth, Emancipator of the Seamen* (1959), and Paul S. Taylor's *The Sailors' Union of the Pacific* (1923).

Oscar Lewis's *The Big Four* (1938) is a critical account of the careers of the founders of the Southern Pacific. Norman E. Tutorow's *Leland Stanford: Man of Many Careers* (1971), and David Sievert Lavender's biography of Collis P. Huntington, *The Great Persuader* (1970), present a more favorable picture. For information on the ferries see George H. Harlan and Clement Fisher, Jr., *Of Walking Beams and Paddle Wheels* (1951). Edgar M. Kahn, *Cable Car Days in San Francisco* (1944), and George W. Hilton, *The Cable Car in America* (1982), deal with Andrew Hallidie's invention. James E. Vance, Jr., *Geography and Urban Evolution in the San Francisco Bay Area,* and Mel Scott, *The San Francisco Bay Area,* include excellent analyses of the impact of early rail and ferry lines.

Irish immigration to the Bay Area has received growing attention recently in such sources as R. A. Burchell, *The San Francisco Irish, 1848-1880* (1980), James P. Walsh, ed., *The San Francisco Irish, 1850-1976* (1978), and William A. Bullough, *The Blind Boss and His City* (1979). New works on Italian immigration are Dino Cinel's *From Italy to San Francisco* (1982), and Deanna P. Gumina's *The Italians of San Francisco, 1850-1930* (1978). Fred Rosenbaum's *Free to Choose* (1976), about the Jews of Oakland, is a model of informative local history. For accounts of San Francisco Jewry also see Rosenbaum's *Architects of Reform* (1980), and Irena Narell's *Our City, the Jews of San Francisco* (1981).

Alexander Saxton's *The Indispensable Enemy: Labor and the Anti-Chinese Movement in California* (1971) is an indispensable book on conflicts between white and Chinese workers. Other sources on the Chinese include Stuart C. Miller, *The Unwelcome Immigrant* (1970), Gunther P. Barth, *Bitter Strength*

(1964), Jack Chen, *The Chinese of America* (1980), as well as eloquent popular works such as Maxine Hong Kingston's *The Woman Warrior* (1976) and *China Men* (1980), and Victor and Brett De Bary Nee's *Long Time Californ'* (1973). The early anti-Japanese movement is chronicled in Roger Daniels's *The Politics of Prejudice* (1978). Also see Harry H. Kitano, *Japanese Americans: The Evolution of a Subculture* (1969), Bill Hosokawa, *Nisei* (1969), and the Japanese American Curriculum Project, *Japanese Americans* (1971).

San Francisco's earthquake era receives a basic interpretation in Judd Kahn's *Imperial San Francisco: Politics and Planning in an American City, 1897-1906* (1979). Different perspectives on the politics of the period are found in Walton Bean's *Boss Ruef's San Francisco* (1952), and the relevant chapters of John Bernard McGloin's *San Francisco* (1978). Also see William Issel, "Class and Ethnic Conflict in San Francisco Political History," *Labor History* (Summer 1977). Beth Bagwell, *Oakland, Story of a City,* includes a chapter on the Frank Mott era. The quake itself is well described in several works, including the official report of *The California Earthquake of April 18, 1906* (1908), and William Bronson's *The Earth Shook, the Sky Burned* (1959). The Bay Area's seismic dangers are spelled out in Robert Iacopi's *Earthquake Country,* Bruce A. Bolt's *Earthquakes* (1978), and Karl V. Steinbrugge's *Earthquake Hazard in the San Francisco Bay Area* (1968).

Peter C. Allen's *Stanford: From the Foothills to the Bay* (1980) is an attractive popular history of the university. Gunther W. Nagel's *Jane Stanford, Her Life and Letters* (1975) is a sympathetic biography. Additional coverage of the Stanford family's role in founding the university is included in Norman E. Tutorow's *Leland Stanford* and Oscar Lewis's *The Big Four.* The University of California's history is covered in Verne Stadtman's *The University of California, 1868-1968* (1970), and Albert G. Pickerell and May Dornin's *The University of*

California: A Pictorial History (1968). We lack a good biography of Phoebe Apperson Hearst, but much of her life is covered in W. A. Swanberg's fine book on her son, *Citizen Hearst* (1961).

For differing views of the Hetch Hetchy controversy see Holway R. Jones, *John Muir and the Sierra Club: the Battle for Yosemite* (1965), and Kendrick A. Clements, "Politics and the Park: San Francisco's Fight for Hetch Hetchy, 1908-1913," *Pacific Historical Review* (May 1979). The Hetch Hetchy conflict is also covered in several national histories of the conservation movement, including Roderick Nash's *Wilderness and the American Mind* (1967). For many years, the *San Francisco Bay Guardian* newspaper has criticized San Francisco for alleged violations of the Raker Act.

East Bay Municipal Utility District history is covered by John W. Noble, *Its Name Was M.U.D.* (1970). Charles M. Coleman's *P.G. & E. of California* (1952) is a sympathetic history of the utility, and Gerald T. White, *Formative Years in the Far West* (1962), covers the early development of Standard Oil of California. George W. Hilton and John F. Due, *The Electric Interurban Railways in America* (1960), are general sources for the development of electric transit systems. Mel Scott, *The San Francisco Bay Area,* and James E. Vance, Jr., *Geography and Urban Evolution in the San Francisco Bay Area,* contain good coverage of the local impact of electric train systems.

Mel Scott's *The San Francisco Bay Area* also describes early road and highway development. For a statewide view see Felix Riesenberg, Jr., *The Golden Road* (1962), and Earl S. Pomeroy, *In Search of the Golden West* (1957). The national picture is included in John C. Burnham's "The Gasoline Tax and the Automobile Revolution," *Mississippi Valley Historical Review* (December 1961), and Frederick L. Paxson's "The Highway Movement, 1916-1935," *American Historical Society Review* (January 1946). For an excellent analysis of the influence of transportation systems on another California metropolitan region, see Robert M. Fogelson, *The Fragmented Metropolis, Los Angeles 1850-1930* (1967).

The basic source for early labor history is Ira B. Cross's *A History of the Labor Movement in California.* Also see Robert E. Knight, *Industrial Relations in the San Francisco Bay Area, 1900-1918* (1960), and David Selvin, *The Sky Full of Storm.* The Mooney-Billings case is covered by Curt Gentry, *Frame-Up* (1967), Richard H. Frost, *The Mooney Case* (1968), and Estolv Ward, *The Gentle Dynamiter: A Biography of Tom Mooney* (1983). The 1934 waterfront strike and its effects are discussed in Charles P. Larrowe's *Harry Bridges: The Rise and Fall of Radical Labor in the United States* (1972), as well as in two contributions by Harvey Schwartz, *The March Inland: Origins of the ILWU Warehouse Division* (1978), and "Harry Bridges and the Scholars," *California History* (Spring 1980). For a statewide view of the politics of the '30s see Robert Burke, *Olson's New Deal for California* (1953).

Among the best discussions of the wartime Japanese relocation are Jacobus Ten Broek, Edward N. Barnhart, and Floyd W. Matson, *Prejudice, War and the Constitution* (1954), and Roger Daniels, *Concentration Camps USA* (1971). Yoshiko Uchida, *Desert Exile* (1982), describes the relocation experience of a Berkeley family.

Roger W. Lotchin discusses military growth in the prewar years in "The City and the Sword: San Francisco and the Rise of the Metropolitan Military Complex, 1919-1941," *Journal of American History* (1979). For widely different views of wartime shipyards see Richard Finnie, *Marinship* (1947), Katherine Archibald, *Wartime Shipyard* (1947), and Joseph Fabry, *Swing Shift* (1982).

The prewar background of Bay Area black history is covered by Douglas Henry Daniels, *Pioneer Urbanites* (1980), and Rudolph M. Lapp, *Blacks in Gold*

Rush California (1977). For a discussion of wartime racial conflict and the growth of the black population see Charles Wollenberg, "James vs. Marinship," *California History* (Fall 1981), and "Blacks vs. Navy Blue," *California History* (Spring 1979).

Berkeley's role in the development of atomic weapons is covered by Nuel Davis, *Lawrence and Oppenheimer* (1968), and J. L. Heilbron, Robert W. Seidel, and Bruce R. Wheaton's *Lawrence and His Laboratory: Nuclear Science at Berkeley* (1981).

Karl Belser's article, "The Making of Slurban America," appeared in *Cry California* (Fall 1970). Also see Richard A. Walker and Matthew J. Williams, "Water from Power," *Economic Geography* (April 1982). Criticisms of California suburban sprawl are contained in Samuel E. Wood and Alfred Heller's *California, Going, Going . . .* (1962), and Raymond F. Dasmann's *The Destruction of California* (1966). Sam Bass Warner, Jr., *The Urban Wilderness,* and David Brodsly, *L.A. Freeway, An Appreciative Essay* (1982), have a more sanguine view of California's automobile suburbs. T. J. Kent, Jr., *Open Space for the San Francisco Bay Area* (1970), argues for a regional "greenbelt," and People for Open Space, *Endangered Harvest* (1980), calls for protection of Bay Area agricultural lands. Bernard J. Frieden, *The Environmental Protection Hustle* (1979), severely criticizes efforts to retain open space and limit population growth, while T. J. Kent, Jr. and Gary E. Pivo defend such policies in "Thinking About Growth . . . ," *Regional Exchange* (June 1982).

Attempts to establish a Bay Area regional government are covered by John C. Bollens, *The Problem of Government in the San Francisco Bay Region* (1948), Mel Scott, *The San Francisco Bay Area,* Stanley Scott and John C. Bollens, *Governing a Metropolitan Region* (1968), and the Association of Bay Area

Governments (ABAG), *Emergence of a Regional Concept, 1910-1976* (1976). For monographs on many aspects of regional government and public policy, see Stanley Scott, ed., *The San Francisco Bay Area* (1966-1972). ABAG's original Regional Plan for the Bay Area was published in 1970. The latest version was issued in 1980. Mel Scott, *The Future of San Francisco Bay* (1963), argues for an agency to control bay fill, and Harold Gilliam, *Between The Devil and The Deep Blue Bay* (1969), describes the save-the-bay campaign and urges adoption of the Bay Conservation and Development Commission's bay plan. Rice Odell, *The Saving of San Francisco Bay* (1972), carries the story into the early 1970s. Frederick Wirt, *Power in the City* (1974), describes the conflicts over San Francisco's Ferry Port Plaza and the US Steel Building. The Dow case is analyzed by Richard A. Walker, Michael Storper, and Ellen Gersh in "The Limits of Environmental Control," *Antipode* (1979), and Anne Jackson in "The Dow Aftermath," *Cry California* (Summer 1977).

Among the books to read on campus upheavals are Seymour Martin Lipset and Sheldon S. Wolin, eds., *The Berkeley Student Revolt* (1965), Steven Warshaw's *The Trouble in Berkeley* (1965), and Kay Boyle's *The Long Walk at San Francisco State, and Other Essays* (1970). For broader interpretation see Irwin Unger, *The Movement: A History of the American New Left, 1959-1972* (1974), and Landon Y. Jones, *Great Expectations: America and the Baby Boom Generation* (1980). Bobby Seale explains the Black Panther movement in *Seize the Time* (1970). The counterculture of the '60s is discussed in Gene Anthony's *The Summer of Love* (1980) and Theodore Roszak's *The Making of a Counter Culture* (1969). Bay Area conflicts over school desegregation are described by Lillian B. Rubin, *Busing and Backlash* (1972), and Charles Wollenberg, *All Deliberate Speed* (1976). Berkeley politics in the postwar period are analyzed from various viewpoints in Harriet Nathan and Stanley Scott, eds., *Experiment and Change in Berkeley* (1978). Eve Bach and others outline a left-oriented political program for Berkeley in *The Cities' Wealth* (1976).

Dirk Hanson's *The New Alchemists: Silicon Valley and the Micro-Electronics Revolution* (1982) is the first book-length study of the subject. The key roles of Stanford and Francis Terman are discussed in Gene Bylinsky's "California's Great Breeding Ground for Industry," *Fortune* (June 1974), and Peter C. Allen's *Stanford: From the Foothills to the Bay* (1980). Many aspects of Silicon Valley development are covered regularly in the *San Jose Mercury News, San Francisco Chronicle,* and John Eckhouse's informative articles in the *San Francisco Examiner.*

James E. Vance, Jr., *Geography and Urban Evolution in the San Francisco Bay Area,* includes a perceptive analysis of both San Francisco's and Oakland's places in the postwar metropolis. San Francisco politics are interpreted in Frederick M. Wirt's *Power in the City.* San Francisco's two daily newspapers, the *Chronicle* and *Examiner,* along with the neighborhood shopping paper the *San Francisco Progress,* have usually supported the downtown-centered development policies. The weekly *Bay Guardian,* however, has been a consistent critic. See particularly the *Bay Guardian*'s book, *The Ultimate Highrise* (1971). Another criticism of recent development decisions is Chester W. Hartman's *Yerba Buena: Land Grab and Community Resistance in San Francisco* (1974). Randy Shilts, *The Mayor of Castro Street* (1982), analyzes the growth of gay political power. Beth Bagwell's *Oakland, Story of a City,* has a very brief summary of postwar Oakland development. Edward C. Hayes's *Power Structure and Urban Policy* (1972) is a radical analysis of decisionmaking in Oakland, while Amory Bradford, *Oakland's Not For Burning* (1968), describes efforts to avoid "another Watts." John Krich's *Bump City: Winners and Losers in Oakland* (1979) is both a critical and affectionate look at the city. Since its sale by the Knowland family in 1979, the *Oakland Tribune* has become more critical of City Hall. The weekly *Montclarion* also often questions official policies.

□ □ □

Bibliography

Allen, Peter C. *Stanford: From the Foothills to the Bay*. Stanford: Stanford Alumni Association and Stanford Historical Society, 1980.

Anthony, Gene. *The Summer of Love: Haight-Ashbury at its Highest*. Millbrae, Calif.: Celestial Arts, 1980.

Archibald, Katherine. *Wartime Shipyard: A Study in Social Disunity*. Berkeley: University of California Press, 1947.

Archibald, Robert R. *An Economic History of the California Missions*. Washington: Academy of American Franciscan History, 1978.

Association of Bay Area Governments. *Emergence of a Regional Concept, 1910-1976*. Berkeley: Association of Bay Area Governments, 1976.

_____. *Regional Plan 1970-1990—San Francisco Bay Region*. Berkeley: 1970.

Bach, Eve, et al. *The Cities' Wealth*. Washington: National Conference on Alternative State and Local Public Policies, 1976.

Bagwell, Beth. *Oakland, Story of a City*. Novato, Calif.: Presidio Press, 1982.

Bakker, Elna. *An Island Called California: An Ecological Introduction to Its Natural Communities.* Berkeley: University of California Press, 1971.

Barth, Gunther. *Instant Cities: Urbanization and the Rise of San Francisco and Denver.* New York: Oxford University Press, 1975.

Barth, Gunther P. *Bitter Strength: A History of the Chinese in the United States, 1850-1870.* Cambridge: Harvard University Press, 1964.

Bay Guardian. *The Ultimate Highrise.* San Francisco: San Francisco Bay Guardian, 1971.

Bean, Walton. *Boss Ruef's San Francisco: The Story of the Union Labor Party, Big Business, and the Graft Prosecution.* Berkeley: University of California Press, 1952.

Beck, Warren A. and Ynez D. Haase. *Historical Atlas of California.* Norman: University of Oklahoma Press, 1974.

Belser, Karl. "The Making of Slurban America." *Cry California* 15(4) (Fall 1970): 1-21.

Bollens, John C. *The Problem of Government in the San Francisco Bay Region.* Berkeley: Bureau of Public Administration, University of California, 1948.

Bolt, Bruce A. *Earthquakes: A Primer.* San Francisco: W. H. Freeman & Co., 1978.

Bolton, Herbert E. *Outpost of Empire: The Story of the Founding of San Francisco.* New York: Alfred A. Knopf, 1931.

_____ . *Wider Horizons of American History.* Notre Dame: University of Notre Dame Press, 1939.

Boyle, Kay. *The Long Walk at San Francisco State, and Other Essays.* New York: Grove Press, 1970.

Bradford, Amory. *Oakland's Not for Burning.* New York: D. McKay Co., 1968.

Brodsly, David. *L. A. Freeway, An Appreciative Essay.* Berkeley: University of California Press, 1982.

Bronson, William. *The Earth Shook, the Sky Burned.* Garden City, NY: Doubleday & Co., 1959.

Bullough, William A. *The Blind Boss and His City: Christopher Augustine Buckley and Nineteenth Century San Francisco.* Berkeley: University of California Press, 1979.

Burchell, R. A. *The San Francisco Irish, 1848-1880.* Berkeley: University of California Press, 1980.

Burke, Robert. *Olson's New Deal for California.* Westport, Conn.: Greenwood Press, 1953.

Burnham, John C. "The Gasoline Tax and the Automobile Revolution." *Mississippi Valley Historical Review* 47(3) (December 1961): 435-459.

Bylinsky, Gene. "California's Great Breeding Ground for Industry." *Fortune* 89(6) (June 1974): 128-137.

California. State Earthquake Investigation Commission. *The California Earthquake of April 18, 1906.* Washington, DC: Carnegie Institution of Washington, 1908.

_____ . Division of Mines and Geology. *Geologic Guidebook of the San Francisco Bay Counties.* San Francisco: 1957.

Camarillo, Albert. *Chicanos in a Changing Society: From Mexican Pueblos to American Barrios in Santa Barbara and Southern California, 1848-1930.* Cambridge: Harvard University Press, 1979.

Camp, William Martin. *San Francisco: Port of Gold.* Garden City, NY: Doubleday & Co., 1947.

Caughey, John. *Gold is the Cornerstone.* Berkeley: University of California

Press, 1948. (Republished in 1976 as *The California Gold Rush.*)

_____ . *Their Majesties, the Mob.* Chicago: Univeristy of Chicago Press, 1960.

Chen, Jack. *The Chinese of America: From the Beginnings to the Present.* San Francisco: Harper & Row Publishers, 1980.

Cinel, Dino. *From Italy to San Francisco: The Immigrant Experience.* Stanford: Stanford University Press, 1982.

Clary, Raymond H. *The Making of Golden Gate Park: The Early Years, 1865-1906.* San Francisco: California Living Books, 1980.

Clements, Kendrick A. "Politics and the Park: San Francisco's Fight for Hetch Hetchy, 1908-1913." *Pacific Historical Review* 48(2) (May 1979): 185-217.

Coleman, Charles M. *P.G. & E. of California: The Centennial Story of Pacific Gas and Electric Company.* New York: McGraw-Hill Book Co., 1952.

Conzen, Kathleen Neils. "Community Studies, Urban History and American Local History." In Michael Kammen, ed., *The Past Before Us: Contemporary Historical Writing in the United States.* Ithaca: Cornell University Press, 1980.

Cook, Sherburne F. *The Conflict Between the California Indian and White Civilization.* Berkeley: University of California Press, 1943.

Cross, Ira B. *A History of the Labor Movement in California.* Berkeley: University of California Press, 1935.

Dana, Richard Henry. *Two Years Before The Mast.* New York: Harper & Brothers, 1840.

Daniels, Douglas Henry. *Pioneer Urbanites: A Social and Cultural History of Black San Francisco.* Philadelphia: Temple University Press, 1980.

Daniels, Roger. *Concentration Camps USA: Japanese Americans and World War II.* New York: Holt, Rinehart & Winston, 1971.

_____ . *The Politics of Prejudice: The Anti-Japanese Movement in California and the Struggle for Japanese Exclusion.* Berkeley: University of California Press, 1978.

Dasmann, Raymond F. *The Destruction of California.* New York: Macmilllan Co., 1966.

Davis, Nuel. *Lawrence and Oppenheimer.* New York: Simon & Schuster, 1968.

Davis, William Heath. *Seventy-Five Years in California.* San Francisco: J. Howell Books, 1929.

Decker, Peter R. *Fortunes and Failures: White Collar Mobility in Nineteenth Century San Francisco.* Cambridge: Harvard University Press, 1978.

Dillon, Richard H. *Embarcadero.* New York: Coward-McCann, 1959.

Donley, Michael W., et al. *Atlas of California.* Culver City, Calif.: Pacific Book Center, 1979.

Egan, Ferol. *Fremont, Explorer for a Restless Nation.* Garden City, NY: Doubleday & Co., 1977.

Ellison, William Henry. *A Self-Governing Dominion: California, 1848-1860.* Berkeley: University of California Press, 1950.

Emparan, Madie Brown. *The Vallejos of California.* San Francisco: Gleeson Library Associates, University of San Francisco, 1968.

Fabry, Joseph. *Swing Shift: Building the Liberty Ships.* San Francisco: Strawberry Hill Press, 1982.

Finnie, Richard. *Marinship: the History of a Wartime Shipyard.* San Francisco: Marinship Corporation, 1947.

Fogelson, Robert M. *The Fragmented Metropolis, Los Angeles 1850-1930.* Cambridge: Harvard University Press, 1967.

Frieden, Bernard J. *The Environmental Protection Hustle.* Cambridge: MIT Press, 1979.

Frost, Richard H. *The Mooney Case.* Stanford: Stanford University Press, 1968.

Gates, Paul W. "The California Land Act of 1851." *California Historical Quarterly* 50(4) (December 1971): 395-431.

Geiger, Maynard J. *The Life and Times of Fray Junipero Serra, O.F.M.* Washington: Academy of American Franciscan History, 2 vols., 1959.

Gentry, Curt. *Frame-Up: The Incredible Case of Tom Mooney and Warren Billings.* New York: W. W. Norton & Co., 1967.

Gilliam, Harold. *San Francisco Bay.* Garden City, NY: Doubleday & Co., 1957.

_____ . *Weather of the San Francisco Bay Region.* Berkeley: University of California Press, 1962.

_____ . *Between The Devil and The Deep Blue Bay: The Struggle to Save San Francisco Bay.* San Francisco: Chronicle Books, 1969.

_____ . *For Better or For Worse: The Ecology of an Urban Area.* San Francisco: Chronicle Books, 1972.

Griswold del Castillo, Richard. *The Los Angeles Barrio, 1850-1890: A Social History.* Berkeley: University of California Press, 1979

Gumina, Deanna P. *The Italians of San Francisco, 1850-1930.* New York: Center for Migration Studies, 1978.

Hague, Harlan. *The Road to California: The Search for a Southern Overland Route, 1540-1848.* Glendale, Calif.: A. H. Clark Co., 1978.

Hanson, Dirk. *The New Alchemists: Silicon Valley and the Micro-Electronics Revolution.* Boston: Little, Brown & Co., 1982.

Harlan, George H. and Clement Fisher, Jr. *Of Walking Beams and Paddle Wheels: A Chronicle of San Francisco Bay Ferryboats.* San Francisco: Bay Books Limited, 1951.

Harlow, Neal. *California Conquered: War and Peace on the Pacific, 1846-1850.* Berkeley: University of California Press, 1982.

Hartman, Chester W. *Yerba Buena: Land Grab and Community Resistance in San Francisco.* San Francisco: Glide Publications, 1974.

Hayes, Edward C. *Power Structure and Urban Policy: Who Rules Oakland?* New York: McGraw-Hill Book Co., 1972.

Heilbron, J. L., Robert W. Seidel, and Bruce R. Wheaton. *Lawrence and His Laboratory: Nuclear Science at Berkeley.* Berkeley: Lawrence Berkeley Laboratory and Office for History of Science and Technology, University of California, 1981.

Heizer, Robert F. and Albert B. Elsasser. *The Natural World of the California Indians.* Berkeley: University of California Press, 1980.

_____ . *The Costanoan Indians: An Assemblage of Papers on the Language and Culture of the Costanoan Indians.* . . . Cupertino: California History Center, 1974.

Heizer, Robert F., ed. *California.* Vol. 8, Handbook of North American Indians. Washington: Smithsonian Institution, 1978.

Heizer, Robert F. and M. A. Whipple, eds. *The California Indians: A Source Book.* Berkeley: University of California Press, 1971.

Hilton, George W. *The Cable Car in America.* San Diego: Howell-North Books, 2nd ed., 1982.

Hilton, George W. and John F. Due. *The Electric Interurban Railways in America.* Stanford: Stanford University Press, 1960.

Holliday, J. S. *The World Rushed In: The California Gold Rush Experience.* New York: Simon & Schuster, 1981.

Hornbeck, David. *California Patterns: A Geographical and Historical Atlas.* Palo Alto, Calif.: Mayfield Publishing Co., 1983.

Hosokawa, Bill. *Nisei: the Quiet Americans.* New York: William Morrow & Co., 1969.

Howard, Arthur David. *Evolution of the Landscape of the San Francisco Bay Region.* Berkeley: University of California Press, 1962.

Hutchinson, Cecil Alan. *Frontier Settlement in Mexican California: The Hijar-Padres Colony and Its Origins, 1769-1835.* New Haven: Yale University Press, 1969.

Iacopi, Robert. *Earthquake Country: California.* Menlo Park, Calif.: Sunset Books/Lane Publishing Co., 1971.

Issel, William. "Class and Ethnic Conflict in San Francisco Political History: The Reform Charter of 1898." *Labor History* 18(3) (Summer 1977): 341-359.

Jackson, Anne. "The Dow Aftermath: Does California Really Mean Business?" *Cry California* 12(2) (Summer 1977): 9-12.

Japanese American Curriculum Project. *Japanese Americans: the Untold Story.* New York: Holt, Rinehart & Winston, 1971.

Jones, Holway R. *John Muir and the Sierra Club: the Battle for Yosemite.* San Francisco: Sierra Club, 1965.

Jones, Landon Y. *Great Expectations: America and the Baby Boom Generation.* New York: Coward, McCann & Geoghegan, 1980.

Jones, Victor. "Bay Area Regionalism: The Politics of Intergovernmental Relations." In Kent Mathewson, ed., *The Regionalist Papers,* 2nd ed. Detroit: Metropolitan Fund, 1978.

Kahn, Edgar M. *Cable Car Days in San Francisco.* Stanford: Stanford University Press, 1944.

Kahn, Judd. *Imperial San Francisco: Politics and Planning in an American City, 1897-1906.* Lincoln: University of Nebraska Press, 1979.

Kemble, John Haskell. *San Francisco Bay: A Pictorial Maritime History.* New York: Bonanza Books, 1957.

Kent, T. J., Jr., and Gary E. Pivo. "Thinking About Growth—for the Bay Area and People for Open Space." *Regional Exchange* (People for Open Space) (June 1982): 1-6.

Kent, T. J., Jr. *Open Space for the San Francisco Bay Area: Organizing to Guide Metropolitan Growth.* Berkeley: Institute of Governmental Studies, University of California, 1970.

Kingston, Maxine Hong. *The Woman Warrior.* New York: Alfred A. Knopf, 1976.

_____. *China Men.* New York: Alfred A. Knopf, 1980.

Kinnaird, Lawrence. *History of the Greater San Francisco Bay Region.* New York: Lewis Historical Publishing Co., 3 vols., 1966.

Kitano, Harry H. *Japanese Americans: The Evolution of a Subculture.* Englewood Cliffs, NJ: Prentice-Hall, 1969.

Knight, Robert E. *Industrial Relations in the San Francisco Bay Area, 1900-1918.* Berkeley: University of California Press, 1960.

Krich, John. *Bump City: Winners and Losers in Oakland.* Berkeley: City Miner Books, 1979.

Kroeber, Alfred Louis. *Handbook of the Indians of California.* Washington, DC: 1925.

Lapp, Rudolph M. *Blacks in Gold Rush California.* New Haven: Yale University Press, 1977.

Larrowe, Charles P. *Harry Bridges: The Rise and Fall of Radical Labor in the United States.* New York: Lawrence Hill, 1972.

Lavender, David Sievert. *The Great Persuader.* Garden City, NY: Doubleday & Co., 1970.

_____ . *Nothing Seemed Impossible: William C. Ralston and Early San Francisco.* Palo Alto, Calif.: American West Publishing Co., 1975.

Lewis, Oscar. *The Big Four: The Story of Huntington, Stanford, Hopkins, and Crocker, and of the Building of the Central Pacific.* New York: Alfred A. Knopf, 1938.

Lipset, Seymour Martin and Sheldon S. Wolin, eds. *The Berkeley Student Revolt: Facts and Interpretations.* Garden City, NY: Anchor Books, 1965.

Lotchin, Roger W. *San Francisco, 1846-1856: From Hamlet to City.* New York: Oxford University Press, 1974.

_____ . "The City and the Sword: San Francisco and the Rise of the Metropolitan Military Complex, 1919-1941." *Journal of American History* 65(4) (March 1979): 996-1020.

Lyman, George D. *Ralston's Ring: California Plunders the Comstock Lode.* New York: Charles Scribner's Sons, 1937.

Margolin, Malcolm. *The Ohlone Way: Indian Life in the San Francisco and Monterey Bay Areas.* Berkeley: Heyday Books, 1978.

McGloin, John Bernard, S. J. *San Francisco: The Story of a City.* San Rafael, Calif.: Presidio Press, 1978.

Miller, Crane S. and Richard S. Hyslop. *California, The Geography of Diversity.* Palo Alto, Calif.: Mayfield Publishing Co., 1983.

Miller, Stuart C. *The Unwelcome Immigrant: The American Image of the Chinese, 1785-1882.* Berkeley: University of California Press, 1970.

Nagel, Gunther W. *Jane Stanford, Her Life and Letters.* Stanford: Stanford Alumni Association, 1975.

Narell, Irena. *Our City, the Jews of San Francisco.* San Diego: Howell-North Books, 1981.

Nash, Gerald D. *The American West in the Twentieth Century: A Short History of an Urban Oasis.* Englewood Cliffs, NJ: Prentice-Hall, 1973.

Nash, Roderick. *Wilderness and the American Mind.* New Haven: Yale University Press, 1967.

Nathan, Harriet and Stanley Scott, eds. *Experiment and Change in Berkeley: Essays on City Politics, 1950-1975.* Berkeley: Institute of Governmental Studies, University of California, 1978.

Nee, Victor and Brett De Bary Nee. *Long Time Californ': A Documentary Study of an American Chinatown.* New York: Pantheon Books, 1973.

Noble, John W. *Its Name Was M.U.D.* Oakland, Calif.: East Bay Municipal Utility District, 1970.

Nunis, Doyce B., Jr., ed.. *The San Francisco Vigilance Committee of 1856.* Los Angeles: Los Angeles Westerners, 1971.

Odell, Rice. *The Saving of San Francisco Bay: A Report on Citizen Action and Regional Planning.* Washington, DC: Conservation Foundation, 1972.

Paul, Rodman W. *Mining Frontiers of the Far West, 1848-1880.* New York: Holt, Rinehart & Winston, 1963.

Paxson, Frederick L. "The Highway Movement, 1916-1935." *American Historical Society Review* 51(2) (January 1946): 236-254.

People for Open Space. *Endangered Harvest: the Future of Bay Area Farmland.* San Francisco: People for Open Space, 1980.

Peterson, Richard H. *The Bonanza Kings: The Social Origins and Business Behavior of Western Mining Entrepreneurs.* Lincoln: University of Nebraska Press, 1977.

Phillips, George H. "Breakdown of the Spanish Mission System." In David Weber, ed., *New Spain's Far Northern Frontier: Essays on Spain in the*

American West, 1540-1821. Albuquerque: University of New Mexico Press, 1979.

Pickerell, Albert G. and May Dornin. *The University of California, A Pictorial History.* Berkeley: University of California Press, 1968.

Pitt, Leonard. *The Decline of the Californios: A Social History of the Spanish-Speaking Californians, 1846-1890.* Berkeley: University of California Press, 1966.

Pomeroy, Earl S. *In Search of the Golden West: the Tourist in Western America.* New York: Alfred A. Knopf, 1957.

Pressman, Jeffrey L. and Aaron Wildavsky. *Implementation: How Great Expectations in Washington are Dashed in Oakland . . .* (3d. ed., expanded). Berkeley: University of California Press, 1984.

Rawls, James. *Indians of California: the Changing Image.* Norman: University of Oklahoma Press, 1984.

Reps, John W. *Cities of the American West: A History of Frontier Urban Planning.* Princeton, NJ: Princeton University Press, 1979.

Riesenberg, Felix, Jr. *Golden Gate: the Story of San Francisco Harbor.* New York: Alfred A. Knopf, 1940.

_____ . *The Golden Road: the Story of California's Spanish Mission Trail.* New York: McGraw-Hill Book Co., 1962.

Robinson, William W. *Land in California.* Berkeley: University of California Press, 1948.

Rocq, Margaret M., ed. *California Local History: A Bibliography and Union List of Library Holdings.* Stanford: Stanford University Press, 1970.

Rosenbaum, Fred. *Free to Choose: The Making of a Jewish Community in the American West.* Berkeley: Western Jewish History Center, Judah L. Magnes Memorial Museum, 1976.

_____ . *Architects of Reform: Congressional and Community Leadership, Emanu-El of San Francisco, 1849-1980.* Berkeley: Western Jewish History Center, Judah L. Magnes Memorial Museum, 1980.

Roszak, Theodore. *The Making of a Counter Culture: Reflections on the Technocratic Society and Its Youthful Opposition.* Garden City, NY: Doubleday & Co., 1969.

Rubin, Lillian B. *Busing and Backlash: White Against White in an Urban School District.* Berkeley: University of California Press, 1972.

Saxton, Alexander. *The Indispensable Enemy: Labor and the Anti-Chinese Movement in California.* Berkeley: University of California Press, 1971.

Schwartz, Harvey. *The March Inland: Origins of the ILWU Warehouse Division, 1934-1938.* Los Angeles: Institute of Industrial Relations, University of California, 1978.

_____ . "Harry Bridges and the Scholars: Looking at History's Verdict." *California History* 59(1) (Spring 1980): 66-80.

Scott, Mel. *The San Francisco Bay Area: a Metropolis in Perspective.* Berkeley: University of California Press, 1959. (Being reissued with a new final chapter.)

_____ . *The Future of San Francisco Bay.* Berkeley: Institute of Governmental Studies, University of California, 1963.

Scott, Stanley and John C. Bollens. *Governing a Metropolitan Region: the San Francisco Bay Area.* Berkeley: Institute of Governmental Studies, University of California, 1968.

Scott, Stanley, ed. *The San Francisco Bay Area: Its Problems and Future.* Berkeley: Institute of Governmental Studies, University of California, 3 vols., 1966-1972.

Seale, Bobby. *Seize the Time: the Story of the Black Panther Party and Huey P.*

Newton. New York: Random House, 1970.

Selvin, David. *The Sky Full of Storm.* San Francisco: California Historical Society, 1966.

Shilts, Randy. *The Mayor of Castro Street: the Life and Times of Harvey Milk.* San Francisco: St. Martins Press, 1982.

Smith, Arthur C. *Introduction to the Natural History of the San Francisco Bay Region.* Berkeley: University of California Press, 1959.

Stadtman, Verne. *The University of California, 1868-1968.* New York: McGraw-Hill Book Co., 1970.

Steinbrugge, Karl V. *Earthquake Hazard in the San Francisco Bay Area: A Continuing Problem in Public Policy.* Berkeley: Institute of Governmental Studies, University of California, 1968.

Stewart, George R. *Committee of Vigilance: Revolution in San Francisco, 1851.* Boston: Houghton Mifflin, 1964.

Swanberg, W. A. *Citizen Hearst.* New York: Charles Scribner's Sons, 1961.

Taylor, Paul S. *The Sailors' Union of the Pacific.* New York: Ronald Press Co., 1923.

Ten Broek, Jacobus, Edward N. Barnhart, and Floyd W. Matson. *Prejudice, War and the Constitution.* Berkeley: University of California Press, 1954.

Thernstrom, Stephen and Richard Sennett, eds. *Nineteenth Century Cities: Essays in the New Urban History.* New Haven: Yale University Press, 1969.

Treutlein, Theodore E. *San Francisco Bay: Discovery and Colonization, 1769-1776.* San Francisco: California Historical Society, 1968.

Tutorow, Norman E. *Leland Stanford: Man of Many Careers.* Menlo Park, Calif.: Pacific Coast Publishers, 1971.

Uchida, Yoshiko. *Desert Exile: The Uprooting of a Japanese American Family.*

Seattle: University of Washington Press, 1982.

Unger, Irwin. *The Movement: A History of the American New Left, 1959-1972*. New York: Harper & Row Publishers, 1974.

Vance, James E., Jr. *Geography and Urban Evolution in the San Francisco Bay Area*. Berkeley: Institute of Governmental Studies, University of California, 1964.

Vallejo, Don Mariano G. "Historical and Personal Memoirs Relating to Alta California." San Francisco: 1875. 3 vols. Manuscript translated by Earl R. Hewitt. Bancroft Library Archives, University of California, Berkeley.

Walker, Richard A. and Matthew J. Williams. "Water from Power: Water Supply and Regional Growth in the Santa Clara Valley." *Economic Geography* 58(2) (April 1982): 95-120.

Walker, Richard A., Michael Storper, and Ellen Gersh. "The Limits of Environmental Control: The Saga of Dow in the Delta." *Antipode* 11(2) (1979): 48-60.

Walsh, James P., ed. *The San Francisco Irish, 1850-1976*. San Francisco: Irish Literary and Historical Society, 1978.

Ward, Estolv. *The Gentle Dynamiter: A Biography of Tom Mooney*. Palo Alto, Calif.: Ramparts Press, 1983.

Warner, Sam Bass, Jr. *The Urban Wilderness: A History of the American City*. New York: Harper & Row Publishers, 1972.

Warshaw, Steven. *The Trouble in Berkeley: The Complete History, in Text and Pictures, of the Great Student Rebellion Against the "New University."* Berkeley: Diablo Press, 1965.

Weintraub, Hyman G. *Andrew Furuseth, Emancipator of the Seamen*. Berkeley: University of California Press, 1959.

White, Gerald T. *Formative Years in the Far West: A History of Standard Oil*

Company of California and Predecessors Through 1919. New York: Appleton-Century-Crofts, 1962.

Wilson, Neill Compton. *Here is the Golden Gate.* New York: William Morrow & Co., 1962.

Wirt, Frederick M. *Power in the City: Decision Making in San Francisco.* Berkeley: University of California Press, 1974.

Wollenberg, Charles. *All Deliberate Speed: Segregation and Exclusion in California Schools, 1855-1975.* Berkeley: University of California Press, 1976.

_____ . "Blacks vs. Navy Blue: The Mare Island Mutiny Court Martial." *California History* 58(1) (Spring 1979): 62-76.

_____ . "James vs. Marinship: Trouble on the New Black Frontier." *California History* 60(3) (Fall 1981): 262-280.

Wood, Samuel E. and Alfred Heller. *California, Going, Going . . .* Sacramento: California Tomorrow, 1962.

□ □ □

Introducing Institute Publications

The Institute of Governmental Studies publishes on a broad range of regional and statewide policy issues that are likely to interest many readers of this book. To receive further information on Institute publications, readers can call or write the Institute of Governmental Studies, 119 Moses Hall, University of California, Berkeley, California 94720. Phone: (415) 642-5537.

The proximity of the Bay, the Delta, and the Pacific shoreline mean that the coastal environment and water policy questions are of prime importance in this region. Institute publications concerning these topics include: Squire and Scott, *The Politics of California Coastal Legislation;* Scott, ed., *Coastal Conservation: Essays on Experiments in Governance;* Storper and Walker, *The Price of Water;* and Dunning, *Water Allocation in California: Legal Rights and Reform Needs.*

The Bay Area's literate and comparatively well-educated public has a sustained interest in the problems of public schools, and a number of Institute publications discuss ways to improve educational performance. Recent examples are Guthrie and Zusman, *Mathematics and Science Teacher Shortages: What Can California Do?* and Stoddart, Losk, and Benson, *Some Reflections on the Honorable Profession of Teaching.*

The diversity of the Bay Area's population and the influx of newcomers from all over the world, especially Latin America, push immigration questions to the forefront. Recent IGS publications are Cross and Sandos, *Across the Border: Rural Development in Mexico and Recent Migration to the United States;* and Fogel and Martin, *Immigration: California's Economic Stake.*

The quality and cost of medical services and health care are universal concerns for all US citizens, and certainly the Bay Area public, which benefits from a comparatively generous pool of hospitals, medical schools, physicians, and health care plans. Many Institute publications deal with the economic and political issues in providing health care and other social services. These studies include Minkler and Blum, *Community-Based Home Health and Social Services for California's Elderly: Present Constraints and Future Alternatives;* Harrington, et al., *Prepaid Long-Term Care Plans: A Policy Option for California's Medi-Cal Program;* and Shonick and Roemer, *Public Hospitals Under Private Management: The California Experience.*

Crossed by many earthquake faults, Bay Area communities are increasingly conscious of seismic safety needs. Institute publications dealing with such issues include the Steinbrugge classic, *Earthquake Hazard in the San Francisco Bay Area;* and Scott, *Policies for Seismic Safety: Elements of a State Governmental Program.*

In addition to books and monographs on these and many other public policy issues, the Institute publishes the *Public Affairs Report* six times a year, and distributes individual copies free on request. The authors are principally University faculty members and researchers with expertise on a wide range of significant topics. Each issue of the bulletin deals with a single topic, exploring policy questions illuminated by current research, and presenting conclusions and recommendations. Recent topics include governmental deregulation, youthful suicide, health policy and the poor, vocational education, biotechnology, California-Mexico trade relations, and native American housing.